THE SELLING
OF 9/11

Dana Heller's previous publications include *The Feminization of Quest-Romance: Radical Departures* (University of Texas Press, 1990), and *Family Plots: The De-Oedipalization of Popular Culture* (University of Pennsylvania Press, 1995). In addition, she is the editor of *Cross Purposes: Lesbians, Feminists, and the Limits of Alliance* (Indiana University Press, 1997).

THE SELLING OF 9/11

How a National Tragedy Became a Commodity

Edited and with
an Introduction by

DANA HELLER

palgrave
macmillan

THE SELLING OF 9/11
© Dana Heller, 2005.

First published in 2005 by
PALGRAVE MACMILLAN™
175 Fifth Avenue, New York, N.Y. 10010 and
Houndmills, Basingstoke, Hampshire, England RG21 6XS
Companies and representatives throughout the world.

PALGRAVE MACMILLAN is the global academic imprint of the
Palgrave Macmillan division of St. Martin's Press, LLC and
of Palgrave Macmillan Ltd. Macmillan® is a registered trademark
in the United States, United Kingdom and other countries.
Palgrave is a registered trademark in the European
Union and other countries.

ISBN 1–4039–6817–9

Library of Congress Cataloging-in-Publication Data is available from the
Library of Congress.

A catalogue record for this book is available from the British Library.

Design by Newgen Imaging Systems (P) Ltd., Chennai, India.

First edition: September 2005

10 9 8 7 6 5 4 3 2 1

Printed in the United States of America.

Contents

For Galya

Acknowledgments

The idea for this collection grew out of an essay I was asked to write for *Topos: Journal of Philosophical and Cultural Studies*, which is published at the European Humanities University in Minsk, Republic of Belarus. I am indebted to Almira Ousmanova, Associate Professor in the Department of Culturology, for extending that invitation to me. Without her encouragement and intellectual camaraderie this book may very well have never been.

Otherwise, I have my writers to thank for their dedication, patience, and unremitting responsiveness. Special thanks go to Bill Hart for his contribution at the eleventh hour. I am grateful as well for the discerning comments of readers and listeners, particularly Amy Kaplan, Robert Wojtowicz, Sangita Gopal, Heidi Schilpphacke, Imke Meyer, and Bish Sen. Farideh Koohi-Kamali, Melissa Nosal, Lynn Vande Stouwe, and the staff at Palgrave Macmillan ministered diligently to the production of this collection in countless major and minor ways. Thanks also go to Marita Sturken, John Rockwell, "the family of Steve Mendelson," and Kevin O'Sullivan at Associated Press. Amanda Bloodgood and Gretchen Edwards provided critical logistical assistance. And I should also acknowledge Old Dominion University for granting me a much-needed sabbatical during the initial stage of cementing the project.

Chapter 1
Introduction: Consuming 9/11

Dana Heller

When it comes to effective marketing, timing is everything. Car salesmen know this, as do stock market analysts, media industry specialists, documentary filmmakers, and White House political advisors. So it came as little surprise when, less than a week before the one-year anniversary of the September 11, 2001, terrorist attacks on the World Trade Center and Pentagon, White House Chief of Staff Andrew H. Card, Jr. publicly revealed a sage piece of the Bush administration's marketing wisdom: "you don't introduce new products in August."[1]

Few would quibble with Card's logic. What was surprising, however, was the "product" that he was marketing: a U.S. military operation against Iraq that would extend America's war on terrorism to the oil-rich heart of the Middle East. With the midterm election season officially under way, Republican political strategists were eager to divert the public's attention from a sagging economy and a seemingly never-ending series of corporate accounting scandals, some of which came dangerously close to implicating administration leadership. As coordinator of the White House effort to "sell" the idea of an Iraqi war to the American people, Card's controversial sound bite was carefully styled and timed to seize the autumn headlines and to generate "buzz," or word of mouth, one of the most effective strategies for alerting potential consumers to the arrival of a new product. His use of advertising rhetoric in promoting U.S. military action seemed, at best, imprudent. Some readers, seeing this as tantamount to an admission of the Bush administration's crude manipulation of public emotion on the anniversary of the 9/11 attacks, were outraged. Political action groups opposed to the Bush team's oil-interests politics and the hawkish militarism that defined its unilateral response in the new war on terrorism seized on Card's remark in order to galvanize resistance to an Iraq invasion. However, administration officials' candid disclosure that the September 11 anniversary had been envisioned as "a centerpiece of the strategy" that would help "sell" the idea of an Iraqi war to the American people was in many ways an amplification of the opportunism that had already transformed 9/11 into a commercial pitch, a slogan that worked its way into the American market lexicon even before Bush policy makers began implementing their plan for Hussein's ouster.[2]

Business as Usual

In the aftermath of a cutthroat presidential campaign that set new records for fund-raising and spending, and triggered controversy with images of flag-draped bodies and disintegrated buildings prominently featured in the Bush team's early reelection advertisements, it seems perfectly clear that Card's 2002 analogy was no mere lapse of official decorum. Indeed, it strikes me as a fairly candid assessment of the post-9/11 political economy, the complex cultural relations of commodification and commemoration, marketing and militarism, commercial patronage and patriotism, that took shape long before American Airlines Flight 11 struck the North Tower, but were brought to the fore and reinvested with nationalist solemnity in that tragedy's wake. The reification of these relations has circulated widely during the past three years through a dazzling proliferation of 9/11 tie-in products, commemorative artifacts, mass media narratives, memorabilia, and kitsch. In some instances, products have been commissioned specifically to rewrite the collective memory of 9/11—such as the George W. Bush Elite Force Aviator action figure, Michael Moore's polemical documentary film *Farenheit 9/11*, and the NBC made-for-television movie *Saving Jessica Lynch*, which depicts the ambush of the 507 Maintenance Company in Iraq and the rescue of nineteen-year-old Pfc. Jessica Lynch from the hospital where she was held prisoner of war. In other instances, products assigned to convey patriotism have no immediate connection to the events of

9/11—Las Vegas casino chips, snow globes, and toilet paper, for example. Products long available to American consumers were refilled with new meanings in the context of the attacks and their aftermath, as in the case of American flag lapel pins and automobile decals, duct tape, and "I ♥ NY" T-shirts. And, in the midst of all this marketing and shopping madness, consumers themselves have often taken the lead in determining the forms and symbolic meanings of 9/11 commodities, sometimes with creative and surprising results.

To the casual observer it might seem that there is no occasion so solemn in the United States—no tragedy so tragic—that it cannot be used for the purposes of short-term commercial profit. Indeed, even the term "9/11" itself, a shorthand that the contributors to this book use throughout to refer at once to the four plane crashes, the thousands of lives lost, and the string of international and domestic actions and events that have resulted from the events of September 11, has attained the cultural function of a trademark, one that symbolizes a new kind of national identification—or national branding awareness, to adopt the jargon of advertising—alongside the almost sublime spectacle of national trauma that forced that brand name beyond the limits of what can fully be absorbed by the mind, seen by the eye, or portrayed by the artist and filmmaker. The industries of marketing and advertising naturally responded to this crisis by refashioning fantasies of coherent, monolithic nationhood and consensual nationalism in accordance with the new post-9/11 economic anxiety disorder. I refer to this response as "natural" because the model of twentieth-century national identity that was challenged by 9/11—the model that we have inherited from our forbearers—is one that mirrors the individual and collective identities of shoppers: that of the American consumer. In 1925, in a speech before the American Society of Newspaper Editors, President Calvin Coolidge proclaimed that "the chief business of the American people is business," thus echoing the triumph of nineteenth-century industrial capitalism and the rise of what Stuart Ewen would famously term "consumer democracy." Driven by the mass marketing of cultural goods and style symbols not limited to an elite class but available to the people at large, the practice of American citizenship became increasingly coextensive with consumer rituals and commercialized myths of self-actualization. The reinforcement of such myths supported not only the advancement of American consumer capitalism, but the symbolic unity and allegorical reproduction of the nation itself, a process as evident in the makeover marketing of "Charles Atlas" (born Angelo Siciliano, an Italian immigrant) and the men's body-building industry he helped spawn, as in the caustic ministrations of the Fab Five on Bravo's *Queer Eye for the Straight Guy* (and now "Girl"), an "Eye" that views the middle-class body as protean and desperately in need of schooling in the manipulation of consumer technologies designed to secure consensual belief in our perpetual personal—and, by extension, national—interest and progress. Indeed, as Ewen points out, in a consumer democracy, "democracy itself becomes style; popular political involvement becomes structured by a pattern of spectatorship and consumption."[3]

With that, let me assure the reader that the writers for this book are not against consumption, either as a necessity of life or as a pleasurable pastime. What we do share are some concerns about the ways that 9/11 has been exploited for profit, hijacked in order to move consumer goods, and, consequently, transformed into a consumer good itself. If that statement seems overly cynical, take a closer look at the 9/11-themed Bush 2004 campaign ad that began airing on national television the week of March 1, 2004. Just as the buff, bald man with the large earring denotes clean floors, and the adorable dough boy denotes a warm, well-fed family, these campaign spots invited us to associate George W. Bush with the nation's response to 9/11, with hopes that fear of subsequent attacks would motivate voters to buy in for another four years. According to some 2004 post-election analyses, that strategy paid off. However, if that reminder seems overly partisan, we might look to the other end of the political spectrum, to Michael Moore's carefully crafted persona of a rumpled, midwestern, blue-collar Everyman armed with little more than a microphone, a film crew, and a talent for splicing together powerful images into narratives aimed at exposing the darkest machinations of American corporate and political power. Not only did Moore's *Farenheit 9/11* immortalize the video footage of George W. Bush's seven minutes of useless torpor following word of the September 11 attacks, but it also demonstrated that documentary films on political themes were potential money makers, at suburban malls as well as urban art houses. The much-publicized disputes over Disney's last-minute refusal to distribute the film only enhanced its box office appeal, as did its well-timed release at the start of the major party convention season. And while it seems doubtful that *Farenheit 9/11* or any of the "doomsday" films released in the months leading up to the November election significantly influenced

the outcome, Moore—as the new voice of the embattled left—
fashioned a sensationalized portrait of presidential ineptitude that
exploited the public's fears of a second Bush term no less than the
right's pointed intimation of terrors that could occur in Bush's
absence.[4]

Fear, as Joe Lockard demonstrates in his essay "Social Fear and
the *Terrorism Survival Guide*," is a forceful marketing tool in the
national effort to secure the homeland from future threats. Even
before September 11, fears of alien invaders who might turn our
own domestic defenses against us have been a driving force in immigration policy debates and in Hollywood cinema, as Bianca Nielsen
shows in her analysis of David Fincher's *Panic Room*. At the same
time, the writers for this volume do not forget what actually happened
on September 11, 2001, and the devastating impact those events had,
and continue to have, on our individual nervous systems and collective sense-making strategies. Consumer goods, objects, commercial
memorabilia can all play instrumental roles in human processes of
reflection, mourning, and healing. With this in mind, the writers
whose work you'll find here grapple with some tough questions:
How might we understand the selling of 9/11 as *both* a cynical
manipulation of consumers engineered by powerful corporate and
political interests *and* a potentially liberating and authentic expression of the people's creative energies in the face of profound grief,
genuine love of country, and sudden fear of national as well as
global instability? How is the marketing of 9/11 indicative of an
effort to construct an economy of symbolic goods that is aligned
sympathetically, on one hand, with respect for human dignity and
suffering, and on the other, with global capitalism's own successful
reproduction and expansion?

"Americana Nervosa" Revisited

This book developed out my sense that it was important to understand the consumer logic of post-9/11 political culture as well as
the political logic of post-9/11 consumer culture. This complicated
"logic" illuminates the invariably contradictory and contentious
processes by which American consumers use, communicate, and
fashion their national identities—their ideas and assumptions about
what it means to be American at this moment in history—with

consumer goods and cultural symbols, all up for purchase. These processes reflect the multiple functions of 9/11-related commodities, among which is the function of barrier to historical understanding, a simplified diversion from the more vexing and complex questions that the attacks have prompted many people to ask, questions such as "Why do they hate us?" At the same time, however, these same commodities may function as instruments of reflection and resistance to the status quo, used by consumers as they negotiate their own strategies for remembering September 11 and for considering an appropriate response, on both individual and collective bases.

In the weeks and months following 9/11, the market for goods representing American patriotic unity and pride expanded dramatically. American consumers both participated in, and bore witness to, a rapid transformation of the World Trade Center attacks into commodities aimed at repackaging turbulent and chaotic emotions, reducing them to a pious, quasi-religious nationalism. An effective displacement of national vulnerability, fear, and demoralization set off a collective compulsion to repeat, to engage in a particular acting out of the trauma through specific practices of consumption that administered to the national hunger for meaning—for images and stories of the attacks. We were, at this time, a nation starved for meaning. But most of what was available for consumption contained no value, only empty calories. The result was a nation suffering from the latest version of the condition that Lauren Berlant and Elizabeth Freeman once termed "Americana Nervosa," "a compulsive self-gorging on ritual images."[5] There is copious evidence to suggest that this condition reached epidemic proportions in post-9/11 American culture, cutting across all social classes, induced by mass media and publishing industry appeals to popular as well as more cultivated manners of consuming 9/11.

For example, a promotional brochure for the Easton Press "leather-bound heirloom edition" of *One Nation: America Remembers September 11, 2001* lures prospective buyers with promises of photographs that capture "American Flight 11 as it approaches and hits the North Tower" and "the agonizing moment the top of the South Tower lists sharply and the building begins to collapse." The copy furthermore guarantees that owners of this "keepsake" will want to reexperience such moments with their children and grandchildren time and again.[6] Here, by representing the attacks as the birthright of future generations, marketers promote the repetition of the traumatic moment as an expression of hope and as a healing ritual that solicits faith in the unity and continuity of the American family.

Such appeals to familial nationalism—or to a country presumably unified less by collective interests than by private investments in the reproduction of future capital—have a long, established place in the rhetoric of American consumerism. However, what is new in the case of 9/11 consumption can be apprehended in a *Publishers Weekly* editorial review for the photographic tribute, *New York September 11*, which hails the book for capturing the "terrible beauty" of 9/11, an appeal to the cultural capital of consumers who have come to regard the visceral shock of the World Trade Center's destruction—the evanescence of these monumental structures into toxic dust—as an aesthetic dilemma.[6] The importance of this aesthetic dilemma to the ethical and ideological conflicts inherent in the commodification of the attacks arises largely out of the recognition, in Wyatt Mason's words, that "the destruction of the World Trade Center is the most exhaustively imaged disaster in human history."[7]

Television images and narratives also played a major role in managing the diaster imagery, as Lynn Spigel demonstrates in her essay on post-9/11 television culture. From the moment Americans became aware that a plane had crashed into the World Trade Center, television intimately directed the sense-making strategies that individuals, coworkers, and communities brought to bear upon the unfolding of events. On average, Americans watched eight hours of television news coverage on September 11.[8] In the days following the attacks, the saturation of everyday life with uniform images of the second plane crash, the firebomb, and the towers' collapse was transformed itself into the uncontested meaning of the event, foreclosing on historical awareness and seeming to preempt any questioning impulses that might have placed the attacks in a broader critical perspective. In the networks' competition for ratings, these television "image-bites" were rapidly integrated into collective memory, not only of the United States but of nations around the world. Nowhere in this volume is the challenge of a global (and global-*ized*) media better expressed than in Yoneyuki Sugita's essay, "Comfort Zones: Japan's Media Marketing of 9/11," which suggests that like the Zapruder footage or like the photo of a Buddhist priest's self-immolation, images have come to define international events, but they often do so out of context, or in contexts that blur the lines between history and the partial truths reiterated by media corporations, news agencies, and their international affiliates.

In other instances, however, consumers took a more active, spontaneous role in the production of 9/11 images. For example, on the morning of September 11, as the attacks on the World Trade Center took place, shoppers who happened to be in or near the Financial District reportedly rushed to purchase single-use cameras with which to photograph the burning buildings. James Jack, the manager of the Duane Reade drugstore located just north of the World Trade Center, witnessed the phenomenon with amazement: "The only thing I sold today was cameras," he reported. "Within an hour of the first initial hit, we sold 60 to 100 cameras."[9] This incident invites us to consider the culturally productive dimension of consumption, or the dynamic, process by which ordinary shoppers seize on opportunities to make and record history with whatever tools or instruments appear within reach. Although each photographer of the burning towers would have had a similar meaning and purpose in mind—to capture a keepsake or memory of a monumental event—here we see an instance where "guerilla" shoppers grab onto that which is mass-produced as a way of contributing to the diverse meanings that the destruction of the World Trade Center would ultimately carry for individual creators, distributors, and consumers of the diaster's image. The single-use camera provides, in this context, an impromptu tactical space of resistance to centralized cultural production.

On September 11, 2001, some people in New York City reportedly began hoarding items related to the World Trade Center towers. In the weeks following the attacks, postcards featuring the WTC towers were in high demand at New York City souvenir stands and tourist kiosks, many of which sprung up around the former site of the towers, a place dubbed "Ground Zero." The lead essay in this volume, by Molly Hurley Depret and James Trimarco, explores the contradictions of trade and tourism at Ground Zero and asks whether the value of the thousands of WTC souvenir paperweights, ashtrays, shot glasses, and T-shirts sold to tourists who came to downtown Manhattan specifically to confront the site of the attacks can be calculated in terms of dollar value alone.

In the immediate aftermath of the attacks, eBay, the world's largest online auction company, allowed registered sellers to auction off 9/11-related material. That same Tuesday, shoppers on eBay apparently began bidding up the prices of World Trade Center memorabilia, many of them hoping to find something with which to remember the buildings. A postcard size drawing of the Twin Towers was priced at $250. A pair of dice with the words "World Trade Center" imprinted on them was priced at $41, even though the dice referred to a casino in Las Vegas that happened to go by that name. Announcing that the company did not want anyone to profit from the tragedy, eBay decided to remove all 9/11-related items from its site until October 1, 2001. When business resumed, 9/11 commodities continued to be sold and purchased on eBay, however, the cultural meanings that traders ascribed to these commodities, as well as to the act of shopping on eBay itself, in no way corresponds with the image of consumers as passive, or unreflective. Some traders consciously viewed their purchases as patriotic gestures, or as political assertions of the enduring vitality and superiority of the American way of life—capitalism. From this perspective, it was not so much the commodity, but the obligatory act of trading itself that carried symbolic meaning. For example, Michael Boyd, a trader on eBay, said he purchased a World Trade Center postcard as a sign of American patriotism. "I began to think that that is what America is all about, free trade," he said. "And that is what these people lost their lives over. Not only their lives but those who have fought for freedom in the past and those who will lose their lives in the future."[10]

Another trader, Cynthia Malaran, is an artist who had spent two years working on a photo project of the Twin Towers. She described her eBay purchase as "a grossly overpriced ($100) poster of the lower Manhattan view, intact." Explaining how she justified the expense, Malaran said that she bought the poster to remind her of the "behavior of humankind." "I am devastated—it is a view I grew up with, and one I never thought would change in this manner. The immeasurable damage and loss stirs up so much emotion inside, from sadness to anger."[11]

Like Malaran's remarks, Mick Broderick and Mark Gibson's essay on eBay's auctioning of 9/11 memorabilia opens the way for a closer consideration of the commodity value of 9/11 goods; the embedding of politics in everyday culture; the contradictory role that critical consumption plays in processes of reaffirming post-9/11 nationalist pieties and in circumventing them; and, the conflation of consumers' sense of personal trauma with historical trauma. While the seemingly limitless variety of subject-object bondings would seem evidence enough that no unified logic or predetermined structure of meaning governs the 9/11 commodity form, we can take Malaran's description of her own capitulation to "gross" 9/11 profiteering as both an authentic expression of desire for some alternative to the official narrative of "us vs. them" and as the compliant recontainment of political ambivalence and dissent within one of the only available forms sanctioned by the culture and not liable to be labeled as unpatriotic.

Thus it seems that we can best apprehend the high-stakes futures game that is "the selling of 9/11" when we retain a sense of the commodity as both a conveyer of corporate, commercial interests, *and* as a tool in a relatively autonomous form of cultural expression. Following this logic, the essays contained in this volume pay close attention to the ways in which 9/11 "things" are consumed at the level of everyday life, and at the same time acknowledge the pressures enjoined upon advertisers and marketers to obfuscate those cultural and social contexts, or to divert shoppers' attentions away from the social relations of production to the thing itself, its popular appeal, its handiness, its value as a status symbol, its tactile, physical allure. This masking of social conditions becomes instrumental in the manipulation of what the critic Jean Baudrillard calls "sign value" (a term that means something very close to "branding awareness"), or the manner in which objects take on the function of symbols in the market, thus inviting consumers to make decisions based on their desires instead of their actual needs.[12] Such diversions remain necessary for the maintenance and growth of global capitalism, and of corporate wealth and power. The problem is that by blinding ourselves to the social dimensions of commodity production, along with the prevailing economic order that stands behind it, we blind ourselves to the very conditions that have mobilized terrorist organizations worldwide to carry out actions against the United States and its global interests.

A Working-Class Hero Is Something to Be

In the weeks and months following September 11, as the nation mobilized for a new war against "terror"—an abstract, placeless, and faceless nemesis—American advertisers and marketers evoked no mythic enemies as it had in wars past: there were no nations to demonize, no despicable Nazis, not even an evil Soviet empire.

What advertisers and marketers did give us was a new breed of American hero. Firefighters, police, and emergency medical workers—ordinary working-class people doing their ordinary jobs—emerged in American culture as extraordinary. More than corporate CEOs, talk-show hosts, or politicians racing to Ground Zero for photo ops, these larger-than-life figures represented, on one hand, a national tribute to those who had made unimaginable sacrifices in the course of their routine labors. The most critically acclaimed documentary film to emerge from the 9/11 attacks, the Naudet brothers' *9/11*, is a film that was originally conceived as a portrait of a NYC firefighter trainee. However, it became a one-of-a-kind historical record of courage under fire. As Øyvind Vågnes argues in his essay, " 'Chosen To Be Witness': The Exceptionalism of *9/11*," this air of exceptionality extends beyond the bravery of the firefighters and beyond the film as a historical document to suggest the exceptional history of a nation, the exceptional professionalism of the filmmakers, and the exceptional value of owning the DVD Commemorative Edition of *9/11*.

At the same time, the post-9/11 working-class hero represented a nostalgic cultural longing for normalcy and simplicity in the face of new extraordinary complexities and uncertainties. This nostalgic wish for a return to a mythic pre-9/11 state of innocence was captured in the lyrics to Alan Jackson's popular country western song "Where Were You? (When the World Stopped Turning)":

> I'm just a singer of simple songs I'm not a real political man/ I watch CNN but
>
> I'm not sure I can tell you/The difference between Iraq and Iran/13

William Hart's essay, "The Country Connection," explores in depth the relation of country music to the crisis of 9/11, but suffice it for now to say that if American country music has always celebrated the suffering of ordinary working-class heroes, Jackson's song elevates the image of an apolitical, geographically challenged American Innocent to the level of gospel. At the same time, the commercial success of Jackson's recording spurred controversy over whether it was ethical for anyone—an individual or corporation—to reap profit from the tragedy of 9/11.

Controversy erupted again in the summer of 2002 when the high-tech company Motorola released its annual report to stockholders.

The report featured a photograph of two New York firefighters posing with the company's radios prominently displayed. That photo sparked outraged reactions from some New York firefighters. Jennifer Weyrauch, Motorola's spokeswoman, was surprised by this angry response. "It was done in a respectful way," she claimed in an interview with the radio news program *Marketplace*.[14] Weyrauch claimed that the photo was not intended as an advertisement, but as a tribute to the New York City Fire Department, one of Motorola's biggest customers. Unmoved by Motorola's defense, New York City firefighters called the company's use of the photo "a disgrace and an offense." Some held the company partially responsible for the death of firefighters during the rescue mission at the World Trade Center. A malfunction with Motorola's radios allegedly made it impossible to hear the evacuation calls that were radioed to firefighters inside the North Tower when it became clear that the structure was going to collapse. Motorola's spokesperson denied such allegations, insisting that there was simply no way to know if the radios had failed, especially given the magnitude of the event. Nevertheless, the photograph aroused suspicion that Motorola had co-opted firefighters in an effort to protect stockholder investments. The photo suggested that Motorola was responsible for saving lives at Ground Zero instead of possibly jeopardizing lives due to defects in their product line.

Hisham Tawfiq, one of the firefighters featured in the Motorola photo, defended the company. The quarrel between Motorola and some firefighters was perplexing to him. In fact, he claimed, it was the New York City fire department headquarters that asked him to do the photo shoot, not Motorola. Moreover, as for the alleged radio malfunction, Tawfig insisted that firefighters had always had problems with them not working well in certain environments. Finally, with so many companies trying to cash in on September 11, Tawfig argued that Motorola's actions could hardly be considered offensive. "I didn't get a dime out of it," he said. "If you're going to point the finger at Motorola, you gotta look at all these other companies that are using firefighters in their ads nowadays, you know jumping on the 9/11 thing, and trying to profit from that also."[15]

Tawfiq had a point. Hailed as America's true heroes in the wake of the attacks, New York firefighters provided American advertisers with the symbolic capital necessary to market products across social and racial boundaries, to target consumers of various market demographics. As urban, working-class hero, the New York City firefighter embodied the political and cultural consensus that was temporarily mobilized by the attacks. In the aftermath of 9/11, this mobilization involved the coming together of various social classes, races, ethnicities, and nationalities into a heterogeneous bloc, created in a sudden and dramatic way by a shared experience of loss, shock, and grief. In this sense, the victims of the World Trade Center attack, unlike the largely noncivilian victims of the Pentagon, could be envisaged as a microcosm of America's multicultural society itself. Of course, such an image obscured real differences of social condition and income level. But for the moment, at least, we could claim that terrorism did not discriminate between office managers and elevator operators, firemen and waitresses, artists and accountants. Nor did terrorism discriminate between legal and illegal immigrants; Hispanics and Asians; Jews and Muslims (although in the days following the attacks, citizens across the nation would discriminate with a vengeance). Although fleeting and never fully stable, the attacks had the effect of creating a tremendous degree of consensual equilibrium between the majority of American social and cultural groups. The power represented in this equilibrium would find embodiment in the figure of the firefighter, a supreme cultural symbol of unity, patriotic courage, and willingness to risk one's own safety for the overall benefit of the nation.

Moreover, as post-9/11 working-class American icon, the firefighter represents a persevering, indefatigable American masculinity. The firefighter image in post-9/11 advertising and mass culture became an important object through which the nation was encouraged to seek compensation for a terrorist act that by its very nature would suggest, even to a non-Freudian, castration of national proportions. In her analysis of the World War II film *The Best Years of Our Lives*, critic Kaja Silverman says that there are historical events of such traumatic magnitude that a nation's men temporarily lose faith in their ability to function as men, and by extension lose faith in the national myths and ideals that bestow their sense of manhood to begin with. When this happens, men experience a crisis of faith so profound that they withdraw their belief in the nation.[16] This concept of historical trauma is useful, I think, in understanding the symbolic meanings that became attached to firefighters in the wake of 9/11. Moreover, the concept allows us to imagine the collective ramifications of individual psychic or physiological shock. In post-9/11 America, marketing strategies and advertising images have played a major role in reaffirming faith in masculinity, and by extension in the nation itself. In the aftermath of 9/11, there was an immediate need to resuscitate masculine confidence as the nation prepared to launch a war in Afghanistan. Thus, the proliferation of advertising images of firefighters and emergency rescue workers cannot be thought apart from collective loss of faith in national myths and cultural efforts to sustain confidence in the coherence of the national body, with heterosexual masculinity as its best line of defense.

At the same time, the firefighter has taken on weight as a symbol of confusion and ambivalence about how much we can—or should—realistically expect of American men in a time of national crisis. Alongside photographic images of firefighters standing atop mountains of steel debris, gallantly hoisting the American flag, some of the most widely circulated (and marketed) images of 9/11 depict firefighters emotionally embracing one another and fighting back tears during memorial services following the attacks. These images, many of them included in commemorative photography books such as *In the Line of Duty: A Tribute to New York's Finest and Bravest*, complicate the category of classic American masculinity.[17] They indicate a willingness to portray a breakdown of masculinity, to reveal the vulnerable humanity that masculine behavior often conceals; at the same time these photographs vigorously reaffirm the adequacy of the American male by consecrating images of those debris-covered, shell-shocked, uniformed "heroes" who were prepared to give their lives to protect civilian society. For example, the photograph of Father Mychal Judge, the Franciscan chaplain of the New York City Fire Department, as he is carried from the rubble of the World Trade Center after being killed by falling debris, has been hailed as a modern pieta. This image, widely circulated on the Internet and included in commemorative photography books, has come to symbolize one of the many crucial links between Christianity and nation, American godliness and American patriotism. The revelation that Father Mychal was gay and a vociferous advocate for homosexual rights has not significantly undermined his popular status as national hero and martyr, although it has politicized the movement to have him declared a saint.

As heroic abstraction, the urban firefighter, fortified by his comrades-in-arms, preserved an image of the nation intact not unlike classic American war photography from generations past. However, in the controversy surrounding the design of the $180,000 memorial sculpture based on Thomas E. Franklin's image of three firefighters raising the American flag at Ground Zero (an image noted for its striking resemblance to the World War II image of six marines raising the flag at Iwo Jima), it became evident that images and myths of the nation's past are inadequate to defining who we are today as a nation, or even more importantly, how we wish to see ourselves. When a clay model of the bronze sculpture was unveiled on December 21, 2001, the three white firefighters of Franklin's photograph had been replaced with one white, one African American, and one Hispanic firefighter. In this way, the ritual consumption of images consecrating the firefighter, heir to the American masculine ideal, became part of the collective process of reimagining social relationships and relations across axes of national power, race, ethnicity, and sexuality. And nowhere in American mass culture was this more apparent than in NBC's popular medical drama, *ER*, which shortly after 9/11 introduced a new character who was a firefighter, a woman, a Latina, *and* a lesbian. In this way, Lieutenant Sandy Lopez became part of the commercial commemoration and reimagining of national identity and heroism in the wake of 9/11, a process by which myths of the past are being rewritten to accommodate new possibilities.

Still the trauma of 9/11 is in large part the trauma of having been abandoned by our fathers, who were unable to prevent the attacks from occurring. The ritual consumption of firefighter images became part of a process of mending the relations between current and future generations, or between the heroic fathers who lost their lives in the attacks and the child-citizens whose futures would now be protected from the violence of terrorism and Radical Islam. Major television networks were quick to exploit the infantile aspects of this emotional framing of the attacks, banking on narratives of oedipal displacement that fashioned George W. Bush as the nation's patriarchal protector, and compensatory narratives of paternal continuity. One of the more sensational examples in this mode of popular programming was "The Babies of 9/11," a production of ABC's evening news magazine, *Primetime Thursday*. The program's host, Diane Sawyer, brought together the widows who had given birth to babies since the deaths of their husbands on 9/11. All in all, sixty-one women participated in the program with sixty-three babies (including two sets of twins).[18] The first part of the program was broadcast on December 20, 2001, with a follow-up segment broadcast on August 29, 2002. The stated goal of the first installment was to gather all of the babies together at the Brooklyn Botanical Garden for a group photograph. According to the follow-up show's promotional copy, the inevitable chaos of trying to "corral 63 infants" would result in "an hour-long show that is full of laughter—and tears." The stated purpose of the follow-up investigation was to revisit these newly single mothers in anticipation of the one-year anniversary of the attacks and find out "how they are coping and whether they've come to terms with their loss and anger."[19]

While the alleged purpose of "The Babies of 9/11" was to offer emotional solace in the face of a national crisis of fatherly loss and defeat, the television news magazine edition was most striking as a staging of anxiety from the nation's collective unconscious. Visually, "The Babies of 9/11" amounted to a spectacle of primordial pandemonium. In the first segment, infants transformed the elegant conservatory at the Brooklyn Botanical Garden into an orgy of cries, shrieks, and gurgles as babies grabbed at one another, chewed on their blankets, crawled persistently out of their designated positions, and passed out on the floor. Cameras highlighted the fast-motion footage of mothers and producers running back and forth, trying to catch the infants and make them sit still for the photo. This comedy of disorderliness, when finally resolved, produced the long-awaited group shot along with the ideal visual metaphor for our national post-9/11 dilemma: "The Babies of 9/11" marketed the poetry of Paradise Regained, heterosexual family life salvaged, and paternal continuity in the face of national tragedy. To emphasize this, interviews with widows about their lost husbands were framed by images of the dead fathers alongside those of their newborn children. These images were juxtaposed to highlight physical resemblances, the passing on of paternal legacies, in an attempt to maintain faith in the solvency of familial—and national—unity.

Red, White, and Wal-Mart

Of the many patriotic commodities that have profited 9/11 merchants, the most ubiquitous and abused has been our own national trademark, "old glory," the American flag.[20] According to published statistics, the total amount of American flag sales in 2001 reached $51.7 million, a record profit. Ironically, according to the same statistics, 67 percent of those flags were manufactured in China, but there is no way to accurately gauge the extent to which this mattered to the consumers who purchased them in record numbers.

What seemed to matter most was participation in the collective compulsion to display the flag, to present it to the public as part of your own unique post-9/11 fashion sense. And Jennifer Scanlon's essay on the nation's largest and most powerful retailer points to the fact that when Americans went shopping for flags they turned to Wal-Mart, which sold 116,000 American flags on September 11, 2001.

The irony here is that in their rush to participate, Americans fashioned their individual patriotisms in precisely the same way: by consuming mass-produced American flag kitsch. In cities and towns, large and small, across the United States, one did not have to look far to find some form of American flag on bold display: merchants adorned their shop windows with flag stickers in order to showcase their unity with the heroes of 9/11, to signal that their businesses are not immigrant-owned, or to demonstrate that immigrant-owned businesses are just as American as any. Commercial, government, and educational web sites exhibited the flag on their home pages. American flag magnets and computer mouse pads adorned file cabinets and work cubicles in offices from Los Angeles to Bangor. After the 9/11 attacks, the four major television networks, ABC, CBS, NBC, and FOX, restyled their network logos, usually visible as transparent fixtures at the bottom corner of the screen, to resemble the stars and stripes pattern, some adding red, white, and blue coloring despite the visual distraction that it imposed. Television talk-show hosts, news anchors, reporters, and even characters on prime time serial dramas and comedies began wearing discrete American flag lapel pins, red, white, and blue brooches, or articles of clothing emblazoned with the flag's trace. Clothing retailers produced shirts, jeans, sweaters, outerwear, sportswear, athletic shoes, and all manner of accessories with American flag patterns and imprints. Top name designers followed the trend, particularly as American consumers began to show a disdain for upscale designer logos in the wake of the attacks, and replaced their own signatures with American flag replica symbols. 9/11 became a fashion event. And American patriots became flag *fashionistas*. Flag-wear became the rage, as it was when, on March 24, 1991, the *Chicago Tribune Magazine* featured the Gulf War as fodder for personal self-expression in a style section titled, "Red, White, and You."[21] In post-9/11 America, these colors underwent a similar cultural remixing in relationship to citizens who are to be addressed strictly as consumers. Marketers depended on the flag for patriotic window advertising, a strategy that invites consumers to become participants in a fashion trend. This strategy effectively empties the flag of any overt political signification and redefines it as a symbol of style and choice, the two key ingredients of marketing success.

In the year following 9/11, on the dirt roads, side streets, and major highways of America, it remained nearly impossible to find a car, SUV, or truck that did not sport an American flag decal on its rear bumper or windshield. Some drivers amplified the effect by attaching plastic flags to their aerial antennas. Some decals were captioned with the words "United We Stand" or the less welcoming, "Stand Back." But despite these choices, which create the appearance of self-expression, the flag auto decal craze represented above all a fantasy of American consensus that denied social as well as political differences. That the driver of a Lexus luxury sedan could just as easily depend on a flag decal for nonpolemical self-expression as the driver of a Plymouth Breeze suggests that patriotic kitsch functions less as a statement of national solidarity than as a capitulation to conformity, with a gag order on expressions of democratic dissent. The flag decal recasts patriotism as a question not of political leaning or political passion but of proper public presentation that proclaims: "I'll wear what they're wearing." In this way, consuming and presenting the flag decal becomes virtually synonymous with pledging one's allegiance to a prepackaged form of silence. Speech, or its illusion, is contained in the fast lane and framed within the context of patriotism-to-go.

In claiming that the American flag functions in such cases less as an expression of national identity than as a national trademark, I am assuming that American patriotism, like American commercialism itself, is based on an illusion of unlimited resources. The transformation of the flag into a national-corporate logo is founded primarily on resistance to the possibility that 9/11 might require a rethinking of our limits, our consumption habits, our domestic values, and our global principles. The American flag loudly proclaims, from the bumpers of gas-guzzling SUVs across the nation, that we will defiantly refuse to question ourselves or engage in enlightened self-reflection of any kind. In this context, the flag erupts upon the national scene like a neurotic symptom, a repetition of our hysterical deafness to any criticism or any idea that might get in the way of our rights to unlimited consumption, and our national duty to employ military measures, if necessary, to protect that right.

At the same time, as I have argued throughout this essay, the political economy exerts only a limited control over the meanings that attach to such commodities. Indeed, some consumers have used flag kitsch to express resistance to self-censorship and to prefabricated political consensus, as in the case of drivers who reportedly attached backwards or upside-down American flags to their automobile bumpers. Some car owners recontextualized the meanings of American flag decals by combining them with other decals depicting the flags of other countries. Such gestures indicate once again that advertisers cannot regulate the uses and meanings of commodities, patriotic or otherwise. Just as a Barbie doll may suggest the joys of growing up female in one context and the horrors of distorted female body-image in another, marketers and advertisers can only attempt to direct consumer desires and sympathies by refocusing the dissonance of consumer energies onto unifying concepts as joy, freedom, healing, and heroism.

Closure through Consumption

"The American Dream: We refuse to let anyone take it away from us."[22]

So read the flagrantly exploitative copy for a General Motors television advertisement for interest-free financing on new GM cars and trucks. It provides a compelling example of American advertisers' evocation of the patriotic mystique, not in the interests of combating terrorism or its root causes, but in the interests of beating the economic downturn and the sharp decline in consumer confidence that resulted from the 9/11 attacks. Although referring in this instance to the automobile, a perennial symbol of American independence, mobility, and glamor, the above motto could just as easily be applied to any of the products that have been sold and consumed in the name of commemorating 9/11.

Of course, in reducing 9/11 to a sales pitch, advertisers need to walk a fine line. Nobody wants to seem too eager to profit from the tragedies, and nobody wants to trivialize the attacks, although some cases, such as the GM ad cited above, test the limits of public tolerance. Most advertisers have exercised at least a modicum of cunning in their profiteering. In linking our national economic recovery with our psychic recovery from the trauma of 9/11, some advertisers found a strategy with which to enhance their profit margins and promote an image of their companies as compassionate patriots, humanized by hardship and overcome with fellow-feeling for American consumers. For example, Spirit Airlines, an economy air carrier, devised a special promotion for the one- year anniversary of September 11, a day when it was generally assumed that few Americans would want to fly. In a press release, CEO Jacob Schorr announced that Spirit was ready to say " 'thank you' to the American public and our valuable customers for flying with us throughout this past year."[23] How were they ready to do this? By allowing passengers to fly free of charge anywhere in the continental United States on September 11, 2002. "These free seats are a token of our appreciation," Schorr explained. In addition, he said that a team of Spirit officials would be "on hand" during the anniversary give-away "to shake hands with passengers."[24]

Spirit Airline's "Freedom to Travel" offer received widespread media coverage, something the small company had never previously enjoyed. "These free seats are a token of our appreciation," Schorr explained. With its pledge of free air travel, Spirit thrust itself into the public spotlight, generating what marketing specialists call "branding awareness," or consumer familiarity with a company trademark. The promotional slogan likened commercial air flight to an exercise of patriotic participation. Spirit's largesse had the effect of making its industry competitors seem tight-fisted by comparison, although few major air companies could afford to match the deal. But even more important, Spirit was able to affect the role of a caring corporation—a humane company whose primary concern is to help fellow Americans recover from the emotional and psychological distress of 9/11. Not surprisingly, two days after announcing the "Freedom to Travel" giveaway, Spirit issued another press release with the headline, "Spirit Airlines Strikes Patriotic Chord." This self-congratulatory document amounted to a litany of appreciative statements from customers moved by Spirit's generosity. "You need to hear the praise and joy that has filled my heart," wrote one thankful respondent.[25]

The Spirit promotion provides a forceful example of a motif that became pervasive in post-9/11 marketing, particularly as the United States approached the one year anniversary: the promise of closure through consumption. Here, product promotion was presented as a humanitarian act motivated by nothing less than the benevolent will and power of companies to heal the nation and help us reclaim our once normal, healthy lives. In another such instance of corporate America–as–cure marketing, Miller Brewing Company ran a television advertisement featuring actual handwritten placards from across the United States. These homemade signs expressed sympathy for the victims of the 9/11 attacks. At the conclusion of the tribute, another sign appeared prominently on screen: a huge, Miller Brewing Company logo. The logo, by association, was transformed into a symbol of national unity and respect for the dead. The brazenness of this spot captured the attention of PBS (Public Broadcasting System) commentator John Ridley, who wryly pronounced Miller's ad the practical equivalent of saying: "there's no better way to salute these heroes than by poppin' a cold one."[26]

Back to Normal?

When David Letterman, the popular comedian and host of the late-night television program *The Late Show*, returned to the air on September 18, 2001, it looked for a moment as if the grand proclamations of the previous week might have come true: the world seemed to have changed. Forsaking his usual wry humor, a solemn Letterman began the program by applauding the firefighters, police, emergency rescue workers, and residents of New York City. "If you didn't believe it before, you can believe it now," he asserted. "New York City is absolutely the greatest city on earth." The audience, needless to say, went wild with applause.[27]

Honoring New York City mayor Rudolph Giuliani's request for people to return to their normal activities following the previous week's attacks, Letterman sat at his desk and asked the audience for their "indulgence" as he struggled for words. "If we're going to continue to do shows, I need to hear myself talk for a few minutes," he said. "We've lost 5,000 New Yorkers . . . and it's terribly sad."[28] Accordingly, Letterman continued with the evening lineup of guests, beginning with CBS television news anchorman Dan Rather. Rather broke into tears as he recalled first learning of the plane crashes. He spoke of his role in the news coverage of the attacks, clutching Letterman's hand across his desk. The second guest of the evening was Regis Philbin, the celebrity host of the morning talk show *Live With Regis and Kelly*. In keeping with the solemn tone of the evening, Philbin first talked about how the attacks had touched him personally. His son, an employee at the U.S. Pentagon, had been sitting in his office talking on the phone with his father about the World Trade Center attacks when the plane crashed into his building. Since his office was on the opposite side of the complex, he was able to escape unharmed. Later in the show, when Letterman asked him if his former co-host, Kathy Lee Gifford, would ever return to the morning talk show, Philbin proposed that the military send her to Afghanistan to exact swift and thorough revenge. "You want a quick end to this," he clowned, "send Kathy Lee over there."[29]

I have summarized a few select moments from this broadcast of *The Late Show* because in them we find the disparate threads that form the tightly stitched fabric of 9/11's marketing: a pious populism celebrated alongside a panel of media elite; self-congratulatory indulgence barely contained by a chastened humility; ritual misogyny and myths of paternal legacy alongside the public spectacle of masculine emotional release between corporate comrades-in-arms; an exhortation to move forward framed by an exhortation to return to an earlier condition of normality. Indeed, as singular event, this *The Late Show* broadcast has come to represent an important moment in the cultural memory of 9/11. For millions of American television viewers who had witnessed a near-complete suspension of the relentless glut and blurt of American commercial broadcasting in the week following the attacks, David Letterman's introspective address, the catharsis performed by his guests (two of the most powerful figures in the news and entertainment corporate industry structure) signaled permission to resume "normal activity." But what on earth could "normal" mean in this context? It certainly could not have meant a return to normal work (indeed, unlike David Letterman, most working Americans had remained at their jobs uninterruptedly during and after the attacks), nor had it signaled a return to normal television viewing, for indeed Americans had done little else but watch television for the entire week following 9/11. Rather what it meant was the resumption of consumer activities, or the uninhibited pursuit of pleasure that marks us as American citizens.

This message was clearly communicated to the American public in the months following 9/11, as official Bush administration statements placed consumer obligation and comfort above historical awareness and at the center of a recovery of national strength, thus linking the redemptive promise of commodities with that of the nation. George W. Bush himself became an unlikely celebrity mouthpiece for the airline and travel industries, which experienced dramatic declines in revenue. Surrounded by uniformed airline employees threatened with job loss, Bush issued a direct appeal to the American public to toss caution to the winds and take the family on a Disney vacation. However, his invitation to forget the trauma of 9/11 by recourse to a Disney-fied version of national normalcy did not effectively abrogate history so much as transplant it to the fashioning of consumer lifestyle practices that replace critical awareness with populist renouncements of history's interruption of pleasure and privilege.

Now, nearly four years after the fact, Americans have begun to exhibit symptoms of "9/11 fatigue," which I believe is less evidence of a limited national attention span than a condition of mental and emotional exhaustion resulting from incessant bingeing and manipulation of evocations of national catastrophe, warnings of future threats, a drawn-out Iraqi military occupation with no visible endpoint, and the continued erosion of civil rights in a fear-saturated, surveillance-obsessed political climate. Moreover, there are signs that the Bush team's overreliance on what Thomas Foster, in the volume's closing essay, calls "cynical nationalism," may be backfiring. Although polls suggest that national support for Bush's "war on terrorism" remains relatively high, his overall job approval ratings slipped significantly and consistently during the summer months leading into the 2004 election, as Americans returned their attentions to domestic issues. And four months after his re-election, a *Newsweek* poll conducted on March 17–18, 2005 shows 48 percent of those canvassed disapprove of the way Bush is handling his job as President, while only 45 percent approve.[30] There is less of a sense of compulsory consensus among citizens on the proper response to 9/11, as declining support for continuation of the USA. PATRIOT Act suggests, and skepticism about the intelligence used to justify the Iraqi war continues to resonate across the nation, as it appears conclusive that no weapons of mass destruction will ever be found. And while it may be too early to fully calculate the impact of September 11, 2001, on U.S. patterns of marketing and consumption, one thing seems clear: the narcissistic wound of September 11—much like the instant in which the mythical Narcissus confronts his watery image—reflected the nation's image back to itself and yet in that moment of self-admiration it became something else. In psychoanalytic writings, the subject of the narcissistic wound exists oddly outside of time, suspended between being and vanishing. And if narcissism has a collective moment in history, it would be a moment similarly suspended in a moment of crisis. Indeed, the moment of narcissism is the moment of trauma, a trauma locked outside of history and time. For this reason, I find that the naming of the event that provides the foundation of this book—"9/11"—as the date of a historical occurrence, is actually a misnaming, a disavowal. In the same sense that Freud understood the enigmatic temporality of war trauma, 9/11 does not belong to past time. Rather, in *Beyond the Pleasure Principle*, Freud claimed that trauma by its very nature exists in the present, insinuating itself into the current moment in place of any immediate experience.[31] Our own experience and vision is blocked by a kind of memory that is not a recollection but a repetition.

The selling of 9/11, as the following essays will show, mime these psychic operations at a social and national level, compulsively interrupting consumers' own experiences with fantasies of desire—the desire for the nation itself—that exists, as myth itself exists, outside of historical time. The selling of 9/11 ensures that the past will be repeated instead of remembered, that the moment of self-reflection, in the commodity form, will function as a disavowal of anything we might not want to see. And it is here that the murky pool of advertising presents itself to citizen-consumers, offering an idealized image of our unshakable national resolve. And it is here, in the idealized fashioning of a perpetual now, that national trauma is transformed into a contractual obligation to congratulate and reward ourselves. We have congratulated our heroes who gave their lives to us; we have congratulated our leaders to whom we give support; and, above all, we have congratulated ourselves simply for being American. But when all is said and done, perhaps the most remarkable thing about U.S. consumer culture after 9/11 is how much it resembles the consumer culture we said goodnight to on September 10, 2001. In a country where patriotism and consumerism are our mutual obligations, the selling of 9/11 would appear to be no more and no less than the latest repackaging of confidence that U.S. marketers, investors, and consumers have long relied upon as we hedge our futures against the limits of a nation that acknowledges none.

Notes

1. Elisabeth Bumiller, "Traces of Terror: The Strategy; Bush Aides Set Strategy to Sell Policy on Iraq," *New York Times*, electronic edition, September 7, 2002. http://www.nytimes.com/2002/09/07/politics/07STRA.html.

2. Ibid.

3. Stuart Ewen, *All Consuming Images: The Politics of Style in Contemporary Culture*. Revised edition (New York: Basic Books, 1988, 1999), p. 268.

4. Such films would include *The Day After Tomorrow* and *The Manchurian Candidate*, neither of which, according to op-ed contributor Jon Margolis, would likely influence public opinion in the long term. See "Box Office Campaigns," *New York Times*, electronic edition, Tuesday, August 17, 2004. http://www.nytimes.com/. (August 18, 2004).

5. Lauren Berlant and Elizabeth Freeman, "Queer Nationality," in *Fear of a Queer Planet*, Michael Warner, ed. (London and Minneapolis: University of Minnesota Press, 1993), 193–229. Citation is from pp. 194–95.

6. Tom Shales, "Anniversary Market: Recalling Tragedy The American Way," *Washington Post*, Thursday, August 29, 2002, p. COI. http://www.iht.com/articles/69763.html. (October 15, 2002).

7. Wyatt Mason, "The Holes In His Head." The New Republic Online. Issue date: September 27, 2004. Post date: September 21, 2004. (Accessed: December 11, 2004.)

8. SunSpot.Net. Source: *Baltimore Sun*, September 11, 2002. http://www.sunspot.net/. (October 15, 2002).

9. "Auction Site Pulls Tower Items," *Wired News*. http://www.wired.com/news/print/0,1294,46736,00.html. (March 21, 2005).

10. Ibid.

11. Ibid.

12. Jean Baudrillard *Selected Writings* (Cambridge: Polity, 1988).

13. Alan Jackson, "Where Were You (When the World Stopped Turning?)," EMI Music/Tri-Angels Music (ASCAP), 2001. http://www.alanjackson.com/cma2001.html. (December 4, 2002).

14. Sam Eaton, "Marketplace," American Public Radio, broadcast Thursday, April 25, 2002. http://marketplace.org/shows/2002/04/25_mpp.html. (December 4, 2002).

15. Ibid.

16. Kaja Silverman, *Male Subjectivity at the Margins* (New York and London: Routledge, 1992), 65–90.

17. *In the Line of Duty: A Tribute to New York's Finest and Bravest* (New York: Regan Books, 2001).

18. According to the *Primetime* web site, this number represented roughly half of the babies born to 9/11 widows. http://abcnews.go.com/sections/primetime/DailyNews/wtc_year_babies_020829.html.

19. "Diane Sawyer Rallies the Widows of 9/11," ET Television: Entertainment Tonight Online, August 29, 2002. http://www.etonline.com/television/a12057.html. (December 4, 2002).

20. SunSpot.Net. Source: *Baltimore Sun*, September 11, 2002. http://www.sunspot.net/. (October 15, 2002).

21. Cited in Berlant and Freeman, "Queer Nationality," 194.

22. John Ridley, "Commentary: John Ridley and the Merchants of Doom," *Now with Bill Moyers*, PBS. http://www.pbs.org/now/commentary/ridley. (October 15, 2002).

23. Thomas Mucha, "Marketing 9/11," Business 2.0: Marketing Focus, AOL Personal Finance, August 15, 2002. http://www.business2.com/articles/web/0,1653,42954,FF.html. (December 4, 2002).

24. Thomas Mucha, "Marketing 9/11," Business 2.0: Marketing Focus, AOL Personal Finance, August 15, 2002. http://www.business2.com/articles/web/ 0,1653,42954,FF.html. (December 4, 2002).
25. Ibid.
26. Ridley, "Commentary."
27. Lillian Kim, " 'Late Show,' 'PI' Make Emotional Return," CNN.com/ Entertainment, September 18, 2001. http://www8.cnn.com/2001/SHOWBIZ/ TV/09/17/gen.letterman.return/. (October 23, 2002).
28. Ibid.
29. Ibid.
30. Polling Report.com. *Newsweek* poll conducted by Princeton Survey Research Associates International. March 17–18, 2005. http://www.pollingreport.com/ BushJob.htm. (Accessed: March 22, 2005).
31. Sigmund Freud, *Beyond the Pleasure Principle* (New York and London: W.W. Norton, 1990).

Chapter 2
Wounded Nation, Broken Time

James Trimarco and Molly Hurley Depret

Introduction

The day was rainy and damp. The mournful melody of "America the Beautiful" emanated from the flute of a lone musician, while a few vendors sold packets of World Trade Center pictures from makeshift tables over public garbage cans. Visitors wandered vacantly past large plaques showing scenes of the World Trade Center being built in stages over time. More interesting were the comments people had written on these plaques—dedications to lost friends, condolences to the city, or urgings toward war. One figure, who we'll call John, drew our attention as he began to loudly point out the exact spot where each of the seven World Trade Center buildings used to stand. A small crowd of tourists and New Yorkers gathered around this former WTC tour guide, desperate for some vision of what the site once held. Because of the spatial confusion caused by sixteen acres of empty space, many people found it difficult to imagine just how the towers stood. How tall were they, really? Where did they stand? How did it feel to walk between them?

A businessman, Matthew, who had worked on the eighty-first floor of the North Tower, stood there listening in silence. After a few minutes he began to speak, lamenting to John that he could no longer remember the halls, stores, and corridors through which he had once traversed daily. "Close your eyes," said John. The crowd looked on as he became a very different sort of tour guide. Matthew almost seemed to enter a trance as he listened to John's photographic recollections of the various hallways, elevators, and shops. "You're getting out of the train," he said. "Now, you're stepping onto the escalator that takes you to the shopping mall. You turn right and see the little coffee place at the corner. Did you used to buy your newspapers there?" Like a Virgil to Matthew's Dante, he played the spirit guide, leading him through a place he could not go alone. Through his stories, he offered a method of healing; guided revisualization of the towers helped visitors to treat this wound on the city's landscape that also afflicted their own minds and memories. This example reveals how trauma and memory help to form people's desire to visit the former World Trade Center site. This chapter will discuss how a similar but much broader dynamic helps create a desire for the site in the minds of many Americans who had little or no personal connection with the World Trade Center.

If larger stories about American history help create a desire to visit Ground Zero, they also create desire among visitors for memories of their trip. Although many dismiss the plastic World Trade Center snow globes and NYPD T-shirts sold around the site as tacky trinkets, it is also true that visitors associate these items with the unique feeling of world-historical *mana* that penetrates Ground Zero. This gives these souvenirs an aura of their own that derives from the place they were purchased. A World Trade Center snow globe bought in Kansas and the same item bought in lower Manhattan are fundamentally different in this sense. As we will demonstrate, such commodities take their value from the larger commodity that is Ground Zero itself. According to Walter Benjamin, part of what granted an object an aura of exceptionality was "its presence in time and space, its unique existence at the place where it happens to be."[1] Our research expands this notion into the practices of tourist consumption, and shows that the object itself need not be unique as long as it was purchased in a sufficiently extraordinary place. Alternatively, for some people visiting the site and purchasing the object there may not be necessary; items from such a site are sold easily on eBay, as Mick Broderick and Mike Gibson describe in this volume.

At Ground Zero, that sense of exceptionality appeared in many forms. We saw it in the media coverage of September 11 and the subsequent patterns of New York tourism. We also saw it in the responses of Ground Zero visitors whom we observed and interviewed in the course of ethnographic research carried out between February and June 2002. Two key themes about Ground Zero's uniqueness consistently appeared in both of these: first, that America experienced September 11 as a national trauma, and second, that flows of time and history were interrupted or stopped. Trauma, time, and history are all tropes that help to construct the paradox at the heart of this essay: How is it that a space widely perceived as sacred is mired in processes of commodification so deep that it becomes a commodity itself? Though this analysis cannot claim to be comprehensive, we seek to outline the ways in which narratives of trauma and history suffuse the former World Trade Center site with a unique aura, and to discuss how this aura interacts with local commercial processes.

Trauma and Historical Consciousness

Noted actor Morgan Freeman, who starred in the terrorism thriller *The Sum of All Fears*, raised a minor controversy in the summer of 2002 when he said that he didn't consider September 11 a "national trauma." In response to a question from a movie critic asking whether Americans were ready for a film about terrorism, Freeman responded with the following statement: "We had a trauma, but it's really not a national trauma. If you were not in New York on September 11, what you saw was an event on CNN."[2] Freeman argues that the effects of September 11 were contained within a particular time and space; in other words, you had to be there. Underlying this argument is the belief that television viewing is not the same as lived experience, so that one who is a witness to an event only through television can make no claim to have experienced that event. On one level, this is undeniably true. Television, radio, and electronic mediums mediate between realities separated spatially and temporally. Yet, in certain cases, the viewing of events through a medium becomes the experience itself.

In recent historical memory most Americans (and others) experienced both the assassination of President Kennedy and the explosion of the Challenger space shuttle as televised tragedies. Media critics Marita Sturken and Lisa Cartwright remind us that "the networks covered the events surrounding Kennedy's death and his funeral over many days with uninterrupted television coverage, making the events a public spectacle and creating an opportunity for mass-mediated participation in the ritual of mourning."[3] Interpreting television viewing as a "ritual of mourning" problematizes the belief that one has to immediately witness events to be affected by them and to thereby have a right to claim victim status. Likewise, we would argue that such a viewpoint was reflected in the U.S. media's immediate extrapolation of traumatized victimhood onto the entire American nation.

In general, most newspapers and television stations labeled the event a national trauma without hesitation or explanation. Much of what has been written about the attacks assumes that the attacks formed a "wound" on the collective psyche of *all* Americans, causing trauma and requiring particular sorts of healing. This framing of September 11 opens the possibility that one need not literally witness an event for it to be traumatic. Yet it is crucial to ask how and why this event was represented as a "national" trauma. Was this a crass political maneuver to create a sense of exclusive nationalism? Or does the dispersal of "trauma" democratize mourning, allowing more people to claim a connection to the site and to feelings of collective loss?

We feel that issues of time and history are central to an understanding of why so many people felt traumatized by the events of September 11 and came to visit Ground Zero in the months that followed. Many media pundits, politicians, and ordinary people agreed that history was forever changed by the deaths of thousands on American soil. They are correct in that tragedies involving thousands of deaths have rarely occurred on American soil, and the number narrows down to a handful when we include only attacks perpetrated by foreign elements. September 11 seems to be in a class by itself, or perhaps with Pearl Harbor, of sudden American tragedies after which history is ostensibly "changed forever." As we will show, the event was isolated in discourse as a traumatic event that shook the nation and altered the course of history.[4] At the same time the former site of the towers, the literal space of trauma, was dubbed "Ground Zero," a term that itself refers to change, disruption, and a break with what has come before: "the point directly above, below, or at which a nuclear explosion occurs; the center or origin of rapid, intense, or violent activity or change; the very beginning: SQUARE ONE."[5] "Ground Zero," then, is defined as the beginning of something new—nothing in the past is entirely relevant to the reality that we find there.

A similar idea crops up again with the notion of trauma, which many psychologists consider to be a disorder in the experience of time. If we keep this in mind, it becomes less difficult to understand the intertwining of the themes of trauma and historical discontinuity that we find in writings about September 11. Later in this chapter we will show some of the ways in which a belief in September 11 as a point of historical crisis and trauma is deeply connected with commodification practices at Ground Zero, which, ironically, are condemned by the same groups that emphasized these themes in the first place. However, before we move on to do that, we need to examine more closely how these themes were articulated concerning Ground Zero.

Constructing a National Trauma

On September 12, 2001, ABCnews.com published "Blow to the Psyche: Americans Will React With Fear, Anger—Danger for Some."[6] According to this article, the destruction of the World Trade Center had already been dubbed an "Attack on America" and journalists were seeking the advice of mental health specialists concerning its effects on America's "psyche." One specialist cited in this article argued that "the trauma of the tragedy will be hard to escape regardless of physical distance from the wreckage in New York or Washington D.C. People who saw it or were part of it will obviously experience some trauma. . . . [T]rauma is experienced vicariously by those who are some distance away."[7] The American Psychological Association (APA) even published an online brochure, "Coping with Terrorism," which stated that affected persons can include "people who experience traumatization from learning of relatives, friends, and acquaintances who were subject to the violence, or from exposure to repeated media accounts of the trauma."[8] An October 8, 2001, report from Intelihealth.com noted that many Americans were finding it difficult to concentrate after watching repeated images of the planes crashing into the World Trade Center towers.[9] They cited a series of recent studies (unrelated to September 11) from a team of University of Essex experimental psychologists, led by Elaine Fox. According to the studies, "anxious people have trouble disengaging their attention from threatening visual images." We cite these studies and media reports not to argue that Americans were traumatized through television, but to show that Americans far from New York City or Washington, D.C., were already being labeled "traumatized" even before psychologists had had time to determine whether there was trauma among the immediate witnesses. These quotes evidence some psychologists' belief in "vicarious" trauma and the media's central role in disseminating and validating this form of trauma.

Roxane Cohen Silver of the University of California at Irvine conducted the most popularly cited study about the effects of indirectly "witnessing" the events of 9/11.[10] She and a team of other researchers developed a survey instrument to test for September 11–related symptoms of "acute stress, posttraumatic stress, and global distress."[11] They were already doing Internet-based research with several thousand people and thus knew "their mental and physical health histories."[12] Their survey was administered via the Internet to 3,496 participants who did not live in New York City, two months and six months after the tragic incidents. From the 2,729 who returned the survey the authors generalized the following results:

> Seventeen percent of the US population outside of New York City reported symptoms of September 11–related posttraumatic stress 2 months after the attacks; 5.8% did so at 6 months. High levels of posttraumatic stress symptoms were associated with female sex . . . marital separation . . . pre–September 11 physician-diagnosed depression or anxiety disorder.[13]

It is important to note that studies such as Dr. Silver's actually help construct the trauma that they claim to be measuring; while they did not *create* the trauma, they re-defined it to include people who did not directly witness it. Both WebMD, a popular healthcare web site, and a September 2002 National Science Foundation press release quoted Dr. Silver's statement that "[t]his investigation demonstrates that the effects of a major national trauma are not limited to those directly affected by it, and the degree of response cannot be predicted simply by objective measures of exposure to, or loss from, the trauma."[14,15] Dr. Silver's study and her statements are fascinating because they reveal that some psychologists were willing to include Americans who were very distant from downtown Manhattan that day. Seventeen percent of Americans stating that they are experiencing symptoms of PTSD should give us pause. How is it that these long-distance "witnesses" appear to share many of the same symptoms with those who witnessed the attacks in real life?

To answer this question we must examine the notion of "trauma," one of the most complex and strangely ideological features in current psychological and popular circulation.[16] According to Allan Young's exhaustive genealogy of Post-Traumatic Stress Syndrome (PTSS), trauma as we know it is also relatively recent: it only began to be used in anything like its modern sense during the last few decades of the nineteenth century. Before this time, the word indicated a physical wound. Moving through a series of interesting intermediary phases, the concept of trauma slowly became more psychological and less physical, particularly in regards to the etiology of the condition. In the case of John Erichsen's 1866 study of "railway spine," for instance, neurological damage stemming from train collisions was thought to cause the onset of illness several days after the accident. But other medical men such as Herbert Page and Jean-Martin Charcot criticized Erichsen for attributing a purely physical etiology to railway spine and argued that extreme fright alone was in many cases enough to damage the organism.[17]

At the same time as these late-nineteenth-century scholars were developing a relationship between psychological and neurological damage, another school of practitioners produced an idea that would become deeply merged with it. This was the idea of the "pathogenic secret," a memory with the power to cause bodily harm. Beginning with the work of Ribot and moving on through Janet and Freud, by the time of 1914 "a number of medical men working in Europe and North America were familiar with the idea that the memory of an experience can produce syndromes resembling hysterical and neurological disorders."[18] While these ideas generated only moderate interest prior to 1914, hundreds of thousands of shell shock cases after the First World War brought about a flurry of publications about postwar traumatic symptoms. These publications generally agreed that the traumatic event had to be so extreme as to be located permanently outside of normal memory, time, and experience—an idea with profound implications for a notion of "national trauma" stemming from the attacks at Ground Zero.

These theories devised around the time of the First World War have remained the basic framework for thinking about trauma until recent times. The notion of being "traumatized" as a kind of harm caused by witnessing violence or abuse has picked up considerable legal and popular currency especially since the 1960s and onward. However, despite a consistent record of publishing on the topic since the time of the First World War, the condition was only officially registered as an independent psychological disease in the third edition of the Diagnostic and Statistical Manual of Mental Disorders (DSM), published in 1980. Before that time it tended to be mixed diagnostically with conditions such as hysteria. After the military debacle and mass unpopularity of the Vietnam War, however, a group of scholars combined the political momentum of the antiwar movement with a slew of new studies on trauma and pushed successfully to have PTSS recognized officially as a separate disorder.[19]

The DSM defines the traumatic experience as involving the following two features:

> Feature 1:   The traumatized person experienced, witnessed, or was confronted with an event or events involving death (either actual or threatened) or serious injury (including threats to the physical integrity of oneself or others). To be "confronted" with traumatic events would include "learning about unexpected or violent death, serious harm, or threat of death or injury experienced by a family member or other close associate."

> Feature 2:   The traumatized person's response to these events involved intense fear, helplessness, or horror.[20]

We ask to what extent those traumatized by September 11 meet the criteria of the definition above. Certainly those who were in downtown Manhattan on that day witnessed many deaths, an experience upon which the first feature hinges. But the extrapolation of this kind of trauma outside of downtown Manhattan involves a reassessment of two key words: "witnessing" and "close associate." Does the television viewing of an event thousands of miles away count as "witnessing" in the same way as the more traditional sort of witnessing through one's own eyes? Similarly, who is a close associate? Must they be a family member or friend, or is the sharing of nationality enough to generate the traumatic response? What about the fear, helplessness, and horror of the second feature? Is fear mediated through the television equally or even comparably as traumatic as a fear invoked by one's immediate surroundings?

To begin to answer these questions we must look to the powerful technologies that help shape Americans' thoughts.[21] At times, elite groups pursuing economic and political goals can manipulate these technologies, playing upon older, already established modes of thought, and particularly on nationalism. The case of President Bush offers an especially clear example of how national sentiment can be manipulated. In a section of CNN.com entitled "America Remembers," a journalist argues that "[a]s a president, Bush found his voice, outlining a battle of good vs. evil and vowing in stark, impassioned terms to win the war on terrorism."[22] A policy analyst from the conservative think tank The Heritage Foundation chimed in, claiming that "[b]asically, we're looking at a wartime president now." While the reelection possibilities for a "war-time president" were surely not lost on the Bush administration, note the power of the underlying narrative of trauma: the nation is wounded, the enemy is evil, history is irrelevant. Radio Netherlands' web site published an article that emphasized this point: "[t]he national trauma makes it very difficult for the president's political opponents to go against him and his argumentation. Both as a statesman and government leader, President Bush has been able to capitalize from 9/11 more than any other politician."[23]

Media and political representations of September 11 as a distinctly "national" attack frame it as an attack that was not only against New Yorkers and Washingtonians, but against all Americans.[24] This conceptualization, which has paved the way for the dispersal of traumatic effects throughout America, has its historical precedents. For instance, in her work on history and memory in postwar Japan, Lisa Yoneyama outlines how the bombings of Hiroshima and Nagasaki have undergone what she calls "the nationalization of memory."[25] In this process, non-Japanese victims of the attacks are played down and the right to claim victimization is extended to the entire Japanese nation, not just to those who lived in the bombed cities. Jack Kugelmass points to very similar processes in action during Jewish tourism to Polish Holocaust sites such as Auschwitz, at which monuments to all Jews indicate that victimhood can be claimed collectively by the entire Jewish nation/religion, even to Jews who lived outside of Europe during the Second World War, or those born many years after its conclusion.[26] In each of the three cases, a tragic historical memory becomes nationalized when seen from the present. Also, in the Japanese and Polish cases, the scholars are careful to point out how the current political goals of many within the national group inform the way memory is shaped and imagined.

While Morgan Freeman's statement at the beginning of this section rejects the idea of a traumatized nation, the attack was media accounts, political maneuvering, and psychological studies have attempted to frame it as exactly that. When trauma is projected onto all citizens of a nation, any attempt to deny it can appear unpatriotic, which partly explains President Bush's ability to implement many controversial policies in a short period of time. However, we do not view trauma simply as a tool unilaterally imposed by an elite-controlled mass media. This explanation misses the emotional draw that these events held for viewers. Sympathy for fellow human beings certainly is not an irrational sentiment, and patriotic feelings may even serve to democratize mourning by giving many different people a claim to the site's memory. Even if the sense of national trauma was constructed through media accounts and shaped by political agendas, this does not mean that people did not experience it, or make it any less real to people scattered throughout the United States who suffered anxiety, nightmares, and general fear.

"A Changed World": Historical Crisis and Traumatic Memory

When a visitor arrives on the CNN.com web site and clicks the button marked "In-depth Special: War Against Terror," she is taken to a section called "America Remembers." Here, she chooses between areas titled "September 11, 2001," "Faces of September 11," "The Cleanup," "Fighting Terror," and "A Changed World." Within each of these sections, temporality and change are central: if she clicks on "September 11, 2001," for instance, she is confronted with this statement: "It began as a sunny day. It ended as the first milestone of the 21st century." The central feature of this page is an illustrated timeline that transports her through key events, quotes, and images, structuring time with the motion of the computer's mouse.

The very title of the last section, "A Changed World," suggests a particular view on history. It takes the visitor to another topic menu, detailing changes in cities, civil liberties, the presidency, the government, and, finally, a button asks that persistent question: "Has the nation really changed?" On this web site, and in much of the discourse about the events of that day, "September 11th" is coded as the extraordinary event that restructures time. "September 10th," likewise, took on a new meaning of "ordinary life before this extraordinary event." Even the dictionary definition of "ground zero" alludes to the sense of out-of-ordinary time and violent, rapid change with which the media imbued September 11. Within this section we explore the problematic of time and history in a situation frequently defined as national trauma.

In a review of the film *Seven Days in September, The New York Times* film critic A. O. Scott refers to a distinction between September 11 and "September 11" first made by Leon Wieseltier, literary editor of *The New Republic*.[27] In Wieseltier's scheme, September 11 referred to "the actual day with its unassimilable horrors" in contrast with "September 11," "the ever-accumulating attempts to assimilate the horror into more normal modes of experience, to make it an occasion for commemoration, reflection and healing." We ask what underlies and unites both of these terms. Three beliefs unite them: that the attack was a unique event, that it inflicted trauma on the nation, and that now it is somehow unrepresentable.

In reference to the exceptionality of the event, James Der Derian holds that September 11 was, in fact, not outside of time, history, or politics, yet journalists and politicians represented it in this light.[28] "After Sept. 11, it became difficult to argue against its exceptionality because of the highly charged political atmosphere."[29] Even Michael Ignatieff argued that the suicide pilots were essentially nihilistic, which "takes their actions not only outside the realm of politics, but even out of the realm of war itself."[30] Ultimately, the events of September 11 were represented with "exceptional ahistoricity," as events "beyond experience, outside of history and between war."[31] The placement of painful events outside of time is what some psychologists argue is a key symptom of traumatized individuals—but can a nation place an event outside "the chains of cause and effect which form" its history? And what are the political implications of doing so?

Construction of the Graveyard Trope

In the weeks and months that followed September 11, people began to speak of the site as a "graveyard." This type of thinking, which had very specific political goals concerning how the site would be used, is the subject of this section. While no one denies the presence of human remains around Ground Zero, nor the fact that people died there, it's important to state that the graveyard trope is not accepted by all. For instance, graveyards are traditionally spaces set aside by groups of people for burial or other disposal of the bodies of the dead, where the living may come to commemorate and mourn them. This is different from a place where many people happened to die—and, as several visitors (especially New Yorkers) told us, if every place where a person had died on Manhattan was a graveyard, the whole island would be off-limits.

New Yorkers tend to respond in this way because they're used to living in a commercial city and not a memorial one. They know that memorial and commercial spaces require very different codes of conduct: Just imagine the reaction you would have if you saw someone setting up a hotdog stand inside the Vietnam Veterans memorial, for instance. The language of "national trauma," however, is powerful enough to unite the memorial and commercial approaches to space at Ground Zero—despite the strong intentions of some who wish to keep them separate.

The central axis of contention at Ground Zero has followed and continues to follow a pattern of argument we refer to, with some irony, as "the carnival versus the graveyard." The carnival represents the festive atmosphere that flourished around the site, complete with Styrofoam Statue of Liberty crowns, honey-roasted peanuts, and a multitude of "Ground Zero" T-shirts. "The graveyard," meanwhile, indicates the solemn attitude of grief and mourning. On one side, then, we find a pattern of tourist and commercial activity that attempts to integrate the site into established patterns of New York and United States secular tourism. Arguments that accompany these attempts include the claim that Ground Zero should be rebuilt primarily as a commercial space, with a limited memorial to mark the "footprints" of the buildings. But it seems impossible for anyone to speak in this way without engendering a counterargument from "the graveyard" side, which describes Ground Zero as "hallowed ground." Horrified by the prospect of Ground Zero's incorporation into secular commercial space, those on this side of the debate position themselves in opposition to the vending of souvenirs at the site and the rebuilding of office buildings there.

We will investigate these lines of argument more closely in the section that follows, both as they appear in their official media forms and as they were articulated to us in conversations with visitors at Ground Zero. However, before we do this, it's important to step back from the highly emotional tenor of the debate to make a few key points. While the carnival and the graveyard may seem to be mortal enemies, they are actually more like Siamese twins—joined in many places, birthed from the same conditions, and entirely unable to exist without the other. The most obvious way this is true is in the dialogue between them: when one side cries "rebuild," the other screams "never!" all the louder.

But the symbiosis in fact goes deeper. In the case of souvenir vending, the problem lies in the consciousness of the average visitor. The powerful desire to shop at Ground Zero is partly propelled by the habits tourists pick up at countless other sight-seeing destinations, in which shopping is normal and perhaps even necessary as a document of one's travels. Because of this context, any sharp distinction between "paying respects" and "shopping" tends to become blurred. Keeping this in mind, we seek to go beyond even the idea of an entanglement between the sacred and profane, and show how the carnival and the graveyard exist as mutually dependent forces at Ground Zero. The storm of controversy about commercialization at the site conceals an underlying harmony—in the current context of twenty-first-century American capitalism—between trade and the construction of a national sacred space.

One way to begin investigation of these problems is to examine the process by which it became natural to call Ground Zero a graveyard in the first place. Writing on New York's special aversion to nonutilitarian memorials, the architect James Sanders offers the following contrast between Washington, D.C., and New York City:

> [T]he civic character of Washington would come to be defined, to a great degree, by its collection of marble and granite monuments, fountains and sarcophagi. Their dignified, somber presence . . . tended (in the opinion of many) to smother or dilute the urban vitality and excitement of the city itself. Its neighbor to the north, by contrast, never paused for reflection. Far from memorializing the past, New Yorkers seemed intent on erasing every trace of it, ruthlessly destroying their most treasured mementos if they happened to get in the way of progress.[32]

In other words, large areas of space designated strictly as memorials are almost nonexistent in New York City, and particularly in Manhattan. Since the political capital was moved to Washington in 1790, the city's self-image has focused on earthier pursuits such as leadership in commercial culture, finance, and trade. In this context the construction of a purely sacred space in the heart of the financial district—defined in opposition to commercial pursuits—would be highly unusual for New York. And yet, the description of Ground Zero as sacred space tends to define its sacredness precisely in opposition to a profane commercialism. This tendency shows up in several spheres of interconnected speech and practice around Ground Zero, including the attitude of the political elite and the press, the comments of visitors to the site, and the behavior of policemen toward vendors in the Ground Zero area. The wider narrative structures pointed to above—radical historical discontinuity along with national trauma—appear, with some differences, in each of these spheres.

Mass media discourse, because of its key role in shaping participants' consciousness of Ground Zero, must be treated first in this case. As noted in the previous section, television and print media was the most direct experience of the attacks accesible to the majority of Americans in the days and weeks that followed. Let's take a look at how the carnival versus the graveyard debate took shape in some of these powerful media outlets.

One of the most strongly worded passages describing Ground Zero as a sacred space and a graveyard appeared on September 1, 2002, in an editorial by former New York City mayor Rudolph Giuliani:

> I am convinced that Ground Zero must first and foremost be a memorial. All other decisions should flow from that goal. If anything else is added to the site, it should complement and not overshadow the memorial. People a hundred years from now should be able to grasp the enormity of this attack by visiting this sacred ground. Ground Zero is a cemetery. It is the last resting place for loved ones whose bodies were not recovered and whose remains are still within that hallowed ground. We must respect the role these events play in our history.[33]

Although the same sentiments had been appearing regularly in the New York and American press, this article stands out for several reasons. First, the authorship of Giuliani, who was widely seen as one of the principal heroes of the attack's aftermath, lends authority to these sentiments (which were later repeated many times in the local New York dailies). Second, he is clear in his imagination of historical consciousness. As outlined above, September 11 was represented and sometimes experienced as a profoundly disjunctive historical event coming from outside of time to usher in a new era in which the older set of traditions that governed politics and culture was no longer relevant, a reading suggested in Giuliani's directive that we emphasize the impact of event on our history. Finally, Giuliani's comments stand out because he self-consciously considers the way that future generations will remember the World Trade Center attack in 100 years. Even then, he argues, they will comprehend the enormity of that particular day.

Giuliani's view of the site as the center of future memory of September 11 is perhaps more politically pointed than the average media depiction of the site's sacredness, which tends to focus on a more purely emotional sense of veneration. The reference may be as brief as a casual description of the site as "hallowed ground," or as involved as a long meditation on the sacredness of the site as we see in a *New York Post* editorial of September 17, 2002.[34] The editorial is addressed to Larry Silverstein and the Port Authority, the site's leaseholder and owner, respectively. The article argues against the construction of office or commercial buildings on the site, and includes the following pledge to avoid the use of such buildings if they are constructed:

> I will never attend a meeting in any building you might construct anywhere on the 16-acre property. Business decisions shouldn't be made in cemeteries.

> I will not eat at any restaurant that chooses to locate in those buildings, nor patronize any place elsewhere associated with that restaurant. People don't party on sacred ground.

> If I'm ever in need of office space, I will not consider those buildings— no matter how cheap the rent. There comes a time in a person's life and in the life of a country when business as usual just isn't good enough.[35]

This statement reveals the author's intense belief in the World Trade Center site's sacredness. Even though the editorial writer describes himself as someone who "usually writes about the importance of money," the graveyard trope asserts a powerfully emotional respect for the dead that out-muscles even the appeal of cheap Manhattan rent.

The same sense of solemnity and respect for the traumatic event has motivated a similar string of press attacks against vendors who sell World Trade Center paraphernalia around the site. These vendors are accused of committing a miniature version of the same trespass that the site's developers are suspected of planning: the contamination of New York's most hallowed site with profane commercial activity. The title of an article in the tabloid press, "How Dare These Ghouls Set Up Their Unholy Shops on this Hallowed Site," bespeaks the derision of vending at Ground Zero.[36]

How is it possible that these arguments for keeping Ground Zero a commerce-free graveyard are connected to the forces that commodify the site? After all, the above pieces argue that because the site was the location of mass death and national trauma, commercial activity must be stopped. However, we would suggest that these arguments contribute to the very commodification they argue against by building up an aura of uniqueness and exceptionality. The historical power of September 11 imbues the site with import and sacredness, and its tourist appeal becomes undeniable.

To see this process in action, we must move from the level of media discourse and investigate the ideas and practices of those who visit Ground Zero. Our choice to interpret Ground Zero commodification in the way we have has been shaped largely by the pattern of visitor responses to the question: "Why did you feel it was important to visit Ground Zero?" Responses to this question could be grouped into three rough categories. The first is a brush-off answer, such as "I was just shopping at Century 21 [a large department store across the street from Ground Zero] and decided to take a look." The second answer offers a personal connection to the site. Perhaps the informant knew someone who had died. One middle-aged man from New Jersey accompanied by his wife and child pointed out that his father had been a steelworker, and had helped construct the Twin Towers. Some simply remembered shopping at the stores beneath the Trade Center and said that the site had "lots of memories" for them.

However, others neither distanced themselves from the site nor connected themselves to it—instead they argued that they had to visit the site because of its importance in history. A woman in her thirties from Connecticut, when first asked why she felt it was important to visit the site, responded offhandedly, "to punish myself." No one had responded this way to our question before; we were curious and somewhat puzzled by her language.

She seems to imply feelings of "survivor guilt," the sense that her life was unjustly spared while someone else's was sacrificed. When asked what she meant, she explained:

> Respondent: A lot of people have a lot of feelings they can't get out. I have my son with me. [It is important to bring him] because it's a big American historical thing.
> Interviewer: Was your experience different from TV? How was it different?
> Respondent: You're here, you're in person, it's more personal.

The respondent justifies her immediate response—that she came to punish herself—by connecting it to her sense of obligation to bring her son to Ground Zero. Even though she does not necessarily enjoy being there, she feels that as a good American parent she should bring him "because it's a big American historical thing." Perhaps this is a rationalization; her son was very young and would probably remember the visit in only the vaguest of terms. Yet we can see something parallel to Giuliani's project of commemoration in her desire to instill historical memories of September 11 in the young. Also, her remark about punishing herself points to a more fundamental reason for her visit to this site of destruction: her separation from the experience of that day. For her, the television representation lacked a human, "personal" element. Are attempts to make the events of September 11 more personal the reason many Americans feel compelled to visit the site in person, to consume this now inaccessible experience?

Tragic History and Touristic Desire

As we examine the role of history in the building of tourist desire to visit Ground Zero, the outlines of a connection between tragedy and commodity begin to emerge, for the conversion of a historical site into a tourist site is a process of commodification. Commodities, for our purposes, are objects of desire that can be, to some extent, possessed and consumed. While Ground Zero itself is not fully consumed by the tourist process, most visits involve the purchase of objects imbued with a slice of the site's aura. And, while an occasional informant bristled at our casual use of the word "tourism" to refer to Ground Zero visitation, students of tourism have been clear on this topic. Donald Horne, for instance, has written that "the tourism of the ceremonial agenda and the tourism of the ceremonial visit to the museum are tourisms of acquisition."[37] Horne suggests that a continuum of acquisition styles, from the crass to the subtle, characterize all tourist practices, including those of visitors who come for cultural or "sacred" reasons, and who may not think of themselves as "tourists."

A gentleman from Boston who was upset by our use of the word "tourism" steamed with anger at this reasoning. In fact, he was horrified and angered by the photography of "Japanese tourists," as he phrased it. He perceived photography as crassly acquisitive. During the course of our research, however, many visitors sought to acquire a memento at Ground Zero. One woman told us that photography was acceptable if you did it yourself, but not if you bought a photograph and money exchanged hands. The conflict between acceptable and nonacceptable forms of acquisition will be treated in more detail below, but for now we want to suggest that the visitor who solemnly abstains from all forms of acquisition is a rare exception, and that most visitors want to acquire commodities, photographs, or, at the very least, memories while visiting.

At times the hunger for a tangible object with which to structure memory can be powerfully emotional. The quote below reveals the depth of personal and national meaning an object can hold:

> Widow Maura Madden said she cherishes her deceased husband's wedding ring, which was found with his body two weeks after the attack. The inscription, "Rich, all my love, Maura," helped medical examiners identify his body, Madden said. "I wear it around my neck with a little red, white and blue flag," said Madden, of Westfield, N.J. "I feel bad for families that don't have anything to remember their loved one by."[38]

The materiality of the object makes otherwise ethereal memories tangible and maintains connection to the past. Though the story and experience of Ms. Madden is more dramatic than those of visitors who come from afar to buy mementos or take pictures, these visitors also seek a material memory. Not all visitors purchase souvenirs around the site; in fact, there has been considerable controversy over vendors, the intermediaries of memory.

Though 9/11 has widely been perceived as a unique historical event, viewing it through the lens of material culture reveals historical parallels otherwise concealed by narratives of exceptionality. We are able to point to any number of other sites where materiality and memory are enmeshed. For instance, anthropologist Jack Kugelmass has explored the desire of Jewish American visitors to Poland to "salvage" pieces of Jewish past.[39] He portrays the purchasing of Jewish memorabilia as a side effect of visitors' need for a tangible object to help structure and sensualize the memory. During the time of his research (late 1980s, early 1990s), the Polish state even "stock[ed] enormous quantities of mass-produced carvings of Jewish peddlers" that were soon copied by local entrepreneurs, not unlike those around Ground Zero.[40] Some visitors sought more rare items, such as objects used in Jewish rituals before the Second World War. Ultimately, Kugelmass argues, "the desire to salvage vestiges of prewar Jewry may even go beyond artifacts to the remains of actual people. At Treblinka, one synagogue youth-group tour leader collected pieces of bone from the surrounding fields. These he placed in a plastic container with the intention of burying them in Israel at the next stage of the tour."[41] The pieces of bone may or may not belong to Jews, but, because of their location, they have become imbued with a strong sense of Jewish sacredness for this youth-group leader.

Mrs. Shirley Thompson's brief online travelogue about Berlin tells a tale even closer to those we heard around the former WTC site.[42] Mrs. Thompson traveled to Berlin in November 1989 specifically to visit the remains of the Berlin Wall. Her motivation to make the trip came during a news broadcast: "[w]atching the BBC News it suddenly struck me that I too could be chipping off a piece of the wall!"[43] She and her husband met a German family (who were also visitors to Berlin) on their walk along the Wall. They gave her their hammer and chisel to chip away a few pieces of concrete, which she was thrilled to have. In addition to these pieces, she bought art from West German art students that was created and sold to aid poor East German art students. Mrs. Thompson says, "I still get a thrill to think that I actually hacked a piece off the great Berlin Wall and have it as a treasured memento in an enameled box in my suburban lounge. We felt that we had truly captured a piece of history—at least in our minds."[44]

Both of these vignettes are connected by the desire for tangible mementos of historical events suffused with a unique aura. Despite the obvious differences between the events, in each of these places people with varying degrees of connection to the site took away souvenirs to capture their experience. The materials within the sites are imbued with significance beyond that of their immediate properties.

In our interviews around the former WTC site, we met a number of people who understood this wish for a material memory. The commodities they purchased included a book entitled *Terror*, which is filled with full-color photos and patriotic discourse, mass-produced photo albums,[45] patriotic teddy bears, and toilet paper bearing the words "wipe out terrorism." The man whose father had helped build the towers told us that "people deal with stuff in different ways. . . . Maybe people need something tangible to help them."

We had a similar conversation with a man from California who had purchased a Ground Zero baseball cap. When asked how he planned to use it, he told us that he would perhaps wear it on the one-year anniversary of the attack on the World Trade Center (which was then about 6 months away). A visitor from England, on a "bonding trip" to New York City with her daughter, told us that "some people need to buy them," even though she insisted that she didn't "think it was good to make money out of tragedy" and thought the viewing platform was "a bit grim." A middle-aged couple from Florida had conflicting opinions about shopping; he found it "tacky," while she had "mixed feelings," stating that "maybe people want a memory of this, but I don't like to see people making a profit off of sorrow."

Another afternoon we began talking with one or two young people from Atlanta, Georgia; before long we had a group of six, all clamoring to give their opinions on the vendors while another member of their party videotaped their responses. They were visiting with their work supervisor, a bespectacled man they called "the philosopher." Within this small group, some were thrilled by the good buys that vendors offered, some were dismissive of the deal-seekers, and others liked the vendors but simply didn't feel like shopping. The first young man we spoke with then told us that he came because the events of September 11 are "something that'll be in a history book" and that Ground Zero was "not real till you see it for your own self." When we asked the rest of the group how they felt about the vendors, one young woman said, "I like the stuff because it's cheap!" The philosopher immediately countered with "She's American. Go to the core of why we're really here."

Underlying these comments, we see that ideas about history and what it means to be American are interwoven. The connections between consumption, history, and patriotism contribute to a desire for souvenirs from the site that seems to enhance, not detract from, the visitors' sense of the site's aura. These visitors do not simply regurgitate the media discourse that opposes commerce and veneration. Instead, consumption itself has become a ritual that does not necessarily detract from the sacred and traumatic character of the site. Much like the woman who said she was visiting to punish herself, many visitors come to the site out of a desire to make history personal and connect with the trauma that all Americans have been told that they are supposed to feel. By placing themselves physically at the site, the flow of history and the charge of trauma become more real, as the young man from Atlanta told us.

In contrast, another group of visitors spoke out angrily about what they saw as the insensitivity and irreverence of street vending around Ground Zero. Take the case of Jerry, an accountant who brought his children from Cleveland, Ohio, to New York City for the first time in March 2002. When we asked what he thought of the vendors of World Trade Center memorabilia, he described them as "disgusting" and forcefully stated, "people shouldn't be making money off this." For an accountant to feel such an aversion to money-making speaks strongly about the conflict caused by sales at this site. However, we should note that a moment later he qualified his initial outrage. Softening his tone, he commented that it is acceptable to sell mementos, "just not so close to where it happened." He then added that "this is America. People can do whatever they want. They could get pine boxes and write FDNY on them and people would buy them. They wouldn't be selling them if people weren't buying them."

Implicit in Jerry's statements is a reverence for this space of tragedy. However, note the interesting connection he makes between economic freedom and American patriotism: "this is America. People can do whatever they want." After a few moments of thought he was able to reconcile an American sense of sacred space and quasi-sacred commercial activity, as long as the sales took place at a distance.

So far we have addressed arguments over whether the space in and around Ground Zero is sacred. These arguments do not occur solely in the statements of city leaders and visitors to the site; they are debated on a daily basis by vendors of World Trade Center souvenirs, by visitors to the site, and by police. Just how far does the "sacred space" extend? How could this space be regulated, since at the time no city laws applied to vending near a space of tragedy? One of the most natural ways to illustrate this would have to be the unique set of rules and regulations experienced by vendors trying to sell in the area around the site from fall 2001 until spring 2004. The actions taken by police at this time show an assumed relationship between increasing proximity to the site and increasing transgression against its purity. In other words, commerce taking place near the site is officially considered contamination, while commerce a few blocks away may not be. The chief consequence of spatial policing has been the maintenance of an elastic "vendor-free zone" surrounding Ground Zero itself. When this research began in February 2002, for example, vending of World Trade Center items was permitted on the near, but not on the far side of Broadway. Essentially, local police had drawn an invisible line down the middle of the avenue, which extended and continued in a large ring around the entire disaster area, separating the vendor-free sacred space that surrounded the site from the mundane and commercial space around it.

Vendors who ignored the regulation and set up on the west side of Broadway were subject to harassment and eviction by police officers.[46] Sammy, a disabled vendor with whom we spoke many times, often ignored this rule. One day, while standing behind his table and listening to him attract customers with his catchy slogans, we noticed a heavyset policeman making the rounds down Broadway. "You're too close to the site," said the policeman, "you'll have to move your table." "I'm a veteran," Sammy responded, refusing to move from his spot. "I have a yellow license."

In this case, the vendor challenged the policeman's conception of the borders of sacred space, claiming that his own identity as a disabled veteran and his holding of an esteemed form of license excused him from the accusations leveled at other vendors. Note how Sammy immediately raised the issue of his veteran status, thereby complicating the usual opposition between "national trauma" and "profiting off sorrow" by emphasizing the sacrifices he has already made for the nation. And indeed, the policeman, although not entirely convinced, was at least willing to let him hold onto his position on the west corner of Broadway.

The invisible boundary around the "vendor-free" zone was not a stationary one. It wandered back and forth across the streets of downtown, moving in harmony with a complex set of external factors. For instance, vendors told us that when Mayor Bloomberg publicly visited Ground Zero on April 6, 2002, the police cleared all of them out of the area. Both sides of Broadway and even surrounding blocks were suddenly off limits. Similarly, vendors with tables were nowhere to be seen on September 11, 2002, although a few determined souls stood on street corners selling handfuls of American flags to the willing crowds. In spite of these periodic expansions, long-term observations reveal a slow, gradual contraction of the vendor-free zone around Ground Zero. While in the first months of the attacks, any sales of such items would have been unthinkable, within a space of four months the line had moved expanded to allow sales on the eastern side of Broadway. By June 2002, we regularly saw vendors on the west side of Broadway and even as close as the eastern side of Church Street, which placed them just across the street from the fence around the construction area.

This is the context in which the police seemed to relax the enforcement of the vendor-free zone somewhat in late 2002 and 2003. However, the state legislature considered and came very close to passing a bill in spring 2003 to restructure vending regulations in New York City and to make vending illegal in all but a small portion of the Ground Zero area. This legislation eventually passed in March 2004, marking a new stage in the codification of moral sanctions about trade in sacred spaces. The web site of the New York Division of Veterans' Affairs ran a press release from Governor Pataki's office entitled, "Governor Signs Legislation to Help Keep New York City Sidewalks Free of Vendor Congestion: New Law Will Protect Interest of Disabled Veteran Vendors."[47] This press release, clearly geared to decrease disabled veteran protest, states that "the new law will protect the interests of disabled veteran vendors by expanding the number of available specialized vending licenses for disabled veterans."[48] However, they would not be allowed in the vicinity of Ground Zero. As Governor Pataki himself states in the release, "[g]iven that the World Trade Center site is sacred ground, we can preserve the area's sanctity by restricting vending in the vicinity of Ground Zero. Visitors from across the country and around the world come to the site to reflect and honor those lost on September 11th. It is fitting that the area around the site should be kept as free as possible from congestion and maintained with dignity." In Pataki's statement, it is clear that the tourist foot traffic is a priority, as is the "area's sanctity," yet he fails to grasp the fact that many of these tourists want to buy mementos from vendors while visiting this sacred site.

Before the March 2004 vending legislation, something that distinguished Ground Zero from other memorial spaces was the NYPD's deep institutional connection with September 11 and its loss of many police in the tragedy. This created an atmosphere in which the police were essentially enforcing respect for their own dead. Their actions fit into the presumed hierarchy of claims to the tragedy, according to which the Fire Department, Police Department, and the families of the victims have claimed special rights over Ground Zero and its future. Because of this hierarchy of claims they feel they have the right to attack those they see as outsiders trying to cash in on a disaster they claim as their own. However, at Ground Zero conflict continues to rage about whether the site belongs to "all Americans," as Giuliani declared when the site was opened for tourism, to all New Yorkers, or if it belongs to the families of the victims first and to everyone else second. The high value of the real estate, of course, hangs over all of this, as a June 2003 article in the *New York Post* demonstrates: "With all due respect, too many of the victims' families have long believed that they have a proprietary claim to Ground Zero. The Twin Towers were attacked because of what they represented, not because of who happened to be inside. And the proper response to that attack is to redevelop the site with an appropriate memorial."[49]

More than two years after the event, the *Post* changes from its established tone of attacking Ground Zero development, and turns its ire on the families' specific claim on the site by arguing that only by accident were their relatives killed or wounded. The true victims are said to be American values ("the Twin towers were attacked because of what they represented") and the site, just like the trauma of September 11, rightly belongs to the American nation and not to any privileged subgroup of it.

Conclusion

After all the battles in words and deeds that have been waged over the fate of Ground Zero, it's telling that no single conception of the site's meaning ever became fully authoritative. When looking across the fence into the gaping emptiness of the site at the time of our fieldwork, many people would agree with a New Jersey man who told us that "We all need to remember this so we'll know why we're at war." For him, the destruction represented an attack on America that demanded immediate, violent retribution. But others interpreted the site differently. One young woman, clearly moved emotionally by the sight of the expansive wreckage, for instance, couldn't help imagining similar wreckage in places like Afghanistan or Iraq. She interpreted the same scene as a statement *against* the horrors of war. Similarly, some see commerce around the site as a proper way to remember, while others see it as irreverent.

These fundamental disagreements show that categories of sacred and profane are constantly shifting and that old-fashioned dichotomies that oppose commercial and venerative activity may not hold in a context of late capitalism. Politicians and other officials utilize these categories when seeking to impose their interpretations, yet, simultaneously, a whole host of divergent readings bubble up in the comments of visitors. Ground Zero, seen as a commodified space, is at once a tool of elite manipulation from above and a canvas on which visitors impose their own impressions of politics and history from below.

Notes

Portions of this essay originally appeared in *Critique of Anthropology* 24, no.1: 51–78, and are reprinted by permission of Sage Publication Ltd. from Molly Hurley Depret and James Trimarco, "Morality and Merchandise: Vendors, Vistors, and Police at New York City's 'Ground Zero' " (© Sage, 2004).

1. Walter Benjamin, *Illuminations* (New York: Harcourt, Brace, and World, 1955), xx.
2. Elizabeth Hays and Jose Martinez with Ralph R. Ortega, "Morgan Freeman's 9/11 Take Panned," *New York Daily News*, June 3, 2002, 4.
3. Lisa Cartwright and Marita Sturken, *An Introduction to Visual Culture: Practices of Looking* (Oxford: Oxford University Press, 2001), xx.
4. Historiographers such as Michael Pocock have attempted to grapple with the theoretical issues underlying the continuousness or discontinuousness of history as imagined by different societies. In *Politics, Language and Time*, for instance, he separates societies that imagine their history as an unbroken line extending into the past from those that trace their beginnings to a founding discontinuous event (Pocock, Chicago: University of Chicago Press, 1960). Much of the thinking about September 11, emphasizing how it has altered history and ushered in a new era, seems to place it in the latter category.
5. *Merriam-Webster's Collegiate Dictionary*, Tenth Edition (Springfield, MA: Merriam-Webster, Incorporated, 1997).

6. Jenette Restivo, "Blow to the Psyche: Americans Will React with Fear, Anger—Danger for Some." http://abcnews.go.com/sections/living/DailyNews/wtc_americanpsyche010911.html. (October 25, 2003).

7. Restivo, "Blow to the Psyche."

8. American Psychological Association, "Coping With Terrorism." [Available online] http://wasearch.loc.gov/sepll/20011004111057/http://helping.apa.org/daily/terrorism.html.

9. Intelihealth.com, "New Study Offers Insight to Why Many are Having Trouble with Concentration and Normalcy After Terrorist Attack." http://www.intelihealth.com/IH/ihtIH/WSIHW000/8271/8014/335055.html. (October 25, 2003)

10. Roxane Cohen Silver et al. "Nationwide Longitudinal Study of Psychological Responses to September 11," *JAMA: Journal of the American Medical Association* 288, issue 10 (2002).

11. Ibid., 1235.

12. National Science Foundation, "People Who 'Gave Up' After 9/11 More Likely to Remain Distressed" http://www.nsf.gov/od/lpa/news/o2/pr0271.htm.

13. Silver et al. "Nationwide Longitudinal Study," 1235.

14. National Science Foundation, "People Who 'Gave Up.' "

15. WebMD Health, "9/11 Still Lingers in Mind and Body." http://my.webmd.com/content/Article/73/88882.htm?pagenumber=2

16. This version of the history of trauma is drawn primarily from Allan Young's exhaustive anthropological study *The Harmony of Illusions* (Princeton, NJ: Princeton University Press, 1995). The intellectual history of such a topic is too complex for this account to be anything more than a sketch.

17. Young, *Harmony of Illusions*, 16–18.

18. Ibid., 40.

19. This effort was aided substantially by the affinity professed by the editors of the manual for the nosological strategies proposed by the German psychiatrist Emil Kraepelin (Young, *Harmony of Illusions*, 94–95). Kraepelin's style features quite rigid categories into which patients are to be categorized through observable symptoms.

20. American Psychiatric Association, *Diagnostic and Statistical Manual of Mental Disorders*, 4th Edition, 1994, 424, 427–28.

21. Phrasing the sentence in this way is begging the question, "Who are Americans?" The short answer would be those who attended school and received most of their socialization within the United States. However, numerous marginal cases exist among immigrant and overseas populations who may be exposed to mainstream American thinking in one aspect of their life (i.e., fashion) but not in another (i.e., notions about gender roles).

22. Sean Loughlin, "Bush Found Voice in Battle Against Terror," September 6, 2002. http://www.cnn.com/2002/ALLPOLITICS/09/04/ar911.changed.presidency

23. Reinout Van Wagtendonk, "9/11, Mr. Bush's Albatross?" September 11, 2002. http://www.rnw.nl/hotspots/html/us030911.html

24. America's diverse ethnic background and vast immigrant population made this claim particularly complex. For instance, while hundreds of Muslim Americans died in the attacks, Muslims have often been framed as the "other," post 9/11, and this group has been singled out for secret arrests and other violations of civil rights. At the same time, Giuliani and Bush have both argued that Muslim Americans are part of the American nation and not to blame as a group.

25. Lisa Yoneyama, *Hiroshima Traces: Time, Space and the Dialectics of Memory* (Berkeley: University of California Press, 1995).

26. Jack Kugelmass, "The Rites of the Tribe: American Jewish Tourism in Poland," in *Museums and Communities*, eds. Ivan Karp, Christine Mullen Kreamer, and Steven D. Lavine (Washington, D.C.: Smithsonian Institution Press, 1992), 382–427.

27. Scott, A. O. "*Film Review, Cameras Were Rolling the Day Time Stopped*," September 6, 2002, *New York Times*, Section E, Column 1, 23.

28. James Der Derian, "*In Terrorem*: Before and After 9/11," in *Worlds in Collision: Terror and the Future of Global Order*, eds. Ken Booth and Timothy Dunne (New York: Palgrave MacMillan, 2002), 101–17.

29. Ibid., 102.

30. Ibid., Ignatieff quoted in Der Derian, 102.

31. Ibid., 103.

32. James Sanders, "The New Ground Zero; Honoring the Dead in the City that Never Weeps," August 31, 2003, *New York Times*, Section 2, 19.

33. Rudolph Giuliani, "Getting it Right at Ground Zero," September 1, 2002, *Time Magazine*. http://www.time.com/time/covers/1101020909/agiuliani.html.

34. John Crudele, "Hey Larry: Build it and I Won't Come," September 17, 2002, *New York Post*, 031.

35. Ibid.

36. Steve Dunleavy, "How Dare these Ghouls Set Up their Unholy Shops on this Hallowed Site?," January 9, 2002, *New York Post*, 004.

37. Donald Horne, *The Great Museum: The Re-Presentation of History* (London: Pluto Press, 1984).

38. Robert Ingrassia, "Tragedy's Lost and Found: City puzzling over trove of rescued 9/11 mementos," January 13, 2002, *Daily News*, 5.

39. Kugelmass, "The Rites of the Tribe."

40. Ibid., 390.

41. Ibid., 393.

42. Shirley Thompson, "And a Wallbreaker Cocktail, Too!" November 25, 1989. http://www.andreas.com/berlin-thompson.html

43. Ibid.

44. Ibid.

45. Several vendors commented that these albums were manufactured in semilegal Chinatown print shops, raising the interesting question of production within the informal economy.

46. However, vendors working for managers always told us the position of their table was a decision of their supervisor, and not their own.

47. New York State Division of Veteran's Affairs, "Governor Signs Legislation to Help Keep New York City Sidewalks Free of Vendor Congestion: New Law Will Protect Interest of Disabled Veteran Vendors," Press Release from the Governor's Press Office. March 5, 2004. http://www.veterans.state.ny.us/PressReleases/2004/prgov030504.htm.

48. New York State Division of Veteran's Affairs, "Governor Signs Legislation."

49. *New York Post* editorial, "An Empty Plan for Ground Zero," June 25, 2003, 028.

Chapter 3

"Chosen to be Witness": The Exceptionalism of 9/11

Øyvind Vågnes

On September 7, 2003, *The New York Times* reported that a videotape of the terror attacks on the World Trade Center two years earlier had recently surfaced. A Czech immigrant construction worker, Pavel Hlava, had intended to make a video postcard to send home, and had accidentally filmed both planes crashing into the towers from the passenger seat of an SUV in Brooklyn. Almost two weeks had passed that September before Hlava realized that he had actually captured the first plane on video, and

> [e]ven then, Mr. Hlava, who speaks almost no English, did not realize that he had some of the rarest footage collected of the World Trade Center disaster. His is the only videotape known to have recorded both planes on impact, and only the second image of any kind showing the first strike. The tape—a kind of accidentally haunting artifact—has surfaced publicly only now, on the eve of the second anniversary of the attacks, after following the most tortuous and improbable of paths, from an insular circle of Czech-American working-class friends and drinking buddies.[1]

A copy of the tape was reported to have been traded by a friend of Hlava's wife to another Czech immigrant for "a bar tab at a pub in Ridgewood, Queens." Hlava and his brother Josef, who had been with him in the car, had tried to sell the tape, both in New York and in the Czech Republic, "[b]ut with little sophistication about the news media and no understanding of the tape's significance, the brothers had no success." Furthermore, the driver of the SUV, Mike Cohen, who incidentally also was Hlava's boss, "had strong objections to releasing the tape." Cohen commented to the *Times*, "[t]hree thousand people died in that place. . . . I told him the day he's gonna sell that film, he's not gonna work for me anymore."

The story of what was considered to be "perhaps, the strangest and most tragic video postcard of all time" is arresting. Hlava had come to the United States in 1999 after years of working in the mines near Ostrava and losing his job, the paper reported. As a recent immigrant story, Hlava's is perhaps not so different from those that abound from earlier times: the cultural logic that transforms his videotape into "haunting artifact" is familiar to those who have grown up knowing such a logic, and foreign to those who are struggling to come to terms with the realities of a different culture. A lack of "sophistication" about the news media is referred to by the reporter; so is, in one and the same sentence, Hlava's limited knowledge of not only the English language (he "speaks almost no English"), but also of specific cultural codes (he "did not realize that he had some of the rarest footage collected"). Indeed, this lack of understanding of the "significance" of the tape is what makes the story entertaining, almost comical. Not only had the tape "bounced around in Mr. Hlava's apartment in Ridgewood," it had also almost been erased, as Hlava had once "noticed that his son was playing around with the video camera and erasing the tape." Hlava had managed to secure the plane's impact just in time, according to the *Times*, who presented the story at their web site accompanied by stills from the tape in "A Rare Glimpse," the kind of audio slide show that is familiar to visitors to the NY Times online.

How can we characterize the "significance" of this tape, as referred to by the *Times*? On one hand, the paper reports, it was hoped that Hlava's images would help federal investigators in studying the collapse of the towers. But it was the economic value of the tape as an artifact, unrecognized until recently by Hlava, that defined its significance as a commodity, and it was Hlava's unawareness of this significance that seemed to astonish and amuse the reporter. Eventually, a freelance news photographer, Walter Karling, had been made aware of the tape, and had brought it to the *Times*; assumedly, it was also he who brought attention to the story. Karling claimed that he was acting as Hlava's "agent," and warned ABC television, which was scheduled to show the tape, not to do so, as the network would be violating copyrights. Hlava obviously needed an agent to translate to him the commodity value of his "haunting artifact."

As the *Times* pointed out, Hlava's tape presented "only the second image of any kind showing the first strike." The first image, not referred to directly in the article, had in fact been shot by another immigrant who had also happened upon the scene accidentally, French filmmaker Jules Naudet, who along with his brother Gedeon had been making a documentary film about James Hanlon, a New York firefighter rookie, and had ended up with *9/11*, the only widely critically acclaimed documentary of the events of September 11 (see figure 3.1). This essay is about that film, but appropriately begins with Hlava. The contrast between his response to that of the Naudet brothers upon viewing the attacks through the lens of a camera is striking, and illustrates the profound difference the professional impulse makes in contemporary documentary filmmaking. Unlike Hlava, the Naudet brothers made efforts to protect their material: they hired the William Morris Agency, known for its "long track

Figure 3.1. Julien Naudet, James Hanlon, and Gedeon Naudet. AP/World Wide Photos.

record of packaging elements from its extensive roster of clients to enhance a project's potential for success in the marketplace."[2]

Equally, the histories of Hlava's tape and the tapes of the Naudet brothers illustrate the importance of claiming "exceptionalism" on behalf of one's work in a consumer culture that thrives on the new and the one-of-a-kind. My argument is this: *9/11* is a film that dramatizes, alongside the tragic events of September 11, 2001, the film's own coming-into-being as an exceptional visual event. *9/11* reasserts this upon its television broadcast as well as with its release as a DVD, made available to the public for homeviewing. The film's design suggests that its exceptionalism—as document of a one-of-a-kind moment—is one with the exceptionalism of the event itself. The filmmakers present themselves as mystically elected to "bear witness" and thus to help a nation remember and honor the past. However, each projection of the film is a new visual event, and when the format changes, *9/11* ultimately negates the very logic that argues for its exceptional status. This is so because different formats invite different ways of watching. Upon its broadcast, *9/11* was one momentous visual event; upon its release as DVD, it doubles as a visual event to be repeated and to be owned as a "commemorative object," a mass-produced artifact.

One of the premises for this essay is that one cannot begin to comprehend the impact of the documentary film *9/11* by studying it as an isolated object. *9/11* is not a film that can be interpreted outside of the historical moment it describes; equally significant, however, it cannot be interpreted outside the moments in which it is *made* and *watched*. In this essay, I do not want to think of *9/11* as a static "text" laid out for academic analysis; I want to think of *9/11*, and of any projection of the film, as alive, as a meaningful lived event. One of the ideas that has helped me in doing so is Mieke Bal's designation of a *visual event* as "what happens when people look, and what emerges from that act."[3] Bal suggests that we consider the event of looking as itself an illuminating object of study. Her proposal flies in the face of traditional art criticism, which ultimately adheres to a consumer logic that treats the moment of watching as singular, as *isolated*.

Of course, art critics have traditionally described the act of looking as a singular visual event, an experience of "absolute presentness," and they will do so even if they look repeatedly, episodically, or only partially. This should come as no surprise, since critics tend to carry with them a sense of how encounters with art objects are traditionally described, and they adhere to those traditions just as novelists adhere to rules of genre.[4] However, the singular visual event as it appears in art criticism is partly fictitious; the moment of seeing is a myth imagined by the critic after the fact. Certainly, we can say the same of television criticism. The broadcast, as singular visual event, is also a convention of that genre, albeit seldom doubted or resisted by critics writing within the genre. This lack of any resistance is largely the result of cultural pressure to treat television broadcasts as grecian urns, or as objects with fixed and immutable meanings. Arguably, every projection of *9/11* is a response to such a pressure, as is, indeed, its production, and only by acknowledging the complexity involved in shifting the focus away from the film to the unfolding and ever-changing conditions in which we view the film are we able to fathom the capacity of *9/11* to shape (and reshape) cultural memory.

When it was broadcast on CBS, on March 10, 2002, with better ratings than the Super Bowl, critics hailed *9/11* as an outstanding visual event.[5] Since television critics had watched it with other critics at a press preview, they wrote about it from that particular and privileged perspective. They prepared the general audience for the "collective experience" of the broadcast by outlining the premises for the public understanding of the event. When audiences at last turned on their television sets in order to watch the broadcast of *9/11*, they were thus prepared for an exceptional documentary narrative.[6]

The challenge that the producers of the broadcast faced was to tell a story that could match not only the gravity of the footage incorporated into *9/11*, but the magnitude of the event documented by that footage. The footage was unquestionably unique, not only because Jules Naudet had captured the only image of the first plane crashing into the North Tower (before Hlava's tape emerged), but because he brought the camera inside the tower and had continued filming as it fell. Naudet thus managed to emerge with the only footage from inside the crumbling WTC. This view from the inside would ultimately lead to *9/11*'s canonization as an antidote to the kitsch that seemed to characterize so many other efforts to represent that tragic day. Its canonization was performed by critics such as Caryn James, who, in the *New York Times*, described the film in terms of what it is not, as much as what it is. She, like many critics, pointed to both contextual and textual factors that determined the success of *9/11*, such as considerations of narrative strategy, or the difficult ethical choices the filmmakers made during recording, production, and post-production. *9/11* was also canonized as exceptional because it did not suggest or argue any explicit political agenda, but remained dedicated to the original story, or at least the original vision, of the filmmakers.[7] It was considered moving, but not overtly sentimental in the moments when it easily could have become just that. Its ommissions were widely considered a demonstration of good taste, in place of a cynical use of the spectacular.[8] In other words, it stood in marked contrast to the many television productions that seemed symptomatic of consumerism's governing ethics and aesthetics.[9] It would not be repeatedly broadcast to the point of numbness, since the Naudet brothers had allowed CBS only two broadcasts. Furthermore, it was considered innovative. In a summary of the year of television in the national Catholic weekly *America*, the broadcast was said to demonstrate what a "new kind" of television "might look like."

Above all else, television critics proclaimed *9/11* an exceptional visual event in its overcoming of the problems of representing death and collective grief on television. It was this aspect of the film that made it different from the kitsch that surrounded it, critics argued. *9/11* is a film that self-consciously acknowledges this possibility, as it records Naudet's response to the extraordinary footage as he captures it. The problem of the representation of death presents itself to the filmmaker in the process of filmmaking with such force that it becomes a central theme of the narrative. The problem is both practical and ethical: How does one record death, and how does one do it in the right way?

Much has been written about the problem of representing death. In one of the classic treatments of the subject, *Camera Lucida: Reflections on Photography* by Roland Barthes, the author is fascinated by his encounter with the past in the recorded image, or with the "return of the dead" that is always present in the photographic image. *Camera Lucida* is a meditation on memory and on death. Barthes's elegant analysis reflects a particular aesthetic: one that revolves around the ability of the recorded image to speak to its own internal contradictions and to startle us, rather than simply shout at us, when doing so; for Barthes, this reflexivity approaches the sublime. And whether one agrees or not with Barthes's response to specific images, one is struck by the implications of his preference for a visual aesthetic of trauma that defies conventional notions of morality or good taste.

When we watch *9/11* we experience, and reexperience, a record of trauma. For historians and psychoanalysts working in the burgeoning field of "trauma studies," the event of death so challenges our notion of representation that it seems unrecordable. In *Trauma: A Genealogy*, Ruth Leys points out that the traumatic scene is, by definiton, "unavailable for a certain kind of recollection."[10] That kind of recollection, when it is to be shared with others, is one that involves language, the uttering of words, the combination of words into sentences. The problem is that we remember in images, and we struggle to translate them into words. We struggle with the limitations of translation. However different the actual witnessing of trauma is from watching recorded images of it, the fundamental problem of how to translate the experience into language is shared.

It is against such a background that the proposed exceptionalism of *9/11* must be considered. Even if we feel that we are at a loss for words, there is the actual publication of thousands of words. Even if we are appalled by the images of trauma, we are nevertheless confronted with them almost every day. We click our way though the *Times*'s slide show of Hlava's images, we turn on our television sets and watch yet another documentary about the events of September 11. And so these images come to surround us constantly, and uneasily, because the mass production and repetitious projection of images is felt to reduce the exceptional into a numbing cliché.

At the same time, in an image-driven culture any traumatic event seems to beg the exceptional representaton of it, the visual event that will stand out among other lesser attempts. After all, if cultural memory in such a culture is archival, we remember the past by watching archived images of it.[11] According to Susan Sontag, to remember is, "more and more, not to recall a story, but to be able to call up a picture."[12] Films and photographs possess the amazing capacity to replace our own memories of an event and to stand in for them, to actually become our memories.[13] A projection of *9/11* has the capacity to help us remember the past, to install memory within us. The film-image may replace the memory-image in a spectator's mind, supplement it, or repress it. The power of the filmmaker is thus tremendous and ethically complex; the documentarist simultaneously invites processes of collective memory and memory distortion.

In an interview with the British newspaper *The Independent*, Philip Roth claimed that he felt that he had witnessed, in the months following the terror attacks of September 11, the "kitschification of 3,000 people's deaths."[14] There had been, he felt, "a great distortion of what happened," as the commemoration of the event had been appropriated so extensively into a range of social and cultural activities that seemed to have little to do with it: "What we've been witnessing since September 11 is an orgy of national narcissism . . . it's impossible to watch a baseball game without having to listen to 'God Bless America' beforehand or without being asked to remember 'our heroes.' I feel like saying: stop, dignity demands that you stop it." The term "kitschification" suggests a particular kind of aesthetization; one that may function as a kind of "anesthetic," one that may numb precisely because of its nonsingularity. I will leave alone the various problems that come with any uniform definition of "kitsch." My point here, rather, is that the extensive image-production of collective trauma creates a longing for an aesthetic sensibility that seems somehow to "do it justice." There is, in other words, a longing for the image or series of images that are *exceptional*, that can "startle," not only "shout." And there is a deeply human need to structure this imagery into coherent narratives, to combine images of what is beyond reason with words that salvage them from incoherence. Among the many television programs produced in the aftermath of the terrorist attacks, only one seemed to meet such an "aesthetic standard" upon its broadcast, namely *9/11*.

9/11 was originally intended to be a documentary about the day-to-day trials of becoming a firefighter. But what it became is as much a documentary about the trials of filmmaking. *9/11* was originally intended to be a film about the ordinary heroism of a rookie. What it became is a film about the heroism of the filmmakers, the Naudet brothers themselves, who are seemingly selected to be "witnesses to history." In his summary for *America*, James Martin concludes that it was difficult not to think "that they were somehow meant to be there: witnesses for the rest of the world, offering a glimpse of the valor of the rescue workers, the sorrow of those who died and the tragedy of terrorism."[15] James Poniewozik of *Time* magazine wrote that the brothers, "who shot tirelessly," became "more like the firefighters they so admired than they could have imagined."[16] Clearly, what we are witnessing when we read these words, is a transfer of heroism.

These sentiments were not merely a reflection of a deeply felt need for exceptional television in the face of kitschification. Indeed, one of *9/11*'s most central and compelling themes is the significance of *seeing*, of bearing witness, and of documenting "history."

Vision serves as a complex metaphor in the film, and carries multiple meanings: to see through a lens while filming is to see future projections of an ongoing event—to see the future construction of the past—and as spectators watching the film, we sense the weight of that, of the dizzying implications of that exceptional gaze for our sense of shared memory. We know, inevitably, that these are images we will come to see again and again. The privileged footage is the footage that is considered exceptional, and thereby secures unprecedented recirculation. In its incorporation of such footage, *9/11* claims an exceptional position in future commemoration.

Of course, there is more than one rhetoric of exceptionalism that the film asks viewers to consider and revisit. Prominent among these would be the notion of American exceptionalism, or the idea that the United States is a chosen nation, a country whose history and unique mission in the world defy comparison. Distinguishing between American freedom-lovers and foreign evil-doers, between "us and them," president George W. Bush called upon the American people to embrace this perspective, and encouraged pride in national identity, in what is "exceptionally" American. An extreme unilateralism soon came to define the "war against terrorism" and what has been referred to as the "Bush doctrine." In early January 2002, Bush stated: "At some point, we may be the only ones left. That's okay with me. We are America."[17] A year after the attacks, he referred to America as "the hope of all mankind" and as the light that "shines in the darkness," echoing, of course, John Winthrop's vision of a city upon a hill. Several critics argued that such rhetoric was evoked for strategic reasons, that it was intended to have a numbing effect on the people of a nation in crisis, and that it was misused in justifying a new political agenda. The television networks did not seem to question this development as much as simply reflect it. In his column in *Harper's*, Lewis Lapham described the ceremonies at the World Trade Center site a year after the attacks, and observed how "the on-air company of talking heads (anchors, learned scholars, distinguished statesmen) held fast to the doctrine of American exceptionalism" and celebrated the "belief in the country's innate goodness and invincible power."[18]

What characterizes such a belief? The revised rhetoric of American exceptionalism in its extreme version is perhaps best expressed by Larry Kudlow, CEO of Kudlow & Co, who on the eve of the second anniversary of the attacks described in the *National Review* a widely felt fear "that another shoe will drop," and complained that "the usual chorus of pessimists and critics of President Bush's resolute wartime policies prey upon [such a fear]. Instead of closure, they seek to reopen the emotional wounds."[19] Kudlow's piece, aptly titled "Faith Over Fear," concluded that "above politics, the much bigger question for this nation is whether faith will triumph over fear. Fear and negativism are just as debilitating for individuals as for nations." Fear, according to Kudlow, "is the Devil's work," and "faith is the Lord's."

Kudlow goes on to quote Ronald Reagan as having said that America is the "last best hope of man on earth," and has a "preordained destiny to show all mankind that they too can be free." "When I think of these words," Kudlow concludes, "I get calmer and my anger begins to recede. The sadness of 9/11 gives way to a sense of mission and purpose." It was this sense of "mission and purpose" that helped the Bush administration rhetorically transform the terror attacks into the exceptional cause for exceptional action in a "monumental struggle of good versus evil." The formula of "exceptionalism plus power equals unilateralism took on new dimensions."[20]

One of the reasons for the widespread interest in "American exceptionalism" is that it defines the collective response of almost every generation, to almost every major event, in American history. The exceptionalist logic of Puritan immigrants developed into a mythology of exceptionalism, and the evangelical metaphors of *vision* and *witness* reemerge whenever this logic is revisited. In contemporary visual culture, these concepts reemerge with new complicated meanings attached. After the events of 9/11, whatever was exceptionally "American" was certainly up for grabs: very quickly the advertising industry began systematically conflating the concept of "exceptionalism," boosting sales by appealing to the tested national spirit. The exceptionalism of America was also reflected in the exceptionalism of American products. It would be misguided to consider the canonization of 9/11 outside these processes. Even if the promotional rhetoric of 9/11 never degenerates into a crude attempt to sell a product, it nevertheless shares the tendency to conflate the exceptionalism of the event it describes with the film's aesthetic of exceptionalism—and it achieves this so effectively that it even manages to convince the critics. Furthermore, 9/11 intentionally conflates both of these concepts of exceptionalism with consumer culture's concept of the exceptional when it is marketed as an "exceptional" DVD, with a waving American flag on its cover: not only the footage in *9/11* is exceptional, so, it would seem, is the documentary, the broadcast, and now the DVD.

The exposition of *9/11* (the first minutes of the documentary in which the spectator is introduced to what is to come) is a good indicator of how the filmmakers understand their own project. The first words uttered by Jules Naudet are: "They say that there is always a witness for history. I guess that day we were chosen to be witness." These twenty words invite several interpretations in their gravity and in their economy; significantly, they are uttered with the benefit of hindsight, and they are themselves interpretative. They propose, in part, that the spectator consider *9/11* as *testimonial*. They certainly address the exceptional role of the filmmaker. What they consider remarkable is not only the actions depicted in the documentary, but also the videotape itself, as a testimony to those actions. Consequently, the film takes on a split or double function, and it cannot stop remarking on this fundamental "doubleness." Moments after Jules Naudet's remarks, James Hanlon, the former firefighter who was involved in the production of *9/11* and is featured as one of the narrators, illustrates this again, when he compares the exceptionalism of the heroism of the rescue workers with that of the footage of the event: "On that day guys from my fire house, my best friends, were some of the firefighters in tower 1 after the plane hit. What they did that day, what everyone there did, was remarkable. And almost as remarkable: it was captured on videotape. Inside the tower. Beginning to end." The tagline-like passage unabashedly claims the exceptional position of the footage you are about to see. The word "captured" suggests a closure: the event was captured, and we are about to see it. We are invited "inside the tower." The footage becomes the physical and symbolic evidence of the professional impulse of the filmmakers, of their fateful presence. Unlike Pavel Hlava, Jules Naudet's awareness of the power of his "eyewitness account" presents the professional impulse as a "gift" to a "seer." It transports not only the gift's recipients, but filmmaking itself into a mythical sphere where concepts such as "the elect" and "redeemer nation" already belong quite nicely. The gift of vision is thrust upon the elected.

9/11 is only able to transport the activity of filmmaking into the mythical because it balances its double impulses in its reflexive presentation, in its persistent dwelling upon the recording of its own footage: in short, upon its depiction of *bearing witness through filmmaking*. The most immediate meaning of a "reflexive" documentary suggests simply that the film invites reflection on itself as a film, on its doubleness. The most obvious, but by no means the most significant, characteristic of such a documentary would be the presence of the filmmaker in the film, in one way or another. For film scholar Bill Nichols, the reflexive mode is most interesting for its progressive political potential, or for the ways in which reflexive documentaries self-consciously yet responsibly interrogate themselves, asking viewers to see them for what they really are: not reality, but a film.

And yet the reflexivity of 9/11 differs from Nichols' conceptualization, because it does not set out to "readjust the assumptions and expectations about the world around us" in the ways that Nichols envisions for the documentaries that he tends to idealize.[21] Instead, the presence of the filmmaker in 9/11 is projected as mythic; it is described by the filmmakers themselves in terms of "fate" rather than "chance" or "professional impulse." This ready eagerness to present an explicit self-interpretation to the spectator tends toward the expository rather than the reflexive, and constantly ejects the Naudet documentary from the reflexive sphere that Nichols describes. We are not so much left to ponder the exceptional footage as we are encouraged to accept it as providence. The narrative strategies of the editing process are transparent in 9/11; even if Jules Naudet truly feels that he was "selected to be witness" at the event, that does not necessitate that the feeling be included in the narrative of the event. Similarly, even if the footage is indeed exceptional, James Hanlon does not need to compare it to the heroism of the firefighters in the commentary.

It is in the editing process that these decisions get made. And in this case, the editing decisions imply that 9/11 is to be understood as an exceptional visual experience, on a number of thought-provoking levels of the meaning of the word "exceptional." Of course, the editing process consists itself of a series of visual events for those involved in filmmaking, the result of what happens when the filmmakers look at their footage. We see, ultimately, what they want us to see in the manner that they want us to see it. However, the ability to foresee the editing process—the ultimate shaping of a narrative—even at the moment of recording, is characteristic of the professional impulse that 9/11 describes. Indeed, the recording moment itself becomes an exceptional visual event, a series of lighting-fast decisions motivated by a particular notion of looking.

On the morning of September 11, Jules Naudet was only practicing his filming, since he had less experience than his brother.

The footage is initially unremarkable, and we see only a little of it; he records what he sees, and the tape is not necessarily meant to ever be projected. He is filming the others casually, following them to a gas leak serveral blocks north of the Trade Center. Questions of editing are as yet hypothetical. However, with the crash of the first plane into the building, the observer is turned into participant; he is *there*, in the midst of it all, and suddenly, that presence is everything. Jules Naudet understands what Pavel Hlava did not: that he is "making history"—and that the film in his camera is a "haunting artifact." The moment suggests to Jules Naudet with immediacy that this is exceptional, and that this *will* be projected; thus, he is forced to consider the future presence of a spectator, a viewer.

Gedeon Naudet finds his way to "the scene," camera in hand, moments later, worrying about his brother. When the first tower falls, both brothers realize that the other might very well be dead. Both remain dedicated to filming, however, and continue to film with separate cameras. Some of the most unforgettable moments of *9/11* are the ones in which both brothers show a concern for their lens, wiping and blowing away dirt in order to secure the quality of the recorded images. Keeping the lens clean became "an obsession," Jules Naudet explains in the commentary; it represented an escape from the reality he was witnessing. The fact that Gedeon Naudet manages to keep on filming even as he worries that his brother may be buried in the rubble, demonstrates his awareness of the need to stay fixed on this exceptional moment, and of a story coming into being as a result of a sudden and dramatic turn of events. Even when he helps a man lying in the street, Gedeon Naudet keeps on filming as he supports him. Moments later he points the camera at himself, and, in disbelief, utters the words "Holy Shit!" "Every single cell of your body was telling you you should not be there," he comments, thinking back. Still he stays, and gets as close as he can to the Trade Center. Despite the fact that he is worried sick about his brother, he keeps on filming, and when he is not allowed into the area with his camera, he returns to the firehouse, where he keeps on taping the emotional responses of the firefighters as they return one by one to find each other alive. Twice in the film Gedeon Naudet explains how the "camera man" took over and "just filmed." Even when Jules Naudet finally returns to the station, and the two brothers are united and embrace in tears, the moment is documented by a third party.

The professional impulse, then, is performed mechanically by the brothers, as an immediately felt "pressure to visualize" the exceptional. The concern for the clean, unclouded image in *9/11* comes to define the film, once again, as double narrative. The "machine-like" response of the brothers, however, is given symbolic meaning in the narrative when it is suggested that they are "selected." Since they are not in control of their own actions, but respond as machines, they are clearly governed by fate.

Here, we should distinguish between watching a broadcast and watching a released version of a documentary, since what emerges when we watch, and watch again, will be different every time. The release of an "enhanced and expanded" version of *9/11* on DVD as a "commemorative edition" invites a spectatorship of the event as formative for cultural memory, and this is different from the event of the television broadcast. It therefore inscribes a new "ethical space." The spectator is free to select from chapters at home, to press "play" again and again, after having brought an object home. The press release from Paramount Home Entertainment Worldwide upon the release of the DVD included comments from the president of Paramount, Eric Doctorow, who claimed that the documentary is "destined to become one of the most important historical records in the history of our country."[22] Doctorow was proud to release the film, as it "honors the memory of those who risked or lost their lives."

The narrative of the DVD does not differ dramatically from that of the broadcast. It is our watching that differs. And there is every reason to think that any change in viewing from one format to another has been well thought over. One such change is evident in the exposition of *9/11*. The broadcast version opens with a crane shot of actor Robert De Niro in an artificially lighted street in downtown Manhattan, where he resides. This is followed by his warnings to viewers of the sometimes harsh language of the firefighters in a moment of crisis. In the DVD version, the actor is replaced by a brief text before the documentary begins, which advises "viewer discretion" because of "strong language and subject matter." Then, a text in white letters rolls up a screen that is otherwise black:

ON SEPTEMBER 11, 2001, THE FIREFIGHTERS FROM ENGINE 7, LADDER 1 RESPONDED TO THE WORLD TRADE CENTER.

THIS IS THEIR STORY.

IT IS ALSO THE STORY OF HOW NEW YORK CITY'S BRAVEST
ROSE TO THEIR GREATEST CHALLENGE.

WHAT YOU ARE GOING TO SEE IS THE ONLY KNOWN
FOOTAGE FROM INSIDE TOWER 1—AN EYEWITNESS
ACCOUNT OF ONE OF THE DEFINING MOMENTS OF
OUR TIME.

The "only known footage" from a "defining moment" plays a central role in the location of that moment within an image-saturated culture. When you watch an "eyewitness account," the distance between the spectator and the event diminishes, or so the rhetoric of the message assumes. The visual event of the broadcast of 9/11 invites the spectator inside the tower, and simultaneously occupies her living room; the opening moments of the DVD celebrate the exceptionalism of that event. The phrase, "What you are going to see is . . ." seems to present to the spectator a prefabricated interpretation, before she has made up her own mind. We are told what to think about 9/11 before we have seen any of the exceptional footage at all.

One can only speculate as to whether this change is a symptom of the fact that the "rawness" of reality TV has changed the aesthetic preferences of television audiences. Was De Niro's presence felt to be inappropriate in the released version? In any event, the distinction between broadcast television and DVD as visual events takes us well beyond such considerations of what we actually see; it calls for an analytical approach to understanding different ways of watching, to the conditions of *visuality* that accompany the viewing of a film released in DVD. Such an approach necessarily begins with considerations of marketing strategies, as Doctorow here defines repeated "watching" as "remembering." The exceptionalism of 9/11 that constituted its anti-kitsch rhetoric is inevitably transformed: it is now packaged and placed among other films on the DVD shelves, where one can look up "September 11 documentaries" at Virgin Megastores or at Amazon.com (where I ordered my own copy) under that very generic description. The film is now positioned permanently in living rooms, where it can be played again and again, and where the projection of the footage is repeated into perpetuity.

Hence, the DVD edition proposes an exceptionalism that is always an option, in which case it would seem to lose something.

But Doctorow's invitation to watch, remember, and honor suggests that 9/11 is still exceptional, and that it should have a privileged position in an ongoing activity of commemoration. That privileged position is confirmed by the sales numbers of the object that is 9/11: The Commemorative Edition. But here we should consider the implications of consuming documentaries that are packaged as "more historical" than other documents. Such claims to historical uniqueness are always controversial, as the historian Dominick LaCapra suggests when he says that it is "best to talk about the distinctiveness of the Holocaust, rather than its absolute uniqueness."[23] The traumatic event should be treated differently than others, but not secluded in a way that renders it beyond comparison: "The difficulty with the concept of uniqueness is that it *can* easily serve identity politics and a certain kind of self-interest, and it can also become involved in what may be termed a grim competition for first place in victimhood. Whose experience was it that was *really* unique?" 9/11 invites us to come closer, to come "inside the tower," in the words of Hanlon, or, as James Poniewozik wrote in his review of the film, to come "inside hell." It enables the spectator to get a sense of the "*really* unique." From this vantage point you are, according to the president of Paramount, able to "honor" the memory of the event collectively. When such claims become integral to an aggressive marketing strategy, we have every reason to reflect on their meaning. Again, according to LaCapra,

> the problems of implication (ideological implication, emotional implication) begin with naming, and certainly with the question of whether or not the event is unique. Whether the name should be unique is closely related to whether the event is unique, and all of these questions of uniqueness and naming necessarily get pulled up into a kind of theological matrix, because it's a question of negative sacralization.[24]

On that note, there are several documentaries that contribute far more to a "negative sacralization" than does 9/11, or that transform the event into what LaCapra calls a "founding trauma." These documentaries, however, are not canonized by a cultural elite as "unique" or "exceptional." Rather, they represent the accumulation of kitsch to which 9/11 is an antidote. However, when 9/11 can be found on a shelf in a Blockbuster store or a Virgin Megastore, its transformation into commodity is obvious; its exceptionalism is more sharply articulated, but less convincing, since it is one of many such objects. If you buy the DVD, you can watch again and again in the name of "honoring memory." The collective experience of a broadcast is transformed, as the individual consumer can press "play" on the machine any time, and as the privileges of consumerism as well as commemoration become available in the form of a memory-object that can be purchased at discount. 9/11 has indeed become the exceptional commodity of the exceptional event, and the producers can have it both ways: it is a critical as well as commercial success.

Such a transformation of the visual event, from the momentary experience of the broadcast to the DVD's promise of infinity, is neither unprecedented nor unexpected; some will claim that it is unavoidable. The first hints of transformation appeared as questions of naming arose. For example, in a piece titled "The Brothers Who Made Ground Zero, The Movie," David Usborne wrote, "[a]lready being dubbed the Zapruder of 11 September (after those famous frames of footage that captured the assassination of President Kennedy on November 22, 1963), the Naudet film is as yet unnamed."[25] The lack of a name made other critics compare the footage to the Zapruder film as well; the footage "may become the Zapruder tape of 9/11," *People* magazine suggested.[26] The process of naming is clearly significant in the canonization of contemporary iconography as exceptional; it also illustrates the objectification of the image, the manner in which it becomes a "haunting artifact" that needs its own name, before it can be mass-produced. To settle on the name 9/11 thus reflects a confidence in the material at hand. Surely, the title suggests that the documentary stands out as *the* defining documentary of the event.

The analogy to "the Zapruder tape" is more profound than it may first seem: the story of the 8 mm film shot by Abraham Zapruder, another immigrant to the United States,[27] proved to be the most contested strip of celluloid in the history of the recorded image. The film is often considered the very epitome of the fethishization of memory as image-object. It has been, in its own way, treasured by the cultural elite. In an interview in 1999 in *The Art Newspaper*, J. G. Ballard called it the "Sistine Chapel of our era," and selected frame 224 as one of seven images that had most inspired him in his writing.[28]

Zapruder sold the graphic 26-second-long film to *Life* on the morning of November 23, 1963.[29] It did not air on television before Geraldo Rivera broadcast a copy on the program "Good Night America" on March 6, 1975. A month later, Time Inc. returned the film and all commercial rights to Zapruder's heirs for the symbolic amount of one dollar. The original has been kept in storage in the National Archives since 1978, never to be projected again. Its reinscription in Oliver Stone's *JFK* (1991) further contributed to its mythic status. In August 1999 the government took possession of the film they already kept in their vaults, after long-lasting negotiations with the Zapruder family. The arbitrators charged with deciding how much the film was worth valued it at $16 million.[30]

Thus we see the transformation of a "haunting artifact" into treasured national object. Mary Panzer, a curator of photographs at the National Portrait Gallery in Washington, D.C., commented in *Art in America* that the legal team of the Zapruder family "located the value of the film not only in its rarity but also in formal attributes such as color and composition, and the sheer emotional impact of its subject matter . . . [and] played a video copy of the film and exhibited color prints of individual frames; some of these images were described as 'haunting and beautiful' and likened to works by Warhol."[31] A well-prepared rhetoric of exceptionalism helped the legal team argue for the central place of the film in the formation of cultural memory: "The Zapruder lawyers pointed to the undeniable power that this artifact exerts over our collective imagination. . . . They asked the arbitration panel to imagine the film as the only repository of the rays of life that shone from the president's limousine and hit the frames of Kodacolor II in Zapruder's camera."[32] It has become impossible to think of the event of the assassination without thinking of the images of the Zapruder film; in many ways the film has become coextensive with the event. The implication of this is that every recollection of Kennedy's death is a visual event, and that the exceptionalism of the image is conflated with the exceptionalism of the event. Zapruder has been called "the most influential filmmaker of the last half of the twentieth century," since the film "established a new code of reality for the representation of violent death."[33] And in 1998, the film was made available worldwide on DVD, digitally enhanced. The DVD release of the Zapruder film paradoxically proposes on its cover that it is "a collector's item for all Americans," thus conflating the exceptionalism of the images with the exceptionalism of national belonging—as, ultimately, 9/11 comes to do.

Pavel Hlava was not aware of the prospects for the "eyewitness account" that he left lying around in his apartment in Queens. When it all happened, he recognized, "on some level at least, that he had created an irreplaceable record."[34] However, Hlava "could not absorb what he was seeing," according to the *New York Times*, and "gamely tried to continue with his video postcard." Most important, Hlava did not understand that the story of his tape had just began, rather than ended, on that morning: " 'It's falling down!' he said in Czech. Then he shouted in English, 'Downstairs, downstairs building,' apparently meaning that it had fallen. They drove on to Pennsylvania." Thus, with the conclusion of Hlava's story in the *Times*, we arrive at the symbolic counter to the triumphant story of how *9/11* continues to project its exceptionalism as well as the mythical exceptionalism of a nation.

Notes

1. James Glanz, "A Rare View of 9/11, Overlooked," *New York Times*, September 7, 2003, late ed., 1.
2. William Morris Agency, wma.com. htp://www.wma.com/0/dept/television.
3. Mieke Bal, "Visual Essentialism and the Object of Visual Culture," *Journal of Visual Culture* 2, no. 1 (2003): 9.
4. David Carrier, *Writing About Visual Art* (New York: Ellsworth Press, 2003), 88.
5. David Bianculli of New York's *Daily News* called it "an astonishing, riveting, remarkable piece of filmmaking" ("Vivid View of '9/11'," *New York Daily News*, March 5, 2002: 74). Caryn James wrote in the *New York Times* that the film was an "important, firsthand piece of history," and "also amazing to watch." The broadcast was "timely because it reveals how quickly even the most horrifying images of Sept. 11 have been absorbed, have come to seem ordinary: a necessary way to grasp a terrible reality but also a dangerously forgetful change. You only have to watch another, more typical documentary to see the difference" ("Experiencing The Cataclysm, from the Inside," *New York Times*, March 6, 2002, late ed., E1). James Poniewozik claimed in *Time* magazine that the documentary "plays more like an independent film than a slick network news special" ("Within Crumbling Walls," Time.com, March 11, 2002. http://www. time.com/time/archive/preview/0,10987,1101020311-214111,00.html).
6. Though critical acclaim dominated the overall response to *9/11*, it did stir some controversy, and some critics addressed it. When Caryn James wrote in her review in the *Times* that "[t]here is nothing here that shouldn't be shown and much that is immensely moving," she referred to a letter from a New Jersey prosecutor, William H. Schmidt, who had asked CBS to consider postponing the program six months, as he felt that "[e]xposure through the media to graphic details can be potentially disruptive to the fragile psychological equilibrium [family

members of victims of the terrorist attacks] are so desperately attempting to regain and maintain" (Jim Rutenberg, "CBS Is Asked to Postpone Showing Tape From Sept. 11," *New York Times*, March 1, 2002, late ed., A13). Gil Schwartz, an executive vice president of CBS, claimed that they would show the film anyway because "those who died that day are better served by keeping our memories and our sense of outrage fresh about what happened." On hearing about the television documentary to be broadcast on CBS, Carie Lemack, president of "Families of September 11," an advocacy group for some relatives of vicims of the attack, whose mother died on American Airlines Flight 11, commented: "They're going to show my mom exploding. . . . We are a country in which we don't show public executions, and that's basically what this boils down to."

7. The "rookie" and the other firefighters the Naudets had been filming were stationed at Engine 7, Ladder 1, in Manhattan. The Naudets had been working on the project for months, and turned down multimillion-dollar offers for the footage because they wanted control over it. When they struck a deal with CBS, the network bought the rights for $1 million, for just two broadcasts, with the brothers retaining copyright and creative control of the project. Although the film hardly can be said to consistently be about the rookie throughout, its main focus remains on the firefighters, and, as will be evident, on the filmmakers themselves.

8. Jules Naudet turned his camera away from burning bodies, thinking spontaneously that no one should see what he saw. Images of bodies hitting the pavement were edited out of the broadcast.

9. Most journalists pointed out that the Naudet brothers donated a portion of the proceeds to the Uniformed Firefighters Association Scholarship Fund, as Paramount Home Entertainment, who released the videocassette and the DVD, and Blockbuster Inc., who offered it for purchase or rental, would also do.

10. Ruth Leys, *Trauma: A Genealogy* (Chicago: The University of Chicago Press, 2000), 9.

11. Many theorists of cultural memory envision it thus, for example Pierre Nora. According to Nora, modern memory is, "above all, archival. It relies entirely on the materiality of the trace, the immediacy of the recording, the visibility of the image" ("Between Memory And History," *Representations* no. 26 [1989]: 13).

12. Susan Sontag, *Regarding The Pain Of Others* (New York: Farrar, Straus and Giroux, 2003), 89.

13. Marita Sturken, *Tangled Memories. The Vietnam War, the Aids Epidemic, and the Politics of Remembering* (Berkeley: University of California Press, 1997), 29.

14. Jean-Louis Turlin, "Philip Roth: I feel like saying: Stop, that's enough . . .'," *Independent.co.uk*, October 16, 2002. http://news.independent.co.uk/people/profiles/story/jsp?story=342912.

15. James Martin, "The Year in TV," *America*, June 17, 2002. http://www.americamagazine.org/gettext.cfm?textID=2003&articleTypeID=37&issueID=376.

16. James Poniewozik, "Within Crumbling Walls," *Time.com*, March 11, 2002. http://www.time.com/time/archive/preview/0,10987,1101020311-214111,00.html.

17. Madeleine Albright, "Bridges, Bombs, or Bluster?" *Foreign Affairs*, September/October 2003. http://www.foreignaffairs.org/20030901faessay82501/ madeleine-k-albright/bridges-bombs-or-bluster.html.

18. Lewis Lapham, "Audible Silence," Notebook, *Harper's*, November 2002: 9.

19. Larry Kudlow, "Faith Over Fear," *National Review Online*, September 11, 2003. http://www.nationalreview.com/script/printpage.asp?ref=/kudlow/kudlow091103.asp.

20. Walter Nichols, "The Bush Doctrine," *Diplomatic History* 26, no. 4 (2002): 550.

21. Bill Nichols, *Introduction to Documentary* (Bloomington: Indiana University Press, 2001), 128.

22. *9/11: The Commemorative Edition* was an anniversary release: it was released worldwide on September 12, 2002.

23. Dominick LaCapra, *Writing History, Writing Trauma* (Baltimore: The Johns Hopkins University Press, 2001), 158.

24. Ibid., 161.

25. Usborne, David, "The Brothers Who Made Ground Zero, The Movie," The Independent.co.uk., February 8, 2002. http://enjoyment.independent.co.uk/film/features/story.jsp?story=118784.

26. Susan Horsburgh and Bob Meadows, "Diary of Valor," *People*, March 18, 2002, 117.

27. Zapruder was born in Czarist Russia, in 1905 (Richard B. Trask, *Pictures of the Pain: Photography and the Assassination of President Kennedy* [Danvers: Yeoman Press, 1994]).

28. William Feaver, "The Film Of Kennedy's Assassination Is the Sistine Chapel Of Our Era," *The Art Newspaper*, July–August 1999, 24–25.

29. Richard Stolley, then reporter of *Life*, describes how Zapruder had told him of a dream he had had: "He was walking through Times Square and came upon a barker urging tourists to step inside a sleazy theater to watch the President die on the big screen. The scene was so vivid it made Zapruder heartsick" ("Zapruder Rewound," *Life* [September 1998]: 43).

30. Panzer, Mary, "What Price History?" *Art In America* (October 1999): 68.

31. Ibid., 69.

32. Ibid., 71.

33. Tom Mullin, "Livin' & Dyin' in Zapruderville," *Cineaction* no. 8 (1995): 12.

34. Glanz, E1.

Chapter 4

Advertisements for Itself: *The New York Times*, Norman Rockwell, and the New Patriotism

Francis A. Frascina

On November 2, 2001, *The New York Times* published a full-page advertisement for itself: a digitally altered color reproduction of Norman Rockwell's well-known painting *Freedom from Fear* (1943) with the byline "Make sense of our times" (B12) (see figure 4.1). The original painting depicts a traditional white American family (see figure 4.2). An attentive mother draws a blanket over two sleeping children, as, by her side, the father gazes at their offspring, while holding his spectacles and a newspaper. The headlines, clearly visible in the painting, read "Bombings," "Horror," and "Women and Children Slaughtered by Raids." The digitally altered image that appears in *The New York Times* advertisement depicts the same family with one crucial change. The 1940s newspaper has been replaced so that the father holds *The New York Times*, dated September 12, 2001, with a photograph of the burning World Trade Center below the headline "U.S. ATTACKED HIJACKED JETS DESTROY TWIN TOWERS AND HIT PENTAGON IN DAY OF TERROR."[1] The altered Rockwell was placed at the end of the section titled "A Nation Challenged" and after the subsection "Portraits of Grief," photographs and personal sketches of those who died in the attacks,[2] both of which appeared daily in *The New York Times* after September 11.

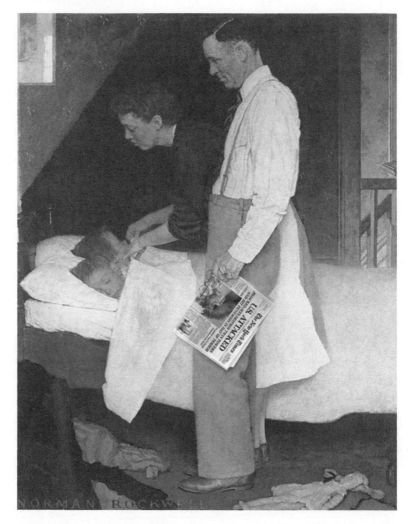

Figure 4.1. "'Freedom from Fear,' a digitally altered version of Norman Rockwell, *Freedom from Fear*, 1943, *The New York Times*, November 2, 2001 (B12)." "©1943 SEPS: Licensed by Curtis Publishing Co., Indianapolis, IN. All rights reserved. www.curtispublishing.com."

Rockwell's *Freedom from Fear*, digitally transformed with the help of a software package, has become a post-9/11 emblem of sentiment, familial security, and the nation under threat. By replacing the World War II newspaper headlines in Rockwell's painting with the headline from September 12, a parallel is forged between America after the Japanese attack on Pearl Harbor and America post-9/11.

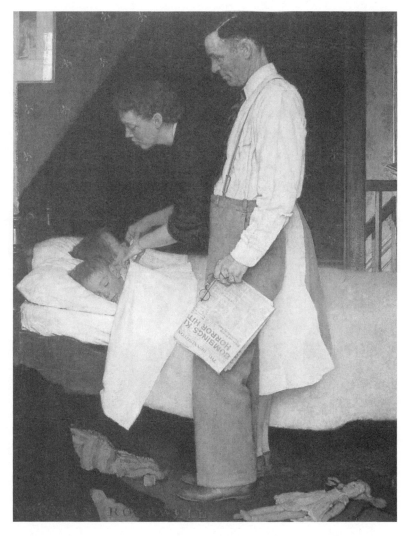

Figure 4.2. "Norman Rockwell, *Freedom from Fear*, 1943, oil on canvas, $45\frac{3}{4} \times 35\frac{1}{2}$ inches, Collection of the Norman Rockwell Museum at Stockbridge, Norman Rockwell Art Collection Trust." "Courtesy of the Norman Rockwell Family Agency."

Between November 2 and December 1, 2001, *The New York Times* included five digitally altered Rockwell paintings on seven separate days (two of the images appeared twice).[3] All of them appeared in the same place, on the last page of "A Nation Challenged" after "Portraits of Grief."

This was a period characterized by an agenda established by President Bush's speech to a Joint Session of Congress on September 20, 2001. On this day he declared a "war on terror" that polarized the world in a new demonstration of American military authority: "either you are with us, or you are with the terrorists."[4] Terrorists, he claimed, "hate our freedoms—our freedom of religion, our freedom of speech, our freedom to vote and assemble." Consequently, "Freedom and fear are at war." He evoked the family, the "true patriot," and announced the creation of the Office of Homeland Security. The speech traded in values as a preparation for radical responses to 9/11. Changes occurred swiftly: On October 7 the bombing of Afghanistan began; on October 8 Governor Tom Ridge was sworn in as head of Homeland Security; and on October 26 the USA PATRIOT Act (Uniting and Strengthening America by Providing Appropriate Tools Required to Intercept and Obstruct Terrorism Act) became law.

The New York Times's choice of Freedom from Fear echoed the text of Bush's speech on September 20. By selecting Rockwell, the newspaper embraced a figure that many regard as the most popular American artist of the twentieth century.[5] He produced work for 322 covers of The Saturday Evening Post from 1916 to 1963, and numerous other illustrations and advertisements. At least four million people across America saw the Post each week. In 2001, the Norman Rockwell brand was reportedly worth between $20 million and $50 million in annual retail sales, with reproductions from The Saturday Evening Post accounting for about 50 percent of that figure.[6] On November 3, the day after the altered Rockwell advertisement for The New York Times first appeared, "Norman Rockwell: Pictures for the American People" opened to the public at the Guggenheim Museum in New York. The traveling exhibition had already reenshrined Rockwell's work within institutionalized definitions of high art, beginning at the High Museum of Art, Atlanta, in 1999. It had also been a financial blockbuster with attendance topping one million. In November 2001 Rockwell's work entered the Guggenheim, a museum traditionally devoted to the representation of abstract art as the major avant-garde phenomenon of the twentieth century. During the 1990s, however, under the directorship of Thomas Krens, the Guggenheim altered its corporate image, bringing in exhibitions such as "The Art of the Motorcycle" in 1998 and a Giorgio Armani fashion retrospective in 2000, which increased its visitor numbers sixfold and provided new funding opportunities: the

Rockwell exhibition and its national tour were made possible by sponsorship from the Ford Motor Company and the Henry Luce Foundation, which also sponsored the catalog. The Guggenheim Museum had opened branches in Berlin, Bilbao, and Las Vegas (in the Venetian Resort Hotel Casino), with another planned for Brazil. In the words of a reporter for *The Baltimore Sun*, the Guggenheim "multinational empire has become the Nike of the museum world: 'Just show it.' "[7]

In the aftermath of 9/11, the Rockwell exhibition and the altered Rockwell images that advertised *The New York Times* were ever more marketable in transformed circumstances, which combined the complexities of national trauma, the new patriotism, and consumerism. One phenomenon of psychological trauma is a longing to return to a vision of the past fashioned by a pleasurable order. The numerous calls for a salve for a wounded people, for healing processes, and for a unified national spirit collided with the externalization of violent retribution, and the impact of job layoffs. Within a few months, posters appeared all over New York City with the image of the Statue of Liberty and the words "Support New York, Shop New York." The "o" of "Shop" was in the shape of an apple enclosing part of the American Flag, draped over the corner of a funeral casket. In a similar pitch to minimize financial losses as a result of falling visitor numbers to New York after September 11, the Guggenheim extended the scheduled Rockwell exhibition by almost four weeks. On a tide of revamped patriotism, this extension supplied a double opportunity. First, it increased the number of visitors desiring cultural comfort. Second, it helped remedy the Guggenheim's financial problems that had resulted in the museum laying off 20 percent of its staff in the wake of 9/11. The Guggenheim thus emerged as cultural ground zero in what one reporter called Rockwell's "enthusiastic reception by an art world, which in a lather of revisionism is falling all over itself to embrace what it once reviled."[8]

"The Four Freedoms"

Freedom from Fear is one of a group of Rockwell paintings, all from 1943, referred to as "The Four Freedoms." The others are: *Freedom of Worship*, *Freedom from Want*, and *Freedom of Speech*. Each painting is a part that stands for the whole four. They are among the most reproduced paintings of all time and have become part of America's "public consciousness and collective memory."[9] There are two early reasons for this. First, the four images were reproduced in color in successive issues of *The Saturday Evening Post*, starting with *Freedom of Speech*, February 20, 1943. Millions of Americans viewed the images, which were received "to wild acclaim"[10] as a "nationwide triumph."[11] Second, the government selected *The Four Freedoms* as the official posters for the second War Bond Loan Drive. Four million posters of the paintings were printed by the Treasury Department. The paintings (and Rockwell himself, in the Hecht Company department store in Washington, D.C., April 26, 1943) went on a nationwide tour in April 1943 to promote the sale of bonds. Newsreel cameras followed, as did further acclaim. Over 1.2 million people viewed the paintings, almost $133 million worth of war bonds were sold, and at least 450 celebrities appeared at ceremonies.

There was not, however, unanimous approval. *Time* magazine published a critical "Art" review in June 1943, shortly after *The Four Freedoms* appeared in poster form. Subtitled "I Like to Please People," a quote from Rockwell, the review claimed that the artist's "popularity is not hard to fathom." His storytelling achieves a "compromise between a love of realism and the tendency to idealize which is one of the most deeply ingrained characteristics of the American people. . . . . Rockwell would probably be incapable of portraying a really evil human being, or even a really complex one—perhaps even a really real one."[12] In the autumn of 2001 this early critique had a reinvigorated relevance. *Time*'s use of the word "evil" in 1943 foreshadowed its extensive use in government and media rhetoric since 9/11. Further, many critics of the Bush administration and of media support of the government had argued that "good" and "evil" were being used in simplistic ways; that a failure to understand the complexities of why the attacks were made risked repeating stereotypical assumptions about Muslims, Middle Easterners, and non-Americans.

In the same issue of *The New York Times* that ran the advertisement version of *Freedom from Fear*, Michael Kimmelman reviewed the Rockwell exhibition at the Guggenheim. He wrote: "in our flag-shrouded anxiety, the cornball sentiments in, say, *Freedom from Fear* . . . seem less remote and contrived than they did before Sept. 11. The picture can make you gulp despite yourself."[13] *Freedom from Fear*, a familiar nostalgic image in collective memory, became newly relevant through the filter of "flag-shrouded anxiety" after 9/11. There is, however, a difference between its generalized appeal, like a commodity capable of being rebranded, and its particular World War II meanings.

In considering this difference there are two issues to highlight. The first is the origin of "the four freedoms" in President Roosevelt's State of the Union address of January 6, 1941. Roosevelt appealed for aid in defense of "the democratic way of life" that had been under assault from "dictators," particularly in Europe, for the last "sixteen long months." He also identified "four essential human freedoms," which he advocated as universal objectives of a better future world: "freedom of speech and expression—everywhere in the world"; "freedom of every person to worship God in his own way—everywhere in the world"; "freedom from want—which translated into world terms, means economic understandings which will secure to every nation a healthy peacetime life for its inhabitants—everywhere in the world"; and the fourth: "Freedom from fear—which translated into world terms, means a world-wide reduction of armaments to such a point and in such a thorough fashion that no nation will be in a position to commit an act of physical aggression against any neighbor—anywhere in the world."[14]

Although Roosevelt praised Rockwell's *Four Freedoms*, the paintings transform the president's emphases on worldwide freedoms into very particular American scenes. The father in *Freedom from Fear* holds an American regional newspaper, from Bennington, Vermont, establishing its New England location. *Freedom of Speech* is obviously set in a town meeting in Vermont, evidenced by the blue-covered "Annual Report" in the foreground. The dissenter is a man in an all-white and predominantly male audience. *Freedom from Want* is less about hunger and poverty and more about the celebration of American Thanksgiving and the image of American abundance in a white, middle-class household. A woman in a cook's apron, overseen by a family patriarch, presents a large turkey-laden plate before the seated family. The immediate symbols of faith in *Freedom of Worship*—a rosary and hands clasped together in prayer—are clearly Christian. So, too, are the clothes of the figure on the right, which are consistent with the Greek Orthodox Church. Significantly this is the only one of Rockwell's *Four Freedoms* to depict a person of color, at top left. Each individual depicted in Rockwell's images, most likely chosen for their canonic generality, stands for a class of individuals within a narrow vision of American belonging.

In retrospect, Rockwell thought *Freedom from Fear* was "based on a rather smug idea."[15] He wrote: "Painted during the bombing of London, it was supposed to say, 'Thank God we can put our children to bed with a feeling of security, knowing they will not be killed in the night.' "[16] For viewers in America it established a geographical distance from the places where war was being waged. Civilian casualties—the deaths of faraway, non-American parents and children—became so abstracted as to be labeled during the Vietnam War as "body count" and during the Gulf War as "collateral damage." Neither phrase would be used to describe deaths in the United States until Timothy McVeigh, convicted of the bombing of the Federal building in Oklahoma City, referred to the deaths of children in his atrocity as "collateral damage." McVeigh, who had learned to kill in the American military during the Gulf War, brought that "distance" to a horrified homeland in 1995.

The second issue to consider is the digital transformation of the Second World War newspaper headline in Rockwell's painting to a scanned-in version of the front page of *The New York Times* dated September 12, 2001 (see figure 4.1). In 1943, Rockwell's parochial image with its New England newspaper was inconsistent with Roosevelt's appeal for a "freedom from fear"—*anywhere in the world*. In 2001, the image was given another narrow focus by *The New York Times*. The horrors of warfare since 1945, including U.S. military actions, kept at a distance by American governments and media, have come "home" through the filter of Rockwell's familiar image of American safety, identity, and domesticity. The filter still assumes racial, heterosexual, and ethnic uniformity against the evidence of a complex multiculturalism in contemporary America. In the aftermath of 9/11, "freedom from fear" now included the proposed need for "homeland security" and the defense of a particular image of the American family. "Fear" was to be transported to those perceived by the United States as enemies: in the words of the president, "either you are with us, or you are with the terrorists." This particular type of American home and family, and the safety of its children, became central to ways in which *The New York Times* encouraged its readers to "make sense of our times."

Representation, Pleasure and Patriotism

Rockwell's representations provide many Americans with pleasurable memories of particular times in their own lives, not least when they recall becoming captivated by the obsessive perfectionism or avid particularizing of one of Rockwell's paintings or *Post* covers. On the other hand, his images are associated with conservative politicians, if not politics. President Ronald Reagan thought Rockwell to be "wonderful" and agreed to chair a fund-raising drive for the planned Norman Rockwell Museum in Stockbridge, Massachusetts; Ross Perot is often photographed in front of his Rockwells. One reason for the appeal of these images is that they are narrative: they tell American stories that offer distraction and absorption, thus absolving viewers from any need for critical analysis of contemporary life and of history. In 1999, Robert Rosenblum, curator of twentieth century art at the Guggenheim, claimed that "just in time for the millennium, we may have a new Rockwell. Now that the battle for modern art has ended in a triumph," which for him took place in the twentieth century, "Rockwell's work may become an indispensable part of art history. The sneering, puritanical condescension with which [Rockwell] was once viewed by serious art lovers can swiftly be turned to pleasure. To enjoy his unique genius, all you have to do is relax."[17] Pleasure and relaxation are the only prerequisites "to love Rockwell for his own sake." Rosenblum wonders how "anybody but the most bigoted modernist could resist . . . the mimetic magic of these paintings."[18] His assertions assume viewers to be passive, unthinking consumers of Rockwell's images and technique rather than active analysts of them as representations. Similarly, Karal Ann Marling, Professor of Art History, and American studies at the University of Minnesota, claimed that, in the 1990s, the artist "stands for something timeless and true, but something always on the verge of destruction—a vision of America that becomes harder and harder to reconcile with rampant crime, urban chaos, and the impersonal age of the computer. To cherish Rockwell can be an act of defiance, a willful retreat into nostalgia and should-have-beens."[19] The appeal to "something timeless and true" proposes that there was once a "vision of America" to be preserved and memorialized. For Marling, Rockwell's pictures take on a life of their own, a peculiar anthropomorphic life: because "Rockwell's pictures lived" in a "world of ordinary things, amid a million other things, they had to select and define, as memory does. They had to accept and cherish. They affirmed precisely what modernism programmatically questions and rejects."[20] However, to discuss pictures in this way, as if they were capable of making choices, is peculiar. Pictures are inanimate; picture makers are not, nor are picture readers.

My point is that pictures produce many possible meanings, which often result in struggles between those meanings that affirm notions of normalcy and those that question normalcy and seek to discover the truths hidden behind such claims. The "reinvention" of meanings for Rockwell's images in a period of patriotic fervor feeds off the myths perpetuated by previous apologists or converts to Rockwell's art as "collective memory." Such meanings also validate a culture deprived of sustained questioning of why certain pictures in American life are hailed as "true."

The terms "normalcy" and "patriotism" with reference to Rockwell's work can be found in an article by Deborah Solomon in *The New York Times* (October 28, 2001) a few days before the opening of the Guggenheim show, Kimmelman's review, and the appearance of the "Freedom from Fear" advertisement. Solomon, a 2001 Guggenheim fellow and author of a biography of Jackson Pollock, was then writing a biography of Rockwell:

> It is odd to think that my generation, the first for whom avant-garde art was not a moral offence but a subject to be diligently studied in college, now finds itself mesmerized by the landscape of patriotism. We who wrote term papers on Andy Warhol's soup cans and barely bothered to look at any flag that did not bear the signature of Jasper Johns are turning for solace to pictorial representations of honor, country and heroism that were born before we were. For years, of course such themes were disdained as artistically incorrect.[21]

Moreover, for Solomon, "[Rockwell] did more to visualize the aspirations of Americans than any other artist of the 20th century. . . . he painted a country whose spirit remained abundantly intact despite two world wars and the Great Depression. In a time when anthrax attacks only intensify our yearning to return to normalcy, Rockwell's pictures of kids, dogs, and uncranky grandmothers might be viewed as normalcy incarnate."[22] Solomon appears oblivious to some vexing and obvious questions: Whose aspirations? Which Americans? What spirit? Whose normalcy? Can anyone speak for "our yearning" without presupposing that difference—social, economic, ethnic, sexual—can be so easily subsumed into her own vision of "normalcy incarnate"?

Solomon singles out Rockwell's *Freedom from Fear* for particular praise as patriotic art, an accompaniment to images of Uncle Sam and Iwo Jima. She does so in terms that portray contemporary "fear" by evoking a racially suggestive "shadow" that causes "the face of American democracy" to "darken": "To see the painting today is to see six decades slip away. We know now what it means to crave freedom from fear, the freedom to walk kids to school and toss a baseball in a park without feeling a shadow of trepidation darken the face of American democracy."[23]

The Guggenheim display of Rockwell's *Four Freedoms* was compatible with Solomon's disturbing characterization. They were housed in a small gallery of their own, a white square room with each painting hung on a separate wall. The effect was chapel-like and the space crowded with craving admirers. An accompanying text panel encouraged visitors to recall the *New Yorker* from 1945, which stated that the paintings "were received by the public with more enthusiasm, perhaps, than any other paintings in the history of American Art." This and other text panels offered visitors in late 2001 and early 2002 a historical rationalization for private consumption. In the large gallery before the one housing the *Four Freedoms*, a text panel, titled "Honoring the American Spirit," stated with uncritical certainty: "Rockwell created images that addressed complex social issues, promoted patriotism, and honored individuals, both celebrated and unknown. . . . Rockwell helped to build a public consensus around national events." The Guggenheim displayed the Rockwells, particularly the *Four Freedoms*, in such a way as to "build a public consensus" around the national event of September 11.

Digital Manipulation and Narrative

On Monday November 5 and Tuesday November 6, a second altered Rockwell appeared in *The New York Times*, again as an advertisement for the paper, with the byline: "Make sense of our times." It was situated in the same place where the altered *Freedom from Fear* advertisement had appeared on November 2 and 4 (B10). This advertisement was based on Rockwell's painting *The Stay at Homes (Outward Bound)* (1927), which is the final work reproduced in the catalog to the exhibition "Norman Rockwell: Pictures for the American People" (186). It first appeared as an illustration for the *Ladies Home Journal* in October 1927. In the painting an elderly mariner rests his left hand protectively on the shoulder of a young boy in a sailor suit; the boy is the right age to be the mariner's grandchild. Accompanied by a dog, they gaze at a sailboat in the distance. The title suggests that they stay at home while perhaps the young man of the middle generation—both son and father—sails away. In the altered version, the advertisement in and for *The New York Times*, the far horizon is replaced by an image of Manhattan, as though seen from the Statue of Liberty, or the Staten Island Ferry, but without the Twin Towers. "They" and "we" look at the cityscape transformed.

In other words, *The New York Times* began to create a visual narrative in the sequence of altered Rockwell images. On November 2 and 4, the headline "events" of 9/11 were established in the image by the placement of the front page of *The New York Times* from the September 12 in the hand of the "father" in *Freedom from Fear*. On November 5 and 6, the hand of the "grandfather" rests on the shoulder of the "grandson" in *The Stay at Homes* (*Outward Bound*), who both gaze at the iconic effects of a Manhattan altered by the destruction of the Twin Towers by hijacked aircraft. In the altered Rockwell, the image of a transformed Manhattan has replaced the image of an expansive sea and a ship sailing to distant shores and *unseen* horrors—the difference for Americans between 9/11 and all wars that came before where horrors were 'elsewere.' Readers of *The New York Times* will have known that many American families had recently gazed at an expansive sea and ships laden with troops and military equipment sailing to distant shores in pursuit of President Bush's "war on terrorism." The bombing of Afghanistan had begun a month earlier, on October 7. The narrative relies, therefore, on a relationship between what is present in the image and what is inferred.

In these two images, *The New York Times* tells an epic story of "cause" (terrorist attacks on the United States), "effect" (deaths of many Americans, destruction of the Twin Towers and their symbolism), and "reaction" (outward bound ships full of military protectors seeking enemies, watched by those who stay at home, the traditional family, characterized by the white grandfather and grandson). Further, the narrative is encouraged by a pun in the byline to the altered Rockwells: "Make sense of our times." The images in *The New York Times* "make sense of our times" by assisting readers and viewers to understand contemporary events within a very limited range of possible conclusions, a range that draws mainly upon the place of Rockwell images in popular understandings of patriotic collective memory. At the same time, the invitation to "make sense of our times" directs readers to consume *The New York Times*.

The following Friday, November 9, a third altered Rockwell appeared in *The New York Times* (B12) (see figure 4.3). This picture was based on *Teacher's Birthday*, which was also a cover for *The Saturday Evening Post*, March 17, 1956 (see figure 4.4). In the original, a teacher stands in front of a blackboard facing a class of children at desks. "Happy Birthday Miss Jones" and other greetings have been chalked on the board. The viewer is positioned to look from behind the children, across their backs to the teacher and blackboard.

In the altered version, a map of Afghanistan hangs in front of the blackboard obliterating the words "Birthday" and obscuring "Surprise Surprise." Readers of *The New York Times* are placed in an imaginative storyline where a lesson about Afghanistan is both part of the myth—enabling American children to "make sense of our times"—and of the sales pitch. Here, *The New York Times* helps "us" to "make sense of our times" and confirms a particular view of education where "we" are freed from the fear of "our" children's ignorance of American conquest and nation-building abroad.

In the narrative sequence, this altered Rockwell has a central function. The children in *Teacher's Birthday*, who can be connected to the children depicted in the two previous altered Rockwells, study a map of Afghanistan in an effort to "make sense of our times." The map becomes a prompt to imagine the next chapter in the narrative constructed by *The New York Times*: cause, effect, reaction, and now retribution. It also prompts a reflection on the previous chapter by providing a visual destination for the mission of the ship, which was erased by a transformed Manhattan in the altered version of *The Stay at Homes*.

The theme of children continued into the next digitally altered Rockwell advert on November 14. Again the image was in full color and on the last page of "A Nation Challenged" (B10). Rockwell's painting *First Love* was originally used as the cover of *The Saturday Evening Post* for April 24, 1926. A young boy and girl sit in a fond embrace on a wooden bench, gazing upon a magnificent sunset. We see their backs, while a dog gazes out at us. In the original the girl holds two flowers. In the altered advertisement, both boy and girl hold American flags—the sort that were sold in Wal-Marts across the United States in the wake of 9/11. In the narrative constructed by *The New York Times* this fourth image associates heterosexual

Figure 4.3. " 'Teacher's Birthday', a digitally a altered version of Norman Rockwell, *Teacher's Birthday*, 1956, *The New York Times*, November 9, 2001 (B12)."

first love with the American flag, and thus with the nation-state. It also takes children, already established in the narrative sequence of *Freedom from Fear, The Stay at Homes* (*Outward Bound*), and *Teacher's Birthday*, into a fond embrace of security, heterosexual love, and the flag.

Following this, on December 1, *The New York Times* used a Rockwell painting on the theme of baseball as an advertisement for itself. The image, titled *Brooks Robinson*, depicts the famous player from the Baltimore Orioles, the team that won the World Series

Figure 4.4. "Norman Rockwell, *Teacher's Birthday*, cover of *The Saturday Evening Post*, March 17, 1956." "Courtesy of the Norman Rockwell Family Agency."

exactly thirty years earlier in 1971—the era of the Vietnam War. In 2001, the World Series with the New York Yankees dominated sports news and briefly revived the spirit of the city. In the original Rockwell, Brooks Robinson signs a ball for a young boy in the crowd. In the altered Rockwell, the player's and the boy's baseball caps are digitally reworked. On Robinson's cap we read the first three letters of the NYPD, the City's Police Department, and on the boy's cap the letters are changed to FDNY, representing the New York City Fire Department. The image serves as a tribute to the hundreds of firefighters, police officers, and emergency services personnel who died at the World Trade Center.

Brooks Robinson appears, as with all of the other altered Rockwells, on the last page of "A Nation Challenged" (B10). In this point in the narrative produced by the sequence of images, children are returned to public pride derived from family enjoyment of sport and sporting personalities. They are now out of the class-room, where, looking at the digitally inserted map of Afghanistan, they learned about the origins and results of "terrorism" and American military reaction. Safe in the knowledge of the latter, they resume "normal" activities of sport and entertainment. At the same time, the letters on the baseball caps are reminders that mourning for the dead at the World Trade Center has become absorbed into the rhythms of American life, in part through the massive increase in post-9/11 merchandising and marketing of items such as the baseball caps that adorn the heads of Robinson and his young fan.

Messages from the White House

On Thursday November 22, the last page of "A Nation Challenged" contained a message from the White House: "Thanksgiving, 2001" signed by George W. Bush and Laura Bush (B10). The message began: "This year we celebrate Thanksgiving still in the shadow of grief." The page served as a text version of Rockwell's *Freedom from Want*, which is the most reproduced of Rockwells's *Four Freedoms*. A week earlier on November 14, *The New York Times* included a "Dining In" section that directly connected the presidential family to Thanksgiving "tradition" and to the name "Roosevelt." A large color photograph of a turkey-laden oval silver plate and a photo-graph of George W. and Laura Bush, dominated the front page. The headline, "Giving Thanks, at the President's Table," was next to an image of a turkey holding an American flag and the subheading "America Reaches for Tradition." Inside, the story continued with a photograph of Laura Bush and the byline "Following Tradition: Laura Bush in the Old Family Dining Room in the White House. On the wall is a portrait of Edith Roosevelt," a figure to whom Laura Bush has been compared (F6). Whether Edith or Eleanor, Theodore or Franklin, the name "Roosevelt" evoked a presidential tradition, a family lineage (Theodore was Franklin's fifth cousin; George W.

is George H. W.'s son), and in the context of post-9/11, triggers associations between "Bush" and "Roosevelt."

The Bush message in the White House Thanksgiving feature in *The New York Times* evoked 9/11: "Thousands of Americans will gather around tables that are missing people who were deeply loved, and who are deeply missed." The message contrasted "suffering and evil" and celebrated "our Nation—its history and freedom, the ideals it embodies, the values it is willing to defend, and the cause for which it is willing to fight." For readers of *The New York Times* the altered Rockwells, previously printed, provided powerful illustrations to this White House advertisement, which ended with "God bless America." The power of "altered eyes" and altered images is carried through in the text with the title "Thanksgiving, 2001," transformed at the bottom of the page to read "Thanks*for*giving" followed by "For ways to help in your community, www.nationalservice.org."[24]

Just over a month after the White House Thanksgiving message, on the final day of 2001, the last page of "A Nation Challenged" contained a message from *The New York Times*. It read, "In a complex world, we wish you simple peace" (B10). For readers and viewers of this paper since the beginning of November the message could be decoded to read: "In a complex world, we wish you a simplistic altered Rockwell piece/peace." Just as Robert Rosenblum encouraged viewers to "enjoy [Rockwell's] unique genius simply by relaxing,"[25] *The New York Times* invited readers to wish for simplicity in the face of the world's complexity.

Noam Chomsky has argued that the interests of power elites who run newspapers need to be examined in conjunction with the function of newspapers as corporations.[26] Editors have to care about advertising revenues as much as they care about the stories they choose to report. The two have a symbiotic relationship with financial profits generated through advertising. After 9/11 major corporations placed large advertisements, many full page, in *The New York Times*. Some participated in expressions of trauma, grief, and patriotic solidarity while also providing corporate information in a time of anxiety; one example is the Bayer Corporation, which produces Cipro, the antibiotic used in treating anthrax.[27]

For Chomsky, corporations advertise in one newspaper rather than another because of mutual associations: a particular way of reporting establishes a site conducive for product placement. For example, on November 14, *The New York Times* published a 150th anniversary section with stories on both its first issue, September 18, 1851 (1, 52), and on the reporting of 9/11 (1, 48), which included a reproduction of the front page of *The New York Times* for September 12, 2001. On November 14 the altered Rockwell advertising the newspaper was *First Love*, in which both boy and girl hold American flags. The 150th anniversary section included a full-page color advertisement placed by Cushman & Wakefield, which is a global real estate services firm with headquarters in New York. Their advertisement was dominated by an image of the American flag flying from a pole and the headline quoting from a famous conventional patriotic phrase ". . . the land of the free and the home of the brave." Cushman & Wakefield congratulate the paper for its years of leading journalism and "shares its dedication and commitment to New York—the financial and business capital of the world. Let freedom ring through the Times" (H11).

The altered Rockwells in *The New York Times* encouraged viewers to associate the post-9/11 journalistic mission with patriotism, patronage, and tradition, one of which is the daily purchase and reading of *The New York Times*. What better advertisement for *The New York Times* than the *Times* itself? The placement of the digitally altered Rockwells also encouraged an emotional response, especially when viewed alongside a page of photographs of those who died in the attacks on September 11.

On September 21 Ariel Dorfman reminded readers of the *Los Angeles Times* of a parallel to the date of September 11—the anniversary of the military coup in Chile in 1973. This coup, sponsored by the United States, brought General Augusto Pinochet to power and resulted in thousands disappearing without a trace. On this anniversary of mourning for Dorfman and millions of other Chileans, he described a situation of parallel suffering, pain, and disorientation: "hundreds of relatives wandering the streets of New York, clutching photos of sons, fathers, wives, lovers, daughters, begging for information, asking if they are alive or dead—the whole United States forced to look into the abyss of what it means to be 'desaparecido,' disappeared, with no certainty or funeral possible for those missing."[28] For Dorfman, these events brought to an "explosive conclusion . . . the United States' famous exceptionalism, that attitude that allowed the citizens of this country to imagine themselves as beyond the sorrows and calamities that have plagued less fortunate people."[29] But American exceptionalism lives on, perhaps more strongly than ever, as Øyvind Vågnes's essay on the documentary *9/11* (contained in this volume) demonstrates. We discover the same impulse in *The New York Times*'s digitally reworked Rockwell images.

Reasons for the effectiveness of President Bush's new patriotism and the compliance of the media are buried deep in *The New York Times*. Here are two related examples. First, on November 3, 2001, the paper carried a report about the novelist Arundhati Roy's essays critical of America's foreign policy, bombing of Afghanistan, and the blowback effects of America's support for the mujahideen and Osama bin Laden after the Soviet Union invaded Afghanistan.[30] Her essays were published in India and newspapers in Europe but "to date, all major American newspapers and magazines have rejected Ms. Roy's new essays on the Afghan war."[31] Second, in *The New York Times* dated November 11, Clyde Haberman noted at the end of "an overview" of the previous day: "the Pentagon is making sure that journalists have virtually no access to independent information about the war [in Afghanistan]. Essentially, all that the American public knows is what the government wants it to know. Some critics ask if the line between information and propaganda has become uncomfortably blurred."[32] There were other resources for journalists.[33] One of them was the Al Jazeera Arabic television network. Established in November 1996 and based in Doha, Qatar, it provided information, film and video footage, interviews, and debates between different representatives, including those from the United States. However, the network's commitment to independence, based on the BBC World Service experience of 60 percent of its staff, was attacked as pro-Islamic by Western media.[34] One example is a highly critical piece in *The New York Times Magazine* by Fouad Ajami, on November 18, 2001, entitled "What the Muslim World is Watching."[35] The front cover of the magazine had a negative combination of headline words "The War They're Watching" and a photograph of villagers in Peshawar, Pakistan, viewing a television program, which clearly shows the face of Osama bin Laden.

I want to conclude by describing the inclusion of the cover of *The New York Times Magazine* containing Ajami's critical report within a photograph of "The First Lady: Laura Bush" by Annie Leibovitz published in *Vanity Fair*, February 2002 (92–93). Coinciding with Bush's State of the Union address on January 29,[36] this was one of several "exclusive" photographs of the Bush administration in a feature article titled "War and Destiny Historic Portraits of the White House in Wartime." In the double-page, posed photograph, dated December 4, 2001, Leibovitz has Laura Bush seated in a chair in the private residence of the White House listening intently on the phone. On her sofa is *The New York Times Magazine*, November 18, 2001, from over two weeks earlier, which appeared in the midst of the visual narrative produced by the altered Rockwells in *The New York Times*. The cover and the words "The War They're Watching" are clearly visible. Here there is a product placement in presidential portraiture, by a celebrated contemporary photographer, which announced that the White House also looked to *The New York Times* to "make sense of our times."

Notes

A longer version of this essay appeared in the *Journal of Visual Culture* 2, no. 1 (April 2003): 99–130, and is reprinted by permission of Sage Publication Ltd. (© Sage 2003).

1. *The New York Times* online store sells a "reprint kit" of that day's newspaper plus the magazine for September 23, 2001, devoted to the aftermath of "September 11." The front cover of the magazine is of "Phantom Towers," which is a digitally manipulated photograph. Does the father in the altered version of *Freedom from Fear* hold the "original" newspaper from September 12 or the merchandised reprint? Original research for this essay was enabled by: an award from the Arts and Humanities Research Board; library resources at Duke University; and the critical support of colleagues in the Department of Art and Art History at Duke. This version was completed while on a Leverhulme Research Fellowship.

2. Eventually collected and produced in an Internet version at *The New York Times* on the web (www.nytimes.com/portraits), and in 2002 as a book (*Portraits 9/11/01: The Collected Portraits of Grief from the New York Times* [New York: Times Books]).

3. In September 2002, Bozell, *The New York Times's* advertising agency, was awarded the $100,000 grand prize in the Athena Awards competition for the "Make Sense of Our Times" advertising campaign with the altered Rockwell images. The Newspaper Association of America and the Newspaper National Network sponsored the competition. The Athena judges noted that "this is advertising at its most potent—a poignant reminder of America's strength and newspapers' power during difficult times."

4. President George W. Bush, Address to a Joint Session of Congress and the American People, September 20, available at the White House web site (www. whitehouse.gov/ . . . /releases/2001/09/20010920-8.html).

5. So opens the preface to Karal Ann Marling, *Norman Rockwell* (Washington and New York: National Museum of American Art, Smithsonian Institution and Harry N. Abrams, 1997), 6. In 1943, *Time* referred to Rockwell as "probably the best loved U.S. artist alive" (in "Art," *Time*, June 21, 1943, 41).

6. According to the vice president for licensing of the Curtis Publishing Company, owner of the *Post*. See Penelope Green, "Rockwell, Irony-Free," *The New York Times*, October 28, 2001, Section 9, 4.

7. Jason Edward Kaufman, "Rockwell Rides A Wave of Patriotism," *The Baltimore Sun*, January 27, 2002 (www.sunspot.net/features/arts/bal-as.rockwell27jan27. story?coll=bal%2Dartslife%2Dsociety).

8. Penelope Green, "Mirror Mirror; Rockwell Irony Free." Also, see my "Revision, Revisionism, and Rehabilitation: 1959/1999: *The American Century, ModernStarts* and Cultural Memory," *Journal of Contemporary History* 39, no. 1 (January 2004): 93–116.

9. Maureen Hart Hennessey, "The Four Freedoms," in Maureen Hart Hennessey and Anne Knutson, *Norman Rockwell: Pictures for the American People* (Atlanta, Stockbridge, and New York: High Museum of Art, The Norman Rockwell Museum, and Harry N. Abrams, 1999), 102.

10. Marling, *Norman Rockwell*, 99.

11. Stuart Murray and James McCabe, *Norman Rockwell's Four Freedoms: Images that Inspire a Nation* (Stockbridge, MA: Berkshire House Publishers and The Norman Rockwell Museum, 1993), 62.

12. "Art," *Time*, June 21, 1943, 41.

13. Kimmelman, "Flags, Mom and Apple Pie through Altered Eyes," *The New York Times*, November 2, 2001, E35.

14. President Franklin Delano Roosevelt, State of the Union Address, January 6, 1941. Speech available at The Franklin and Eleanor Roosevelt Institute web site (www.feri.org/fdr/speech03.htm).

15. Rockwell quoted by Hennessey, "The Four Freedoms," 102.

16. Rockwell quoted by Marling, *Norman Rockwell*, 100.

17. Rosenblum, "Reintroducing Norman Rockwell," in Hennessey and Knutson, *Norman Rockwell: Pictures for the American People*, 185.

18. Ibid., 183.

19. Marling, *Norman Rockwell*, 7–8.

20. Ibid., 8.

21. Deborah Solomon, "Ideas & Trends: In Time of War; Once Again, Patriotic Themes Ring True as Art," *The New York Times*, October 28, 2001, Section 4, 14.

22. Ibid.

23. Ibid. On October 29, Solomon's article was placed in the Education section of *The New York Times* on the web as a resource for students and parents.

24. The web reference is for the Corporation for National and Community Service, USA Freedom Corps (AmeriCorps, SeniorCorps, and Learn and Serve America).

25. Rosenblum, "Reintroducing Norman Rockwell," 185.

26. See Noam Chomsky, *Understanding Power: The Indispensable Chomsky*, edited by Peter R. Mitchell and John Schofield (New York: The New Press, 2001), chapter 1, especially 18–24. The New York Times Company, with 2002 revenues of $3.1 billion, includes *The New York Times, International Herald Tribune, Boston Globe*, sixteen other newspapers, eight network-affiliated television stations, two New York City radio stations and more than forty web sites, including nytimes.com and boston.com.

27. For one example see the full page ad in *The New York Times*, November 1, 2001: A17.

28. Ariel Dorfman, "Commentary; America Looks at Itself Through Humanities Mirror," *Los Angeles Times*, September 21, 2001, Section 2, p. 15.
29. Ibid.
30. Celia W. Dugger, "An Indian Novelist Turns Her Wrath on the U.S.," *The New York Times*, November 3, 2001, A3. Roy's articles were published in European newspapers, including *The Guardian*. See: Arundhati Roy, "The Algebra of Infinite Justice: As the US Prepares to Wage a New Kind of War," *The Guardian*, September 29, 2001, (www.guardian.co.uk/saturday_review/story/0,3605,559756,00.html) and Arundhati Roy, "Brutality Smeared With Peanut Butter," *The Guardian*, G2, October 23, 2001 (www.guardian.co.uk/g2/story/0,3604,579191,00.html). Both of the Roy texts can also be found in Arundhati Roy, *Power Politics*, expanded edition (Boston: South End Press, 2002). For a critique of Roy see Tod Gitlin, "The Ordinariness of American Feelings," October 10, 2001, opendemocracy.net (www.opendemocracy.net/debates/article-2-47-105.jsp).
31. Dugger, "An Indian Novelist Turns Her Wrath on the U.S."
32. Clyde Haberman, "An Overview: Nov. 10, 2001: Bush's Exhortation at the U.N., and Firing Up the Hollywood Canteen," *The New York Times*, November 11, 2001, Section 1, B1. See the careful piece by Elizabeth Becker, "In the War on Terrorism, A Battle to Shape Opinion," *The New York Times*, November 11, 2001, front page and Section 1, B4, B5.
33. For example, Marc W. Herold, *A Dossier on Civilian Victims of United States' Aerial Bombing of Afghanistan: a Comprehensive Accounting, December 2001* (Durham, NH: unpublished manuscript, Department of Economics and Women's Studies, University of New Hampshire) (pubpages.unh.edu/~mwherold).
34. Information from Ibrahim Helal, editor-in-chief of the Al Jazeera newsroom, lecture, Duke University, February 6, 2002. For a report by a former BBC journalist, and now a senior producer at MSNBC.com, see Michael Moran, "In Defense of Al-Jazeera," October 18 (www.alied-media.com/aljazeera/msnbc.htm).
35. Fouad Ajami, "What the Muslim World is Watching," *The New York Times Magazine*, November 18, 2001, 48–53, 76, 78. For a critique see: Rime Allaf, "Qatar's Al-Jazeera is not pro-Zionist enough for New York Times's Foud Ajami's Taste," *The Daily Star* (Lebanon), November 20, 2001 (www.dailystar. com.lb/opinion/20_11_01_b.htm) or (www.mafhoum.com/press2/71P21.htm).
36. Available at (www.whitehouse.gov/news/releases/2002/01/20020129-11.html). For a critique see Rahul Mahjan, "The State of the Union and the New Cold War," January 31, 2002, *Counterpunch* (www.counterpunch.org).

Chapter 5

The Comfort Zone: Japan's Media Marketing of 9/11[1]

Yoneyuki Sugita

The 9/11 terrorist attacks were of course big news in Japan. And it was made bigger still by the Japanese mass media's efforts to market 9/11 by placing the attacks into a context that would excite the emotions of the Japanese people. However, reporting the 9/11 attacks and subsequent related events presented a problem for the Japanese media for two reasons. First, the media was at a loss to explain what had actually happened. Second, and more fundamentally troublesome, was how to understand the significance and meaning of the attacks through the lens of Japanese society. The value of 9/11 as a media commodity depended on the Japanese mass media's abilities to locate the comfort zone, or to package these events and their meanings in a manner that the Japanese public would find compelling and comprehensible. In the process of tackling these problems, the media passed through a period of situating and resituating the shocking images of airline passenger planes smashing into the World Trade Center towers, buildings that were very familiar to the millions of Japanese tourists who had visited New York City or to the many Japanese moviegoers who knew the New York City skyline from watching Hollywood films.

"When confronted by a culturally exotic enemy, our first instinct is to understand such conduct in terms that are familiar to us—terms that make sense to us in light of our own fund of experience," writes Lee Harris, as part of his attempt to chart the West's course of action in response to 9/11.[2] When the term "enemy" is replaced with "event," Harris's comment becomes an accurate description of the situation that the Japanese mass media faced in the wake of 9/11. The Japanese media tends to confine major news events, especially news about an overseas crisis (usually read as a crisis involving the United States), within certain categories of understanding that the Japanese public are long familiar with. The Japanese mass media long ago convinced itself that it had to set the agenda for how major news items, especially items that suggest the need for response to foreign policy challenges, would be presented to the Japanese public. For example, if North Korea were to test launch a ballistic missile, broadcast TV would immediately start showing new or stock video of the missile leaving the launch pad, complemented by an overlay of ominous-sounding background music to deepen the impression of danger and threat, with the rest of the media echoing this style of reporting. Above all, media outlets across the board could be relied on to follow the time-tested formula of analyzing the implications of the launch for Japan's safety within the context of the U.S.-Japan bilateral security agreement. No major or popular mass media outlet would think of discussing the possibility that North Korea might have legitimate state interests that its government decided to protect, as any country with a functioning central government would consider doing, and that ballistic missiles might represent a defensive counterthreat to any country contemplating military aggression against North Korea (usually read as the United States, but sometimes understood to include Japan).

In short, the Japanese mass media considers news items not as reportage of political, economic, social, or business events, but as information products to be sold to the Japanese public. The best marketing strategy is to fit these news items into test-marketed categories, or "comfort zones," by which I mean the categories of collective understanding that Japan's mass media assumes the public is comfortable with. The media as an organ of propaganda serving government and/or corporate interests is not my concern here. While propaganda in support of state or corporate interests occurs to a significant degree on a daily basis, the Japanese media is less nervous about government ministerial or business agents looking over their shoulder and more concerned with how news items can be presented in ways that are appealing and familiar to the public and that fit preexisting popular notions of Japan's place in the world.

As a story about a major overseas event, 9/11 was at first difficult for Japan's mass media to cover. While it was soon reported that the terrorists who hijacked and flew the airliners were apparently from Middle Eastern countries, the attacks themselves did not immediately fit into any category of understanding about the Middle East region, or any other global situation already familiar to the Japanese media. Consequently, the media found that it had to experiment for a period of time with different ways of marketing 9/11-related news. Generally speaking, the marketing of 9/11 proceeded initially through four coverage themes: (1) constant repetition of the spectacular images of the attacks (the airplane crashes into the World Trade Center) in a fairly decontextualized, apolitical, and dichotomous fashion (innocent New Yorkers victimized by crazed terrorists); (2) the positioning of the 9/11 terrorist attacks within the context of Islam and the Middle East, a religion and a region unfamiliar to most Japanese prior to 9/11; (3) expressions of sympathy for Americans and praise for America's greatness as represented by its ability to quickly get back on its own feet; and, (4) reports about what seemed to be a resurgence of American nationalism, which were coupled with reports of sudden and jarring American demonstrations of a consensual desire to rail against and kill all terrorists.

Finally, after the launch of the U.S. attack on Afghanistan in October 2001, the Japanese mass media found a way to present 9/11 in a way that fit into the nation's comfort zones, or preexisting sense-making categories that both the media and the public are at ease with. These categories were based on:

(a) The Japanese public's understanding of the protection provided by the United States, in the form of the more than fifty-year-old U.S.-Japan bilateral security agreement, which operates not only to provide Japan with security but that has also provided, historically speaking, room for Japanese companies and government ministries to pursue enrichment and economic growth;
(b) Ambivalent pacifism, a belief structure in Japanese society that houses two opposing popular desires: (1) a strong emphasis on Japan's newfound postwar interest in pacifism and (2) the desire for Japan to play a more substantial role in international affairs.

This chapter demonstrates that in the case of 9/11 the Japanese mass media believe that success as agenda-setters for the public, along with commercial success (after all, with the exception of

Japan's public broadcasting station, the media consists of for-profit commercial entities), depends on keeping the news confined to these categories. When the Japanese mass media linked 9/11 to the U.S.-Japan alliance, it realized that it had finally found a groove that could supplant earlier nerve-wracking reporting attempts. When this happened, the mass media was able to prolong public interest in 9/11 beyond the temporarily arresting images of suicide airplane attacks. Once 9/11 was linked by the media to the U.S.-Japan alliance, there was room for opinionated disagreement among, for example, those who support the alliance and those who do not; those in favor of dispatching Japan's Self Defense Forces (SDF) to Afghanistan's coastal waters in support of America's military campaign, and those who stand against it. But unquestioned itself was the U.S.-Japan alliance, which Japan's mass media used as the overriding lens for viewing 9/11 and explaining its ramifications for Japan to the Japanese people. Any other analytical option, even the obvious one of attempting to understand how the Arab world's growing hatred for the United States had contributed to 9/11, was scarcely considered.

As this discussion concerns the Japanese mass media and its role of translating the meaning of 9/11 to the Japanese public, the main focus will be on television news and news shows broadcast by commercial television stations (with the exception of NHK, Japan's public broadcast station), major nationwide newspapers, tabloid newspapers, popular magazines with large circulations, books published by mass-market publishers, and polls. The manner in which Japan's television stations and leading mass-media writers covered 9/11 will be surveyed in order to arrive at a general understanding of the prevalent mass-media strategies for marketing the 9/11 attacks.

Spectacular Images and Simplistic Viewpoints

In Japan, it was evening when the first aircraft crashed into the North Tower of the World Trade Center. Japan's mass-media coverage of the 9/11 attacks began with dramatic, Hollywood-style images on the TV screen. As in the West, commercial TV stations in Japan continuously replayed the spectacular images of the jet crashes to keep viewers riveted to the screen. The public was informed by these fast-paced, shocking images rather than by detailed and objective commentaries. While this approach was understandable given the absence of explanatory facts during the early days of 9/11 coverage, the news bureau director at Nippon Television (NTV), one of Japan's three major commercial broadcasters, readily admits that at the outset, commentary about 9/11 (explanation and analysis) was kept to a minimum and served mainly as an organizational device to help viewers process the far more important video images. As the NTV news director put it: "We all know that the public was interested in knowing the facts immediately after the incident took place. Broadcasting, however, needs a series of attractive flows: a live broadcast, a report, a summary, and a commentary. When we have the right rhythm of flow, our audience will not change the channels. Commentaries are necessary to keep the flow moving."[3] The emphasis was on big-picture drama and action. Echoing this preference for visual as opposed to analytical content, the chief news executive at another major commercial network, Fuji Television Network, said he wanted "images of the scene rather than people's faces." The NTV news director claimed that his station was giving the public what it wanted. "What matters most is what the viewers wish to see. Of course, that is footage of the scene," he said.[4]

Only one of Japan's three commercial networks, NTV, broadcast an extended special (lasting two hours) the night of 9/11. The NTV program, which was titled "Exclusive: Worldwide Simultaneous Exposition-09/11 Camera was Inside the Building," converted the attacks into aesthetic commodities, accompanied by such window-dressing features as exclusive video shots from all sorts of angles, constant replays of the most dramatic images, a succession of well-thought descriptions of visual elements, and other sophisticated visual presentation techniques. Absent, however, was analytical substance or any serious attempt to explain why the attacks had happened. Thus, it can be argued that NTV's news special was quite successful at dramatizing 9/11, especially as teary relatives of the victims and heroic activities by firefighters pulled at the heartstrings of Japanese audiences. Indeed, NTV registered a TV rating of 30.4 percent of all households for this program, an astonishing success given that in Japan even popular TV entertainment shows rarely command ratings of higher than 18 percent, and very few programs have reached 30 percent.[5] The shocking scenes presented in this program undoubtedly upset many viewers and produced anger at the still-unknown assailants, but viewers were presented with no objective analysis of who might have been responsible for the attacks, or why.[6]

During the two-hour news special, NTV paraded various "experts" across the screen, but the result was only speculation and superficial examination. The main job of these experts was to break the silence of watching the nonstop onscreen horrors with provocative remarks. In contrast, Japan's public broadcasting station, NHK, tried to fulfill its mission of presenting only the objective facts without any spectacular enhancement. As part of its coverage, NHK opted not to invite outside experts but to rely solely on its in-house staff. NHK's editor-in-chief later said, "In this kind of ongoing emergency, the mission of the public broadcasting station is to convey only the facts. Consequently, we focused on live footage from the scenes and reports from NHK's correspondents. At that particular time, we did not have much background information about the incident. We came to the conclusion that it was too early to invite external experts for commentary."[7]

In short, eye-popping scenes initially had a startling impact on Japanese television viewers, but otherwise the public did not know what to make of 9/11. The continuous broadcast of these scenes did not fall within a comfort zone. There was no immediately available category of understanding that could be referenced, and hence speculation about 9/11 was rife, not only on TV but also in the print media. The excitement generated by the initial coverage of 9/11 quickly began to die down as there was no central news focus and the public became inured to burning and collapsing buildings. To maintain interest in 9/11, the Japanese mass media began searching for sound bites. When President George Bush announced that the 9/11 attacks meant that the United States was at war, the Japanese media jumped immediately on his words. They quickly and uncritically accepted Bush's simplified explanation of what had happened and how America would respond: A terrorist group called "Al Qaeda" was responsible for the attacks. Osama bin Laden is their leader. Both fundamentalists and protectors of fundamentalists are the bad guys while Americans are innocent victims. This would be a war on terrorism, and the fight against terrorism would be a righteous crusade.

War, especially a war declared by the world's only superpower, is guaranteed to arouse public interest and generate media coverage in any country. But Bush's sudden war rhetoric struck a chord that was more familiar in Japan than in most other countries, especially when one considers that Japan's memory of its wartime defeat is only a half-century old and that since that time there has been a steady drumbeat of war-related concerns in the context of the generally quite prominent coverage Japan's mass media gives to the implications of any change in Japan's security relationship with the United States. The war rhetoric helped transform 9/11 into an information product that the mass media felt it could market more easily, especially as it was becoming evident that the Japanese people were hungering for a more meaningful explanation of what happened and its ramifications. Not only did the Japanese mass media need to find the right explanatory format, it also needed to distill information into simple black-and-white terms, to make 9/11 consistent with the usual approach to reporting major foreign policy stories in Japan. The war rhetoric that started to flow from the Bush administration and its Manichean view of evildoers vs. innocent victims exactly suited the Japanese mass media's need to roll out a different category of understanding.[8]

Focus on the Middle East

In the wake of the 9/11 attacks, mass media outlets such as newspaper tabloids, popular magazines, and publishers of general-interest books began marketing 9/11 from a different perspective. Because the terrorist attacks were executed by Islamic fundamentalists, there was a sudden surge of interest in the Middle East and Islam, made more intense by the fact that most Japanese barely had any knowledge of the region and its leading religion. A number of popular books on Islam and the Middle East, not to mention maps of Afghanistan, experienced a strong surge in sales.[9]

Keeping in step, Japan's commercial TV networks began to air programs that dealt primarily with Islam and the Middle East. Beyond this thirst for basic knowledge, the question underlying these TV programs, and the information in the press, was whether Japan, too, might become the victim of terrorist attacks by Islamic fundamentalists. Whether it was ignorance or a preference for simpleminded explanations, the tabloids, popular magazines, and TV gossip programs chose to represent the Islamic world as monolithic and essentially different from the modern Western world (which for the purposes of this reporting included Japan), and therefore mysterious and dangerously "other." Osama bin Laden, whom the United States regarded as the terrorist mastermind behind 9/11, was described as the leader of a global Islamic terrorist network. In short, bin Laden and the Islamic world were paired and presented as treacherous and evil, dangers to those living in the West—and possibly in Japan.[10]

From the outset of the Japanese mass media's focus on Afghanistan, which the U.S. government had decided to confront militarily, the Taliban were essentially described as alien beings, liable, Japanese viewers were told, to behave immorally. Following up on Bush's declaration of a "war on terrorism," the Japanese media decided that it had to make clear to the public who the enemy was. Taking their cue from U.S. assertions of the nature of the terrorist threat, the Japanese mass media in short order went along with designating the Taliban as the primary enemy target, though there was no independent Japanese government official report or Japanese media investigation to confirm whether this determination was warranted. With this biased presumption now in hand, the Japanese mass media thought it would be much easier to find an audience-pleasing way to report on the next 9/11 event, which was the start of military operations in Afghanistan. From a business-marketing standpoint the sensible course of action was to report the attack on Afghanistan in uncomplicated, dichotomous "good vs. evil" terms.[11]

With the start of military operations, this was also a time for some of Japan's Middle East scholars to sell their knowledge to media outlets and, in some cases, become celebrities. It did not take much to encourage this kind of opportunism, as various mass-media outlets wanted to utilize expert opinion to buttress the credibility of their TV and print reporting. What the mass media really wanted, however, was not scholarly exposition but well-dressed eggheads who would provide undemanding explanations of current affairs and, if possible, sensationalized accounts of future scenarios that made sense to Japanese TV viewers and newspaper readers. The usual question asked of these experts was, "Why did Islamic fundamentalists attack the United States?" The experts provided several possible answers, such as a long history of conflict between the Islamic world and the West, or, alternately, confrontation between a traditionalist Islamic-based civilization and a liberal/consumption-oriented American civilization, the negative effect of globalization upon the Islamic world, and the loss of Islamic tradition because of American influence, etc. Another often-asked question was: "When [not "whether"] will the United States retaliate militarily?" The assumption was that it was logical for the United States to retaliate, and that retaliation was simply a matter of time.[12]

In Japan, academics were often put before the cameras or their views presented on newspaper op-ed pages to explain 9/11. But these scholars, while reputable in their academic fields, were in this instance asked to perform as fortunetellers. For example, before the military campaign in Afghanistan started, scholars were often asked to speculate about strategies and tactics. Their remarks were not only speculative but also often wide of the mark. One prevalent expectation was that the United States would be bogged down in Afghanistan just like Great Britain was in the nineteenth century and the Soviet Union in the late twentieth century. Contrary to this expectation, it took little more than a month for the United States to rout out a significant number of Taliban and send the rest into hiding. Even the most talented scholars are not necessarily good fortunetellers. In exchange for fame and financial compensation, many initially reluctant academics provided viewers with half-baked opinions and erroneous judgments.[13]

The Japanese mass media again successfully sold the 9/11 attacks not by promoting a genuinely deeper understanding of historical events in the Middle East or the global Islamic community, but by renting professional scholars and asking them to present generally uncomplicated, audience-pleasing, black-and-white explanations. Still, even though the commercial mass media was trying to maintain the discussion at the mostly superficial level, they found themselves fumbling about to put post-9/11 events into a framework that would make the Japanese public comfortable. In other words, images of the 9/11 airplane crashes, collapsing skyscrapers, clouds of debris, and the personal testimony of the victims needed very little Japanese context, because these were just the raw, visceral images of a catastrophe that needed no filtering as it passed to the brain. But as America started down the road to retaliation, eager to unleash the might of its military, the possibility of consequences could no longer be ignored. The enemy had at first been clearly articulated—Al Qaeda, the Taliban, Osama bin Laden, or all three—but as the war on terrorism became a war increasingly framed in global terms, it became clear that countries other than the United States would have to make choices. As it dawned upon the Japanese that these choices would probably involve their country, a sense of unease took hold. Accordingly, the Japanese public began to look for more than news, which up to this point had mainly emphasized a war against terrorist evil and the tactics and strategies needed to win that war. Again, Japan's mass media had to search for a different way to market the news. The right "comfort zone" for 9/11 and its aftermath had not yet been found, so this called for another change in news reporting.

The Rise of American Nationalism and Patriotism

Alongside the negative reporting on the Islamic world, some mass-market books and entertainment magazines featured light, cheerful commentary and essays by Japanese authors who looked favorably upon the post-9/11 resurgence of American nationalism and who praised America's greatness as demonstrated by its ability to bounce back quickly. One such Japanese author, George Itagoshi, a popular writer in Japan who often explains America to Japanese readers, wrote that the damage caused by 9/11 was much worse than anything America had experienced during World War II, but that its resilience enabled it to rise again like a phoenix.[14]

Fukiko Aoki, an international freelance journalist who writes popular books and essays on a variety of subjects, was in New York City at the time of 9/11, and was thus able to convey vivid descriptions of how New Yorkers suffered. Though she was sometimes critical of the United States after 9/11, particularly with respect to its unilateral political response and arrogant dismissal of other countries, her reports frequently expressed a strong belief in and respect for the vitality and power of American democracy. This belief was often coupled with denouncements of Islamic fundamentalists, but with no attempt to understand who might have been behind the 9/11 attacks and for what reasons.[15]

Sadahei Kusumoto, chairman emeritus of the Japanese American Association of New York (one of the most influential Japanese-American societies in the United States), argued in the mass circulation magazine *AERA* that the U.S. attacks against Al Qaeda in Afghanistan had the backing of all Americans. According to Kusumoto, President Bush had not manipulated the American public, nor had he led the country into a war on terrorism; instead, he believed that in some sense Americans pushed Bush to take revenge. In his view, the Bush administration was merely acting as expected, in response to the popular will, without actually explaining how the "will of the people" had been communicated or interpreted by U.S. leaders.[16]

An energetic journalist who is quite familiar with the American media, Michelob Nakamura, admitted that some U.S. mass-media outlets, especially TV broadcasters, covered 9/11 in such a way as to deliberately fuel the rise of American nationalism. She wrote that during the first three months following 9/11, the U.S. mass media was extremely one-sided, accentuated the ominous, and was unreceptive to opinions from scholars, students, critics, or journalists who held any opinion that challenged the views of the Bush administration. But Nakamura found this stifling of antigovernment criticism to be a temporary phenomenon, as she believed that America had returned to its core values of freedom, liberty, and democracy. She became convinced that the United States had not lost its ability to criticize and analyze itself, and she affirmed the underlying strength of American democracy.[17] Ryu Murakami, a best-selling novelist and essayist, was impressed with the diversity, flexibility, and perseverance of American behavior as a whole, such as when American leaders asked their fellow Americans to return to a life of normalcy after the terrorist attacks.[18]

Because 9/11 was a violent catastrophe, the Japanese people were quick to sympathize with the United States, as did many other countries. At the same time, Japanese writers recognized that 9/11 had sparked a resurgence of U.S. nationalism and patriotic pride, a resurgence that they regarded, albeit vaguely, as "important." These two currents were bound to collide, as the sympathy felt by the Japanese people, while undoubtedly endearing to many Americans, did nothing to help the Japanese themselves better understand the U.S. response to 9/11. The sympathy phase proved to be short-lived, and in fact was soon followed by a strong backlash in Japan against the United States when military action began. While domestic U.S. polls showed the Bush administration getting high marks from the American public for its war on terrorism, the Japanese began to reveal a growing feeling of revulsion toward the United States once the bombing campaign in Afghanistan started and media stories about the plight of war victims started to appear. As the backlash took hold among the general public, the Japanese mass media elected to downplay feelings of sympathy toward the United States and began backing away from their earlier endorsements of the U.S.-led military intervention in Afghanistan.

Emerging Criticism of America's Reaction to 9/11: The Dangerous Rise of American Nationalism

As the United States started its military campaign against Afghanistan, the Japanese mass media swiftly changed its 9/11-related news coverage. Confronted by images of bombs dropping and of U.S. soldiers in full battle gear, the mass media realized that a sympathetic view that celebrated the virtues of American society was no longer tenable for the Japanese public. The media promptly started to criticize the immaturity and barbarity of U.S. military actions, decried the dangers inherent in rising American nationalism, and found fault with American arrogance. The Japanese mass media began to ask the question: "Why is the United States hated so much, particularly by people in the Middle East?" Manabu Miyazaki, a popular and outspoken nonfiction writer, compared the United States to an adult who acts with the mind of an infant, unable to take into account other people's perspectives. This infantilized adult did not doubt his omnipotence or his own sense of justice; he became violent if his desires could not be satisfied. According to Miyazaki, it was unfortunate that this infantilized adult had been invested with the strongest power of any country in the world.[19]

On November 10, 2001, President Bush addressed the United Nations. At that point the U.S. military was occupying Afghanistan. Evidently, this victory gave Bush the confidence to demand that all nations identify whether they were friends or enemies of the United States, stating: "[For] every regime that sponsors terror, there is a price to be paid. And it will be paid. The allies of terror are equally guilty of murder and equally accountable to justice."[20] Gen Nakayama, a prominent Japanese translator, intellectual, and writer who regularly addresses comments to the Japanese public through the Internet about the 9/11 attacks, appears to have been the first person in Japan to call Bush's pronouncement the "Bush Doctrine." Taken literally, this doctrine could be interpreted to declare that the United States considered itself to be the world's sole sovereign nation, and that only Bush, as the sitting U.S. president, possessed the right to exercise that sovereignty. Bush has restricted important civil liberties in the United States, with surprisingly little criticism by the American mass media. Nakayama expressed his contempt toward U.S. arrogance about its power and its egocentric behavior.[21]

This contempt, and the contempt that would be voiced by numerous Japanese critics whose opinions now mattered to the mass media, was largely a response to President Bush's simplistic articulation of America's war on terrorism. Because innocent people had been killed on American soil as a result of vicious terrorist attacks, it was ostensibly just for the United States to retaliate against Afghanistan, the nation that housed Osama bin Laden who was believed to be responsible for 9/11. Thus, the formal military dimension of the "war on terrorism" began. And while people the world over were generally convinced that acts of terrorism are unforgivable, Osamu Nishitani, a well-known social critic and professor at Tokyo University of Foreign Studies, sounded a dissenting voice, asking what gave Bush the right to determine who the terrorists are. The United States selectively chose who the terrorists were, he claimed, and later easily expanded the scope of the term "terrorist" to those who presumably protected terrorists and to those who did not support the United States.[22]

This critical tendency found well-received, powerful expression in Tetsu Nakamura, a Japanese physician who has been operating hospitals in remote Pakistani and Afghan villages for seventeen years, and who occasionally writes for both Japanese mass media and non–mass market publications. He wrote that the construction of a "righteous America" in opposition to a "satanic Taliban" was sheer nonsense, and he pointed out that this simplistic Manichean view was merely American propaganda that Japan had uncritically accepted. On the basis of his long experience as a physician working closely with Afghanis, he expressed the belief that ending starvation in Afghanistan rather than military retaliation would be the quickest way to eradicate any support for terrorism in that country.[23]

In September 2002, *Shukan SPA!* [*Weekly SPA!*], a popular general-interest weekly magazine, posed a series of straightforward questions that it believed ordinary Japanese people were asking: Can the Japanese people trust so-called American justice? Has Osama bin Laden been proven guilty? At this time, the possibility of a U.S.-led invasion of Iraq was starting to get attention in Japan, and so another question was asked: Can Iraq be censured for its possession of weapons of mass destruction? And, if so, how can America's use of such cruel weapons as depleted uranium armaments and cluster bombs go unchallenged?[24] One of Japan's most prominent newspaper commentators, Yoichi Funahashi, an internationally known foreign policy journalist who writes for the *Asahi*, asked a straightforward question: "Why does only the United States have the right to carry out preemptive attacks?" If every country followed this logic, offense would always be the best defense. Funahashi argued that such logic would result in global chaos, thereby elevating rather than reducing the threat of attack by one country against another. His conclusion was that U.S. leaders were obsessed with the idea that time is on the enemy's side: the longer the United States waits to act the more dangerous the world becomes. Funahashi asserted that the United States was in danger of becoming a paranoid nation, a font of unending warnings about imminent terrorist attacks.[25]

In October 2001, with President Bush enjoying a 90 percent domestic approval rating, the USA PATRIOT Act (Uniting and Strengthening America by Providing Appropriate Tools Required to Intercept and Obstruct Terrorism),[26] which has a built-in five-year expiration clause, was passed into law with virtually no debate in the U.S. Congress. Akio Akagi, a former NHK TV network commentator, denounced the PATRIOT Act as uncharacteristic behavior by the country renowned as the leading advocate of liberty and freedom. In his view, passage of the PATRIOT Act should be regarded as an infamous black mark in the history of America's democracy. Akagi also wrote that the PATRIOT Act disqualified the United States from any future preaching about human rights to other countries.[27]

The Japanese mass media, in an effort to capitalize on the growing anti-Americanism among Japanese, ratcheted up its criticisms of the U.S. military attacks against Afghanistan and at the same time began to acknowledge the antiwar movement that had developed within the United States itself. As part of a first-anniversary commemoration of the 9/11 attacks, *Shukan Kinyobi (Weekly Friday)*, a trendy weekly general-interest magazine, reported that protests against the war on Afghanistan had started in New York City and were taking root elsewhere in America. The magazine reported that among the U.S. antiwar critics, some charged the United States with excessive reliance on military power to solve complex international problems. These antiwar activists argued that the United States itself has a history of involvement with various terrorist groups, and that 9/11 represented "blowback" (to use a now-famous term) from previous U.S. military and intelligence actions. *Shukan Kinyobi* rounded out its report on U.S. antiwar activism with the thoughts of a retired seventy-one-year-old American university professor, who believed that Americans should inquire more deeply into why global hatred of the United States had become palpable.[28]

Munesuke Mita, a noted sociologist and social critic, as well as former Tokyo University professor, expressed surprise that so many Japanese had been astonished by the nature of the 9/11 attacks. Given the inequities in the world and the current imbalance of power in the international system, Mita claimed that it was all too predictable that Islamic fundamentalists would resort to something like suicidal airplane attacks. Based on the results on the ground, generated by the late 2002 military campaign in Afghanistan, the United States had been successful in the first round of the war on terrorism, but Mita believed that this would only encourage martyrs and other anti-American extremists to carry out acts of retaliation. America's war on terrorism could therefore easily slip into an ever-accelerating spiral of revenge. So long as U.S. leaders sought to stamp out terrorism by resorting to wars of revenge, no matter how many victories are gained, Americans would never be liberated from the nightmare possibility of anti-America fanatics employing suicidal attacks involving nuclear, biological, or chemical weapons somewhere on U.S. soil. Moreover, Mita argued that worries about terrorism had already started to displace forms of democratic control in the United States. Ever since 9/11, American society had moved steadily in the direction of a security-first, control-from above governmental approach. Mita's view in January 2003 was that it remained an open question as to whether or not the United States would come back from the 9/11 shock as a liberal, open, and democratic country.[29]

Most of the criticisms summarized in the sections above were concerned with the impact of 9/11 on domestic political values in the United States. While some mass-media commentators were critical of America's military excesses or infantile behavior in relation to the war on Afghanistan, the only consequences of the war considered were those that might have the effect of reducing democratic freedoms for Americans. Hardly any mention could be found of the consequences of U.S. actions for the inhabitants of Afghanistan, for other countries in the Middle East that might be accused of harboring terrorists, or for Japan or developed European nations friendly to America should U.S. actions make them blowback targets. What these criticisms represented was a groping attempt in the mass media to strike the right chord for the Japanese public, or to find a balance between Japan's sense of security in its alliance with the United States and its right to openly criticize its ally. Indeed, despite some occasional disputes between America and Japan over goals and process, the Japan-U.S. alliance has been the dominant reference point in Japan's conceptions of its relationship with the United States for roughly fifty years. As such, it has come to provide a category of understanding that the mass media returns to again and again, to explain both U.S. actions and the implications of those actions for Japan. Once Japan's mass media harnessed the alliance to 9/11, the interpretation of 9/11 in Japan began to settle into a more established framework, less troubled by some of the criticisms of America's post-9/11 foreign policy reviewed above. The dominant question now became, What role, especially what kind of military role, could Japan play within the framework of the U.S.-Japan alliance now that a "war on terrorism" was underway?

Linking 9/11 with the U.S.-Japan Alliance

After the United States began its military attack against Afghanistan in October 2001, the Japanese mass media primarily focused attention on issues related to U.S.-Japan relations. One especially dominant issue was whether Japan should dispatch a contingent of its Self-Defense Forces abroad, and whether Japan should amend Article Nine,[30] the war-renouncing clause in the nation's constitution.[31]

In December 2001, the Hakuhodo Institute of Life and Living (HILL), a think tank established in 1981 by Hakuhodo Inc., Japan's second-largest advertising agency, conducted a public opinion poll in metropolitan Tokyo regarding the 9/11 terrorist attacks. Of 381 people surveyed (ages 18 to 76), 86 percent replied that Japan should play a positive role in promoting world peace, but within that group, 58 percent said: "It is necessary to dispatch Japan's Self-Defense Forces," while 56 percent said: "It is appropriate for Japan to make contributions other than dispatching Self-Defense Forces," which means that 14 percent of those who believe Japan should take positive steps toward world peace harbored contradictory views of what kind of positive role Japan could in fact play. This survey result is an excellent example of how Japanese people sometimes try to wiggle between two diametrically opposed choices as regards foreign policy matters.[32]

On October 14, 2001, the *Mainichi Newspaper* reported its own public opinion survey of Japanese attitudes toward American military action against Afghanistan. Fifty seven percent supported the U.S. attack and 55 percent agreed with Prime Minister Junichiro Koizumi's statement of positive support for the U.S. military campaign. Also, 57 percent supported sending SDF troops to cooperate with U.S. military forces, but only 12 percent thought that Japan should implement wide-ranging (including military) cooperation with the United States. On the other hand, 42 percent favored non-military cooperation with the United States. Another 42 percent believed that Japan should seek a conflict resolution through the United Nations. One of the most important foreign policy questions in Japan since the end of the post–World War II U.S. occupation is whether Japan should eliminate the current constitutional constraint on exercising the right of collective self-defense. Even after the 9/11 terrorist attacks and U.S. military retaliation against Afghanistan, the majority of respondents (56 percent) felt that Japan should keep that constraint in place.[33] This result indicates that while a majority of those surveyed believe something needs to be done to stop terrorism, including cooperation with the United States that extends to support for U.S. military attacks, many also hold the conviction that Japan itself should not take an active military role in the international community.

The Japanese mass media has a strong inward-looking tendency to analyze foreign affairs issues in the domestic context.[34] Japanese society consists of groups that are based on close and direct ties among group members. In order to belong to a group, the Japanese place enormous stress on the importance of maintaining harmony. Issues concerning the Japan-U.S. alliance, however, are an exception, often going against the grain of Japanese society by creating division. The division caused by the alliance results from an uneasy coexistence between Japanese pacifists and hawks in the postwar period. In the wake of defeat, Japan's complete demilitarization, the bitter and agonizing wartime memories held by the population, and the insertion of Article Nine into Japan's postwar constitution helped to firmly establish pacifist sentiment among the Japanese people. But counteracting this pacifism was the Cold War and the phoenix-like rebirth of Japan as a leading economic and military power. With the Cold War over, the new threat of terrorism has helped push hawkish

Japanese political leaders to the forefront, especially the hawks of a younger generation that did not experience the misery of war but rather promotes the idea of Japan playing a more active military role in the international arena.

In the United States, individualism remains an important creed. But when facing a national crisis, Americans are known for rallying around the flag and uniting against whatever foe is seen to be threatening the American way of life. In contrast, even though the Japanese are believed to be group-oriented, when faced with a national crisis they tend to suffer a weakening of their seemingly strong forms of unity. Japan consists of individual citizens each with his or her own domestic agendas, without possessing a strong sense of identity as a nation-state.[35] When Japan faces an international crisis, the Japanese mass media tend to analyze and interpret the crisis conditions in such a way as to provoke ideological cracks and divisions. When this occurs, it dramatically stirs Japanese public opinion and turns the public media sphere into a madhouse of conflicting views.

Part of the problem was this: although Japan was quite sensitive to the post- 9/11 American mood, as a country it lacks a strong sense of responsibility for international society. In the Japanese press, it was suggested that this lack was of considerable concern to the Japanese government. Specifically, the government worried that Japan might fall into the same trap it fell into during the Gulf War. If Japan did not dispatch the SDF but made only a financial contribution to the military campaign against Afghanistan, Japan might again be publicly criticized by the United States and by the political leaders of other countries, as happened in 1991. Japan had to find a way to demonstrate its determination to eradicate terrorism, aligning itself as a positive member of the international community, yet without appearing to be unthinkingly in accord with U.S. military interventions. In other words, Japan tried to create an image of itself as exercising individual will in cooperative international relations.[36]

In October 2001, the Japanese Diet passed three so-called terrorism-related bills, enabling the Japanese government to dispatch the SDF abroad for the first time in history, to provide the United States with logistical support. Yoichi Masuzoe, a former associate professor of International Relations at Tokyo University and currently a very active critic of Japanese foreign policy as well as a member of the upper house in Japan's parliament, pointed out that these laws are full of shortcomings. He insisted that no alliance should exist without the right of collective defense. As a result, he believes a full revision of Article Nine is inevitable.[37] Nevertheless, at the same time that the alliance with the United States is seen as essential to national security, an anti-alliance tradition is also firmly rooted in postwar Japanese society. Prime Minister Koizumi's dependence on the United States has remained an easy target of criticism. *Shukan Post (Weekly Post)*, which has the largest circulation among weekly magazines in Japan (890,000), has severely criticized Koizumi, stating that his decision to assist the U.S. military intervention in Afghanistan in the form of a dispatch of SDF forces was out of control. The publication has also disagreed with Koizumi's statement that "regardless of legal constraints, we must do it through political determination," by which he commits to standing alongside the United States whenever it sees the need to take military action.[38]

Further, Masahiko Hisae, a Kyodo News foreign correspondent in Washington, D.C., critically contends that Koizumi has repeatedly responded to a series of post-9/11 crises in an impromptu manner and without sufficient debate. Although fundamentally adhering to statements by successive cabinets in the Diet in support of Article Nine, he has nevertheless responded favorably to Washington's strong pressure to dispatch forces to post-9/11 military conflicts initiated by the U.S. government. At first, the Japanese government dispatched their SDF fleet to the Indian Ocean for the purpose of "collecting information." When the Anti-terrorism Special Measures Law was enacted, the purpose of the SDF fleet dispatch became "assistance to the United States." Koizumi expanded the interpretation of laws without debate in order to give preference to cooperation with the United States.[39]

In its efforts to market 9/11 to the Japanese public, the Japanese mass media waged a prolonged search for the most appropriate framework to capture the disagreements and criticisms that surfaced in Japan in response to U.S. actions in the aftermath of 9/11. The Japanese mass media's linking of the 9/11 attacks with the U.S.-Japan alliance constituted a contradictory yet critical comfort zone for the Japanese people as they sought to derive meanings from the 9/11 attacks that were appropriate to their own sense of Japan's place in the world. This was primarily because of the Japanese people's ambivalent emotions toward the United States in the postwar era. The Japanese mass media, once it found this zone, succeeded in marketing the 9/11 attacks as a matter in which Japanese people had reason to invest. And it suggests that there may not be a clear-cut

conflict between those who seek to strengthen the alliance with the
United States and raise Japan's military profile in the international
arena, and those who seek to abolish the alliance to make Japan a
more independent force in the world community. One can easily
argue that both views share the same root belief. Japanese can
empathize emotionally with Americans during a crisis, while simultaneously seeking to shape their own national identity by becoming
sharply critical of U.S. foreign policy. A study of the Japanese
mass-media response to 9/11 reveals this ongoing, contradictory
process.

Notes

1. I would like to extend my special thanks to John McGlynn for his excellent
   research assistance. His suggestions and criticisms of an earlier version of this
   chapter were invaluable. My profound thanks also go to Dana Heller, who provided me with thought-provoking comments and invaluable pieces of advice,
   and patiently worked with me.
2. Lee Harris, "Al Qaeda's Fantasy Ideology," *Policy Review*, August/September
   2002.
3. Yumiko Hara, Maki Shigemori, and Yuji Suzuki, "Sono Yo, Hitobito wa Terevi
   wo do Mitaka: 9.11 Doji Tahatsu Tero no Shicho Kodo Bunseki" ["How Did
   People Watch TV on That Night? An Analysis of Viewing Behavior of the 9.11
   Terrorist Attacks"] *Hoso Kenkyu to Chosa* 52, no. 3 (March 2002): 26–32.
4. Ibid., 32–33.
5. http://www003.upp.so-net.ne.jp/kaori_a/drama/ranking_history.html
6. Keizo Sawaki, " '9.11' wa Dou Katararetaka" ["How '9.11' Was Mentioned"]
   Zenei, November 2002.
7. Hara, Shigemori, and Suzuki, "Sono Yo, Hitobito wa," 26–32.
8. Hidetoshi Sotooka, Koichi Edagawa, and Kenji Muro eds., *9gatsu 11nichi
   Media ga Tamesareta Hi [September the 11th, the Day the Media Was Tried]*
   (Tokyo: Trans Art, 2001), 3–4.
9. Tadashi Karube, "Konton heno Shiza: Kokka to Boryoku wo Megutte,"
   ["Perspectives On Chaos: On State and Violence,"] *ΑΣΤΕΙΟΝ* 57 (2002): 52;
   Kobe Newspaper, November 15, 2001. http://www.kobe-np.co.jp/kobenews/
   sougou/011115ke29800.html.
10. Masatake Matsubara, ed., *Jinari suru Sekai: 9.11 wo dou toraeruka [Earth
    Sounding World: How Should We Understand 9.11?]* (Osaka: Kosei Shuppan,
    2002), 43–44, 91–92.
11. Ryu Murakami, *Shushuku suru Sekai, Heisoku suru Nihon 9.11 [Constricted
    World, Blocked Japan, Post September Eleventh]* (Tokyo: NHK Shuppan,
    2001), 111.
12. Matsubara ed., *Jinari suru Sekai*, 92–93.
13. Ibid., 92–93.

14. George Itagoshi, *Graund Zero [Ground Zero]* (Tokyo: Fushosha, 2002).

15. Fukiko Aoki, *Mokugeki Amerika Hokai [Witness: Destruction of America]* (Tokyo: Bungei Shunju, 2001).

16. Sadahei Kusumoto, "9.11 Jiken to Masukomi: Genchi kara Mita Amerika to Nihon no Hodo" ["The 9.11 Attacks and Mass Media: American and Japanese Mass Media from New York's Perspective"] *AERA* 152 (April 2002).

17. Michiyo Nakamura, "Hihan Seishin Ushinawanai Amerika" ["An America That Does Not Lose Its Critical Mind"] *Shimbun Kenkyu* no. 614 (September 2002).

18. Murakami, *Shushuku suru Sekai*, 50.

19. Manabu Miyazaki, *"Seigi" wo Sakebu Mono koso Utagae [Question Those Who Insist on "Justice"]* (Tokyo: Diamond sha, 2002), 30.

20. "Remarks by the President To United Nations General Assembly," November 10, 2001. http://www.whitehouse.gov/news/releases/2001/11/20011110-3.html.

21. Gen Nakayama, *Atarashii Senso? 9.11 Tero Jiken to Shiso [A New War? 9.11 Terrorist Attacks and Thought]*, (Kyoto: Tokyusha, 2002).

22. Osamu Nishitani, *"Tero tono Senso" towa Nanika: 9.11 Igono Sekai [What is the "War on Terrorism": Post 9.11 World]*, (Tokyo: Ibunsha, 2002), i–ii.

23. Tetsu Nakamura, "Kiga Jotai no Kaisho ga Tero Konzetsu heno Chikamichi" ["Relieving Starvation is the Shortest Way to Eradicate Terrorism"] *Ushio* (December 2001).

24. " 'Amerika janai Gawa' no 9.11," "9.11: A 'Non-American' Perspective," *Shukan SPA!*, 81–84.

25. Yoichi Funahashi and Jitsuro Terashima, "Amerika wa Dokohe Iku" ["Where Will America Go?"] *Ushio* (October 2002): 80–81.

26. http://www.epic.org/privacy/terrorism/hr3162.html.

27. Akio Akagi, *Jikai suru Amerika [Self-destructing America]* (Tokyo: Chikuma Shobo, 2001), 23–25.

28. Muneo Narusawa, "Tada 'No' to Ieba ii" ["Just Say 'NO' "] *Shukan Kinyobi*, no. 428 (September 20, 2002).

29. Munesuke Mita, "Apokaripusu" ["Apocalypse"] *Ronza* 92 (January 2003): 51–52.

30. Article Nine: Aspiring sincerely to an international peace based on justice and order, the Japanese people forever renounce war as a sovereign right of the nation and the threat or use of force as means of settling international disputes.
    In order to accomplish the aim of the preceding paragraph, land, sea, and air forces, as well as other war potential, will never be maintained. The right of belligerency of the state will not be recognized.

31. Murakami, *Shushuku suru Sekai*, 102.

32. The Hakuhodo Institute of Life and Living (HILL), "Survey on Post-9.11," conducted in December 2001. http://www.hakuhodo.co.jp/news/20020125-2.html.

33. A nationwide public opinion survey by telephone of the special counterterrorism bill. Conducted by the *Mainichi Newspaper* on October 14, 2001.

34. Akio Takahata, " 'Taningoto' no Ninshiki wo Aratameyou" ["Let's Change Our Consciousness as 'Idle Spectators' "] *AERA* 152 (April 2002): 8.

35. Nikkei Business, et al., eds., *Tero to Global Shihon Shugi no Asu [Terrorism and the Future of Global Capitalism]* (Tokyo: Nikkei BP, 2001), 122–23.

36. Masayuki Yamauchi and Jitsuro Terashima, "Jindo to Bunmei Shakai heno Chosen" ["The Challenge Against Humanity and Civilized Society"] *Ushio* (November 2001).

37. Yoichi Masuzoe, *Atarashii Senso to Nihon no Koken [New Wars and Japan's Contribution]* (Tokyo: Shogakkan, 2002), 150, 167.

38. *Shukan Post [Weekly Post]*, October 12, 2001.

39. Masahiko Hisae, "9.11 Igono Nichibei Kankei" ["Japan-U.S. Relations after 9.11"] *Hon* 27, no. 9 (September 2002).

Chapter 6

Entertainment Wars: Television Culture after 9/11

Lynn Spigel

After the attacks of September 11, traditional forms of entertainment had to reinvent their place in U.S. life and culture. The de rigueur violence of mass media—both news and fiction—no longer seemed business as usual. While Hollywood usually defends its mass-destruction ethos with claims to "free speech," constitutional rights, and industrywide discretion (a la ratings systems), in the weeks following September 11 the industry exhibited (whether for sincere or cynical reasons) a new will toward "tastefulness," as potentially trauma-inducing films like Warner's *Collateral Damage* were pulled from release. On television, violent movies also came under network scrutiny. USA cancelled its primetime run of *The Siege* (which deals with Arab terrorists who plot to bomb New York). At TBS, violence-packed films like *Lethal Weapon* were replaced with family fare like *Look Who's Talking*. TNT replaced its 1970s retro lineup of *Superman*, *King Kong*, and *Carrie* with *Close Encounters of the Third Kind*, *Grease*, and *Jaws* (although exactly why the blood-sucking shark in *Jaws* seemed less disturbing than the menstruating teen in *Carrie* already begs questions about exactly what constitutes "terror" in the minds of Hollywood executives).[1]

But it wasn't just the "hard" realities of violence that came under self-imposed censorship. Light entertainment and "diversions" of all kinds also didn't feel right. Humorists Dave Letterman, Jay Leno, Craig Kilborn, Conan O'Brien, and Jon Stewart met the late-night audience with dead seriousness. While *Saturday Night Live* did return to humor, its jokes were officially sanctioned by an opening act that included a somber performance by Paul Simon, members of the New York City Fire Department, and Mayor Rudolph Giuliani himself. When producer Lorne Michaels asked the mayor if it was okay to be funny, Giuliani joked, "Why start now?" (implicitly informing viewers that it was, in fact, okay to laugh). In the midst of the new sincerity, numerous critics summarily declared that the attacks on the Pentagon and World Trade Center had brought about the "end of irony."[2]

Despite such bombastic declarations, however, many industry leaders were actually in a profound state of confusion about just what it was the public wanted. Even while industry leaders were eager to censor out trauma-inducing images of any kind, video outlets reported that when left to their own discretion consumers were eagerly purchasing terrifying flicks like *The Siege* and *The Towering Inferno*. One video retailer noted an "uneasy" feeling about consumer desire for films like *The Towering Inferno*, and one store owner even "moved such videos so they were arranged with only the spines showing, obscuring the covers."[3] Meanwhile, Internet companies worried about the hundreds of vulgar domain names for which people applied in the hopes of setting up web sites. One major domain name reseller halted auctions for several names it considered tasteless, including "NewYorkCarnage.com."[4] As these cases suggest, the media industries had to balance their own public image as discriminating custodians of culture with the vagaries of public taste.

Given its historical status as a regulated private industry ideally meant to operate in the "public interest," television was the most hard hit by this conflict between maintaining the image of "public servant" and the need to cater to the public taste (or at least to what advertisers think the public likes). Getting back to the normal balance between their public service and entertainment/commercial functions posed problems for broadcasters and cablers alike.[5] In the midst of the turmoil, the Television Academy of Arts and Sciences and CBS postponed the Emmy Awards ceremonies twice.

To be sure, television executives' nervous confusion was rooted in the broader havoc that 9/11 wreaked on television, not just as an industry, but also as "a whole way of life."[6] Most fundamental, on September 11, the everydayness of television itself was suddenly disrupted by news of something completely "alien" to the usual patterns of domestic TV viewing.[7] The nonstop commercial-free coverage, which lasted on major broadcast networks and cable news networks for a full week, contributed to a sense of estrangement from ordinary life, not simply because of the unexpected nature of the attack itself, but also because television's normal routines—its everyday schedule and ritualized flow—had been disordered. As Mary Ann Doane has argued about television catastrophes more generally, not only television's temporal flow, but also television's central narrational agency breaks down in moments of catastrophe.[8] We are in a world where narrative comes undone and where the "real" seems to have no sense of meaning beyond repetition of the horrifying event itself. This, she claims, in turn threatens to expose the underlying catastrophe of all TV catastrophes—the breakdown of capitalism, the end of the cash flow, the end of the logic of consumption on which U.S. television is predicated.

By the weekend of September 15, television news anchors began to tell us that it was their national duty to return to the "normal" everyday schedule of television entertainment, a return meant to coincide with Washington's call for a return to normalcy (and, hopefully, normal levels of consumerism). Of course, for the television industry, resuming the normal TV schedule also meant a return to commercial breaks and, therefore, TV's very sustenance. Already besieged by declining ad revenues before the attacks, the television industry lost an estimated $320 million in advertising revenue in the week following the attacks.[9] So, even while the media industries initially positioned entertainment and commercials as being "in bad taste," just one week after the attacks the television networks discursively realigned commercial entertainment with the patriotic goals of the nation.[10] In short—and most paradoxically—entertainment and commercialism were rearticulated as television's "public service."

By September 27, Jack Valenti, president and CEO of the Motion Picture Association of America, gave this "commercialism as patriotism" ethos an official stamp of approval. In a column for *Variety*, he wrote, "Here in Hollywood we must continue making our movies and our TV programs. For a time, during this mourning period, we need to be sensitive to how we tell a story. But in time—and that time will surely come—life will go on, must go on. We in Hollywood have to get on with doing our creative work. . . . The country needs what we create."[11] Valenti's message was part of a much older myth of show business—a myth that ran through countless Depression Era and World War II musicals—a myth of transcendence in which showbiz folks put aside their petty differences and join together in patriotic song. If in the 1940s this myth of transcendence emboldened audiences for wartime sacrifice, now, in the twenty-first century, this transcendent myth of show business is oddly conjoined with national mandates for a return to "normal" consumer pleasures. In a bizarrely Baudrillardian moment, President Bush addressed the nation, begging us to return to normal life by getting on planes and taking our families to Disneyland.[12]

In fact, despite the initial tremors, American consumer culture and television in particular did return to normal (or at least a semblance of it) in a remarkably short span of time. Yet, while many people have noted this, the process by which this happened and the extent to which it was achieved beg further consideration. Media scholarship on 9/11 and the U.S. attacks in Afghanistan has focused primarily on print and television news coverage. This important scholarship focuses on the narrative and mythic "framing" of the events; the nationalist jingoism (for example, the use of flag graphics on news shows); the relative paucity of alternative views in mainstream venues—at least in the immediate weeks following the attacks; the role of alternative news platforms—especially the Internet; competing global news outlets—particularly Al Jazeera; and the institutional and commercial pressure that have led to "infotainment."[13] Despite its significant achievements, however, the scholarly focus on news underestimates (indeed, it barely considers) the way the "reality" of 9/11 was communicated across the flow of television's genres, including its so-called entertainment genres.[14] The almost singular focus on news fails to capture the way television worked to process fear (even fear trumped up by the media) and return the public to "ordinary" life (including routine ways of watching TV). The return to normal has to be seen from this wider view, for it was enacted not just through the narrative frames of news stories, but through the repositioning of audiences back into television's fictive time and places—its familiar series, well-known stars, favorite characters, and ritualized annual events (such as the Emmy Awards).

In the following pages, I explore how an assortment of television genres—dramatic series, talk shows, documentaries, special "event" TV, and even cartoons—channeled the nation back to normalcy, or at least to the normal flows of television and consumer culture. I am particularly interested in how these genres relied on nationalist myths of the American past and the enemy/"Orient." But I also question the degree to which nationalist myths can sustain the "narrowcast" logic of today's multichannel television systems (and the more general movement of audiences across multiple media platforms). In other words, I want to interrogate the limits of nationalist myths in the postnetwork, multichannel, and increasingly global media systems.

Admittedly, the fate of nationalism in contemporary media systems is a huge question that requires perspectives from more than one field of inquiry. (For example, we would need to explore the impact of deregulation and media conglomeration; the dispersal of audiences across media platforms; competition among global media news/entertainment outlets; relations between local and global media flows; audience and interpretive reception contexts; and larger issues of national identity and subjectivity.) My goal here is not to provide exhaustive answers to all of these questions (no one essay could do so), but rather to open up some points of interrogation by looking at post-9/11 media industry strategies, the discourses of the entertainment trade journals, and especially the textual and narrative logic of television programs that channeled the nation back to commercial TV "as usual."

History Lessons after 9/11

Numerous critics have commented on the way that the attacks of 9/11 were perceived as an event completely outside of and alien to any other horror that ever happened anywhere. As James Der Derian notes, as a consequence of this rhetoric of American exceptionalism, "9/11 quickly took on an *exceptional ahistoricity*," as even many of the most astute critics refused to place the events in a political or social context from which they might be understood. Der Derian argues that when history was evoked in nonstop news coverage of destruction and loss, it appeared as nostalgia and analog, "mainly in the sepia tones of the Second World War—to prepare America for the sacrifice and suffering that lay ahead."[15] But, at least after the initial news coverage of which Der Derian speaks, history was actually marshaled in a much more contradictory field of statements and images that filled the airwaves and ushered audiences back—not just toward nostalgic memories of World War II sacrifice—but also toward the mandates of contemporary consumer culture.

On television these "contradictory" statements and images revolved around the paradox of the medium's twin roles as advertiser and public servant.

In the week following 9/11, television's transition back to normal consumer entertainment was enacted largely through recourse to historical pedagogy that ran through a number of television genres, from news to documentaries to daytime talk shows to primetime drama. The histories evoked were both familiar and familiarizing tales of the "American experience," as newscasters provided a stream of references to classroom histories, including, for example, the history of U.S. immigration, Pearl Harbor, and Vietnam.[16] They mixed these analogies to historical events with allusions to the history of popular culture, recalling scenes from disaster film blockbusters, science fiction movies, and war films, and even referencing previous media events, from JFK to Princess Diana. Following 24/7 "real time" news strategies that CNN developed in 1991's Gulf War, major news networks provided a host of "infotainment" techniques that have over the past decade become common to war reporting (i.e., fast-paced "MTV" editing, computerized/game-style images, slick graphics, digitized sound-effects, banter among "experts," and catchy slogans).[17] On September 12, CNN titled its coverage, "The Day After" (which was also the title of the well-known 1980s made-for-TV nuclear disaster movie). Fox sported the slogan, "America Strikes Back"—based, of course on the *Stars Wars* trilogy. Meanwhile, the FBI enlisted the television show *America's Most Wanted* to help in the hunt for terrorists.[18] As we searched for familiar scripts, the difference between real wars and "made-for-TV" wars hardly mattered. History had become, to use Michel de Certeau's formulation, a heterology of science and fiction.[19]

But what did this turn to familiar historical narratives provide? Why the sudden appeal of history? Numerous scholars, from Roland Barthes to Marita Sturken, have analyzed the ways in which history and memory serve to produce narratives of the nation. This work has shown how media (from advertising to film to television to music) play a central role in conjuring up a sense of national belonging and community.[20] Certainly, after 9/11, the media's will to remember was connected to the resuscitation of national culture in a country heretofore divided by culture wars and extreme political partisanship. However, for the culture industries, the turn to history was not only connected to the resuscitation of nationalism; history was also connected to the parallel urge to restore the business routines and marketing practices of contemporary consumer media culture.

At the most basic level, for television executives who were nervous about offending audiences, history was a solution to a programming dilemma. History, after all, occupies that most sought-after realm of "good taste." It is the stuff of PBS, the Discovery Channel, the History Channel—it signifies a "habitus" of educated populations, of "quality" TV, of public service generally. History's "quality" appeal was especially important in the context of numerous critical attacks on television's lack of integrity that ran through industry trade journals and the popular press after 9/11. For example, Louis Chunovic, a reporter for the trade journal *Television Week*, wrote, "In the wake of the terrorist attack on the United States, it's hard to believe Americans once cared who would win *Big Brother 2* or whether Anne Heche is crazy. And it's hard to believe that as recently as two weeks ago, that's exactly the kind of pabulum, along with the latest celebrity/politician sex/murder/kidnapping scandal, that dominated television news." Chunovic therefore argued, "We cannot afford to return to the way things were."[21] Ironically, however, the industry's post 9/11 upgrade to quality genres—especially historical documentaries—actually facilitated the return to the way things were. Historical documentaries served a strategic role in the patriotic transition back to "normalcy"—that is, to commercial entertainment and consumer culture.

Let's take, for example, ABC's programming strategy on Saturday, September 15. On that day, ABC became the first major network to return to a semblance of normal televisual flow. Newscaster Peter Jennings presented a children's forum, which was followed by an afternoon lineup of historical documentaries about great moments of the twentieth century. The lineup included episodes on Charles Lindbergh, the Apollo crew and the moon landing, and a documentary on the U.S. press in Hitler's Europe. Interestingly, given the breakdown in surveillance, aviation, and communication technologies that enabled the attacks, all of the chosen histories were about great achievements of great men using great technologies—especially transportation and communications technologies.[22]

Meanwhile, from an economic point of view, these historical documentaries were first and foremost part of the contemporary network business strategy that industry people refer to as "repurposing." The documentaries were reruns repackaged from a previous ABC series narrated by Jennings and now "repurposed" for patriotism. This is not to say that Jennings or anyone else at ABC was intentionally trying to profit from disaster. Certainly, Jennings's forum for children provided a public service. But, as anyone who studies the history of U.S. television knows, the logic of capitalism always means that public service and public relations are flip sides of the same coin. In this case, the public service gesture of running historical documentaries also served to transition audiences from TV news discourse and live reportage back into prerecorded narrative series. Similarly, with an even more bizarre resonance, on the evening of September 15 NBC ran a special news report on *Dateline* followed by a rerun of the made-for-TV movie *Growing Up Brady*.

More generally, history was integral to the transition back to entertainment series programs. On October 3, 2001, NBC's *The West Wing*, one of television's premiere quality series, preempted its scheduled season premier to provide a quickly drafted episode titled "Isaac and Ishmael." On the one hand, the episode (which teaches audiences about the situation in the Middle East) was clearly an earnest attempt by the cast and creator–executive producer Aaron Sorkin (who wrote the script) to use television as a form of political and historical pedagogy.[23] On the other hand, the episode was also entirely consistent with contemporary business promotional strategies. Like the ABC strategy of repurposing, the NBC network followed the business strategy of "stunting"—or creating a stand-alone episode that attracts viewers by straying from the series architecture (the live episode of *ER* is a classic example of the technique). In this case, *The West Wing* was in a particularly difficult position—for perhaps more than any other network series its "quality" appeal lies in its "timely relevance" and deep, if melodramatic, realism. (The series presents itself as a kind of parallel White House universe that runs simultaneously with the real-life goings-on in Washington.)[24]

The credit sequence begins with successive headshots of cast members speaking to the audience in direct address (and in their celebrity personae). Martin Sheen welcomes viewers and announces that this episode is not the previously scheduled season premiere. In a subsequent headshot, another cast member even refers to the episode as "a story-telling aberration," signaling its utter discontinuity from the now routinely serialized/cumulative narrative structure of contemporary primetime "quality" genres. Meanwhile, other cast members variously thank the New York Fire and Police Departments, while still others direct our attention to a phone number at the bottom of the screen that viewers can call to donate money to disaster relief and victim funds. In this sense, the episode immediately asks audiences to imagine themselves foremost as citizens engaged in an interactive public/media sphere. Nevertheless, this "public service" ethos is embroiled in the televisual logic of publicity. The opening credit sequence ends with cast members promoting the new fall season by telling audiences what kinds of plots to expect on upcoming episodes. The final "teaser" comes from a female cast member (Janel Moloney) who hypes the fall season by promising that her character will have a love interest in future shows.

After this promise of titillating White House sex, the episode transitions back to its public service discourse. Essentially structured as a teach-in, the script follows a group of high school students touring the White House and caught in the west wing after a terrorist bomb threat. Attempting to calm the nerves of the students, various cast members lecture this imaginary high school class about the history of U.S.-Middle East relations. In an early segment, Josh Lyman, a White House "spin doctor," lectures the frightened students on terrorism and Middle East animosity toward the West. After a wide-eyed female student asks, "Why is everyone trying to kill us?" Josh moves to the blackboard, where he begins his history lesson. While he admits that the United States is somewhat to blame (he mentions economic sanctions, occupation of Arab lands, and the U.S. abandonment of Afghanistan), he says all of this at such rapid-fire speed that there is no in-depth consideration of the issues. Instead, the scene derails itself from its "teaching" mission by resorting to the colonialist rhetoric of "curiosities." The scene ends with Josh telling the students of his outrage over the cultural customs of Islamic extremism. The familiar list of horrors—from the fact that women are made to wear a veil to the fact that men can't cheer freely at soccer games—redirect the episode away from ethics toward an ethnocentric celebration of American cultural superiority.[25] Josh ends by reminding the students that, unlike Islamic extremists, Americans are free to cheer anything they like at football games, and American women can even be astronauts.

In this regard, the episode uses historical pedagogy to solidify American national unity *against* the "enemy" rather than to encourage any real engagement with Islam, the ethics of U.S. international policy, or the consequences of the then impending U.S. bomb strikes. Moreover, because the episode's teach-in lectures are encompassed within a more overarching melodramatic rescue narrative (the terrorist bomb threat in the White House), all of the lessons the students (and by proxy, the audience) learn are contained within a narrative about U.S. public safety. In other words, according to the logic of this rescue narrative, we learn about the "other" only for instrumental reasons—our own national security.

In all of these ways, *The West Wing* performs some of the fundamental precepts of contemporary Orientalism. First, as Edward Said suggests, in the United States—and in particular after World War II—Orientalism retains the racist histories of "othering" from the earlier European context, but becomes increasingly less philological and more concerned with social scientific policy and administration that is formulated in federal agencies, think tanks, and universities that want to "know" and thus police the Middle East. In this configuration, the production of knowledge about the Middle East is aimed at national security and the maintenance of U.S. hegemony. And as Said suggests, this kind of social scientific knowledge orientalizes the Middle Eastern subject and demonizes the Arab as "other"—as the antithesis of Western progress and humanity.[26] Indeed, when Josh details the cultural wasteland of Islamic extremism, he enacts one of the central rhetorical principles of Orientalism. For as Said argues, the "net effect" of contemporary Orientalism is to erase any American awareness of the Arab world's culture and humanity (its poets, its novelists, its means of self-representation), replacing these with a dehumanizing social-scientific index of "attitudes, trends, statistics."[27]

The fictional schoolroom on *The West Wing* performs this kind of social scientific Orientalism in the name of liberal humanism. And it does so through a pedagogical form of enunciation that places viewers in the position of high school students—and particularly naïve ones at that. The program speaks to viewers as if they were children, or at best, the innocent objects of historical events beyond their control. The "why does everyone want to kill us?" mantra espoused by *The West Wing*'s fictional students becomes, to use Lauren Berlant's phrase, a form of "infantile citizenship"[28] that allows adult viewers comfortably to confront the horrors and guilt of war by donning the cloak of childhood innocence (epitomized, of course, by the wide-eyed figure of President Bush himself who, in his first televised speech to Congress after the attacks, asked, "Why do they hate us?").

In the days following the attacks, the Bush administration spoke often of the eternal and "essential goodness" of the American people, creating a through-line for the American past that flattered a despairing public by making them the moral victims of a pure outside evil.[29] In a similar instance of denial, commentators spoke of "the end of innocence"[30] that the attacks ushered in, as if America had been completely without knowledge and guilt before this day.[31] Not surprisingly, in this respect, the histories mobilized by the media after 9/11 were radically selective and simplified versions of the past that produced a kind of moral battlefield for "why we fight." As Justin Lewis shows in his survey of four leading U.S. newspapers, print journalists writing about 9/11 tended to evoke World War II and Nazi Germany while "other histories were, regardless of relevance, distinctly less prominent." Lewis claims that "the more significant absences [were] those histories that signify the West's disregard for democracy and human rights [such as] the U.S. government's support for the Saudi Arabian Theocracy."[32] He argues that the history of World War II and Nazi Germany was mobilized because of its compelling narrative dimensions—especially its good vs. evil binary. While this creation of heroes and villains was also a primary aspect of television coverage, it seems likely that many viewers weren't really looking for "objective truth" so much as narrative itself. In the face of shock and uncertainty that seemed to make time stand still, these narratives offered people a sense of historical continuity with a shared—and above all, moral—past.[33]

The need to make American audiences feel that they were in the correct moral position ran through a number of television's "reality" genres. One of the central ways that this moral position was promoted was through the depiction of women victims. In her analysis of news coverage of 9/11, Jayne Rodgers argues that the news tended to frame stories in "myths of gender," and, she claims, one of the central trajectories of these myths was a reversal of the gendered nature of heroism and victimization. Rodgers points out that even while "male deaths from the attacks outnumbered female deaths by a ratio of three to one," news narratives tended to portray men as heroes (firemen, policemen, Giuliani) and women as victims (suffering and often pregnant widows). Despite the fact that there were thirty-three women firefighters and rescue workers on duty on September 11, the media portraits of heroism were mainly of men, which, as Rodgers aptly argues, worked to "restore gender, as well as social and political order."[34]

On television, these myths of gender were often connected to age-old Western fantasies of the East in which "Oriental" men assault (and even rape) Western women—and more symbolically, the West itself. (Cecille B. DeMille's *The Cheat* [1915] or Rudolph Valentino in *The Sheik* [1921] demonstrate the longevity of this Orientalized "rape" fantasy.) In the case of 9/11, the United States took its figural place as innocent victim in stories that interwove myths of gender and the Orient. Both daytime talk shows and nighttime news were filled with melodramatic tales of women's suffering that depicted women as the moral victims of Islamic extremism. And "women" here meant both the women of Afghanistan who live under Taliban rule and American survivors (the widows) who lost their husbands during the attack. While, of course, these women are at one level real women who really suffered, on television they were fictionally rendered through melodramatic conventions that tended to elide the complexity of historical causes for the tragic circumstances the women faced.

For example, in the weeks following the attacks, *Oprah* included episodes featuring pregnant survivors who had lost their husbands. These episodes intertwined personal memories (via home videos of the deceased) with therapy sessions featuring the traumatized women. In these episodes, the "talking cure" narrative logic of the talk show format was itself strangely derailed by the magnitude of events; the female guest was so traumatized that she was literally unable to speak. In one episode, for example, a young pregnant woman sits rigidly on stage while popular therapist Dr. Phil tells her about the twelve steps of trauma (and Oprah interjects with inspirational wisdom). The episode presents this woman as having lost not only her husband, but also her voice, and with that her ability to narrate her own story. In the process, the program implicitly asks viewers to identify with this woman as the moral and innocent victim of *chance*. In other words, any causal agent (or any sense that her suffering is actually the result of complex political histories) is reduced to the "twist of fate" narrative fortunes of the daytime soap.

Writing about the history of American melodramas, Linda Williams argues that this theme of the "suffering" moral victim (particularly women and African Americans) can be traced through cinematic and televisual media representations (including depictions of American historical events). Williams claims that victim characters elicit our identification through sentiment (not only with them but, allegorically, with historical injustices they face). Following Lauren Berlant and Ann Douglas, she cautions that sentiment and vicarious identification with suffering—in both media texts and politics more generally—are often stand-ins for actual social justice, but, that importantly, sentiment is not the same as justice. By offering audiences a structure of feeling (the identification with a victim, their revealed goodness, and their pain), melodrama compensates for tragic injustices and human sacrifice. Or as she puts it, "Melodramatic climaxes that end in the death of a good person—Uncle Tom, Princess Charlotte, Jack Dawson (in *Titanic*) offer paroxysms of pathos and recognitions of virtue compensating for the loss of life."[35] In political melodramas (like the stories told of 9/11's female victims), pathos and virtue can often be an end in itself; the spectator emerges feeling a sense of righteousness even while justice has not been achieved in reality, and even while many people feel completely alienated from and overwhelmed by the actual political sphere.

Addressing the public with this same kind of sentimental/compensatory citizenship, President Bush used the image of female suffering in his first televised address before Congress after the attacks. Harking back to Cold War paranoia films like Warner Brother's *Red Nightmare* (which was made with the Defense Department and showed what a typical American town would look like if it were taken over by "commies"), President Bush painted a picture of the threat that terrorism posed to our freedom. "In Afghanistan," he claimed, "we see Al Qaeda's vision of the world," after which he listed a string of daily oppressions people might be forced to face should Al Qaeda's vision prevail. First on his list was the fact that "Women are not allowed to go to school." The rhetorical construction here is important because by suggesting that Al Qaeda had a vision for the world, President Bush asked TV audiences literally to imagine themselves taken over by Al Qaeda and in the women's place—the place of suffering. Having thereby stirred up viewers' moral indignation and pathos, he then went on to justify his own plan for aggression, giving the Taliban a series of ultimatums. Whatever one thinks about Bush's speech, it is clear that the image of suffering female victims was a powerful emotional ploy through which he connected his own war plan to a sense of moral righteousness and virtue (and it is also clear that we had never heard him speak of these women in Afghanistan before that day).

A more complicated example is CNN's airing of the documentary *Beneath the Veil*, which depicts the abuses that women of Afghanistan suffered under the Taliban. Originally made in the spring of 2001 for Britain's Channel 4, *Beneath the Veil* was produced "under-cover" by Saira Shah (who grew up in Britain but whose father is from Afghanistan), and with considerable risk to the film-maker (photography was outlawed by the Taliban, and the fact that Shah is a woman made the whole process doubly dangerous). *Beneath the Veil* not only outlines the Taliban's oppression and cru-elty, but also global neglect and responsibility, as well as the need for immediate political action. Shah is careful to reflect on her own Western assumptions about women, feminism, and Islam. She avoids—as much as possible—the narcissism inherent in her docu-mentary and aims to rescue these women by showing that it was the Afghan women themselves—a group known as the Revolutionary Association of the Women of Afghanistan (RAWA)—who were the first to fight against the Taliban.

Beneath the Veil opens with footage shot (via hidden cameras) by RAWA. There are images of women huddled in a pick-up truck and being brought to a football field turned public execution arena. They are killed for alleged adultery. Interspersed throughout the film are images of and dialogues about the women's oppression, RAWA's own efforts to liberate women, and Shah's documentary witnessing of the events. An accompanying web site (still up) provides numer-ous links to information and zones of action and participation. The program and its web site constitute an important political use of electronic media. While there are images of female suffering, the pathos elicited by the pictures is organized around the desire for action (which Williams reminds us can also be part of melodrama) rather than just sentiment as an end in itself.

However, when rerun and repurposed by CNN in the context of the post-9/11 news coverage, the politics of *Beneath the Veil* were significantly altered. In the two months following the attacks, CNN reran *Beneath the Veil* so many times that it became a kind of daily documentary ritual. Although it was certainly important for audi-ences to learn about this human rights disaster, we should never-theless wonder why Western eyes were willing to look at this documentary with such fascination after 9/11 (as opposed to, say, on September 10). First, it should be noted that in the wake of 9/11 documentaries of all sorts (but especially ones about terrorism) were, according to *Variety*, a "hot property" in the television industry.[36] Second, whatever the original achievements of the program, in this new context audiences were led to make easy equivocations between the kind of oppressions the women of Afghanistan faced and the loss of innocent life on American soil on September 11. In the context of CNN's programming flow we saw *Beneath the Veil* adjacent to news footage depicting Ground Zero, stories of American victims and heroes, anthrax attacks, public safety warnings, mug shots of the FBI's most wanted terrorists, and war footage depicting a bizarre mix of bombs and humanitarian aid being dropped on Afghanistan.[37] In this programming context, *Beneath the Veil* could easily be read as a cautionary tale (like *Red Nightmare*) and a justification for the U.S. bombings in Afghanistan. In other words, it might well have conjured up national unity for war as a moral position.

In the midst of the U.S. bombings, Shah produced a follow-up film, *The Unholy War*, which aired on CNN in mid-November 2001. This film documented the lives of women (especially three young Afghan girls) in the midst of the U.S. war against the Taliban. The film showed the destruction caused by bombings, the problems entailed in building a post-Taliban regime, and Shah's own failures in trying the save the lives of the three girls (she attempts to get them an education) whose father rejected her humanitarian efforts. *The Unholy War* disrupted the "flow" of CNN's rotation of *Beneath the Veil*. It also punctured President Bush's melodramatic rescue/war narrative, and questioned (the usually unquestionable) ideologies of "humanitarianism" that legitimated the U.S. bombings. As Shah said in an interview with Salon.com:

> I couldn't believe that we couldn't help them and that money wouldn't solve their problems. . . . That was a real revelation for me. I rather arrogantly, in a very Western way, assumed that I could solve their problems because I had good will and money. It taught me that their problems are more complex. It also taught me a lot about what's needed in Afghanistan, and how frustrating it is rebuilding a country that's been destroyed to the extent that Afghanistan has.[38]

Event TV and Celebrity Citizenship

While Shah's *Unholy War* suggests that there were indeed counternarratives and antiwar messages to be found on the airwaves and on web sites like Salon.com, the news images of unfathomable destruction that aired on 9/11 resulted in industry attempts to match that spectacle with reparative images on a scale as great as the falling towers. In this respect, "Event TV" (or television programs designed to take on the status and audience shares of media events) flourished after 9/11, and with this another staging of national unity after the attacks.

The first of these was the celebrity telethon, *America: A Tribute to Heroes*. Telecast live from New York, Los Angeles, and London on September 21, 2001, at 9 PM, the 120-minute program was simulcast on more than 320 national broadcast stations and cable networks. According to the Nielsen ratings, the program garnered a 65 share of U.S. households, making it one of the most-watched programs of the year, behind only the Super Bowl.[39]

America: A Tribute to Heroes featured an overwhelming community of stars recounting the stories of those who died or risked their lives in the struggle. These eulogies were interspersed with musical performances of popular hits from the baby boom to post-boomer past (the assumed generations of donors). Like all televised funerals, this one deployed television's aesthetics of liveness to stave off the fear of death. In other words, not only the "live" feed, but also the sense of unrehearsed spontaneity and intimate revelations, gave viewers a way to feel that life will go on in the present. The ritualistic and funereal atmosphere resurrected the recently dead for the living, restoring faith not only in spiritual terms but also in terms of the medium itself. (In other words, it was that most "degraded" of media—television—that brought us this powerful sense of healing and community.)[40]

While certainly designed to be a global media event, this was a deliberately "understated" spectacle, achieved through a deliberate display of "star capital" minus the visual glitz and ego. Staged with "zero degree" style (just candles burning on an otherwise unadorned set), the program appealed to a desire to see Hollywood stars, singers, and sports heroes reduced to "real" people, unadorned, unrehearsed (or at least underrehearsed), and literally unnamed and unannounced (there was no variety "host' presiding over the entertainment, no identification of the stars, and no studio audience). This absence of style signified the "authenticity" of the staged event, thereby giving stars the authority to speak for the dead. So, too, the actual mix of stars (for example, Mohammad Ali, Clint Eastwood, Paul Simon, Julia Roberts, Enrique Iglesias, Bruce Springsteen, Celine Dion, Chris Rock, Sylvester Stallone) combined what might otherwise have been a battle of stars semiotics (given their often at-odds personae and historical associations) into a compelling—and for many people, moving—site of mourning. The program's "interactive" aspect further strengthened the telethon's aura of community as on-demand celebrity phone operators, from Goldie Hawn to Jack Nicholson, promised to reach out and touch us. In all of these ways, *America: A Tribute to Heroes* is a stunning example of how post-9/11 television has created not a public sphere per se, but rather a self-referential Hollywood public sphere of celebrities who stand in for real citizens, and who somehow make us feel connected to a wider social fabric.

The 53rd Annual Emmy Awards ceremony—which was twice delayed because of the attacks—is another example. Jack Valenti's "show must go on" ethos was everywhere in the publicity leading up to and culminating in this yearly television event. Somehow the industry was convinced that the airing of the Emmys was so important to America that any sign of celebrity resistance to gather (whether for fear of being attacked or fear of looking crassly self-absorbed) would somehow be tantamount to "letting the terrorists win." As the Academy of Television Arts and Sciences chairman Bryce Zabel told viewers, canceling the Emmys "would have been an admission of defeat. Like baseball and Broadway, we are an American tradition."[41]

It seems just as probable, however, that the Academy and CBS were also worrying about their own commercial viability in the post-9/11 climate. In other words, canceling the Emmys would not just be an admission of the defeat of the nation; it would also be an admission that the consumer logics of TV—its annual ceremonies and self-congratulations—had been defeated. In this regard, in the wake of 9/11, the Emmys also came to signify the degree to which the televisual and marketing scene could be revitalized. The broadcast, which took place on November 4 at Los Angeles's Shubert Theatre (almost two months after the originally scheduled broadcast), was carefully orchestrated in this regard. Although there were more "no-shows" than usual, and while the area outside the theater was reportedly a "surreal" scene of rooftop sharpshooters, the Emmy producers encouraged the stars to perform their roles in the usual fashion. Before the broadcast, executive producer Gary Smith coached the stars, "Don't be afraid to be excited. . . . That's what people are looking for."[42]

The Emmy Awards program was another self-referential celebrity public sphere, this time constructed through appeals to television and Hollywood history. The opening sequence begins with Christian trumpet player/singer Phil Driscoll doing a bluesy rendition of

"America the Beautiful" with a backup choir of students from different colleges across the country. The national unity theme is underscored by a large-screen display of video images (everything from the flag and the Statue of Liberty to historical footage of Charles Lindbergh's lift-off and civil rights protests to landscapes of prairies and cities, all spliced together in a seamless quilt of meaning). This is followed by a female voice-over that announces, "Tonight television speaks to a global audience as we show the world images of an annual celebration. Our presence here tonight does more than honor an industry, it honors those cherished freedoms that set us apart as a nation and a people." After this, the scene cuts to veteran newscaster Walter Cronkite, who appears via satellite from Toronto. Cronkite directly addresses the camera and narrates a history of television's importance to American politics and culture. Evoking the words of the World War II broadcaster Edward R. Murrow, Cronkite says, "Television, the great common denominator, has lifted our common vision as never before, and television also reminds us that entertainment can help us heal."

The Driscoll performance, the video-backdrop, the female voice-over, and finally the widely respected Cronkite provide a prelude to what will be the night's apologetic theme: the ritualistic honoring of stars is not narcissistic commercialized self-indulgence, but instead a public service to America and its image in the world.[43] The opening sequence then transitions to host Ellen DeGeneres, who delivers her monologue as the cameras cut back and forth to a bevy of Hollywood stars seated in the audience. Significantly, among those singled out are stars associated with Hollywood liberalism—including the cast of *The West Wing* and Bill Maher (who had already been in trouble with his sponsors for what they perceived to be unpatriotic comments). In other words, as with the telethon, the Emmy ceremony was not simply "right-wing" in its approach to patriotism; it presented well-known Hollywood liberals (including a grand finale by Barbra Streisand and, of course, DeGeneres herself) as part of a national community who leave their identity politics at home to join together and defend the larger American cause. Drawing attention to the patriotic mission of this liberal constituency, DeGeneres humorously asks the audience, "What would bug the Taliban more than seeing a gay woman in a suit surrounded by Jews?"

While the opening act establishes television as its own historical reference and television stars as their own public, a sequence near the end of the broadcast is even more blatant in its self-referential memories of Hollywood nationalism and celebrity citizenship. And while the first act uses network era "hard" newsman Cronkite (who is in Toronto and far removed from the pomp and pageantry), this later segment features the ultimate postnetwork celebrity journalist, Larry King (who is dressed in a tuxedo and is obviously part of the Hollywood community). King introduces a montage of vintage footage portraying Hollywood's efforts in wartime (e.g., the Andrew Sisters; Betty Grable's legs; Bugs Bunny; Bob Hope and the USO; Marilyn Monroe posing for the boys and kissing a wounded GI; Frank Sinatra signing an autograph; Harpo Marx clowning on stage; Hope and a bevy of sexy starlets in Vietnam; Hope, Steve Martin, and Jay Leno in the Gulf interspersed with Vietnam footage of Hope and Phyllis Diller as well as black-and-white images of Nat King Cole and Milton Berle performing for the troops). The rapid, decontextualized series of star fetish icons, the musical accompaniment (from the Andrew Sisters's World War II hit "Boogie Woogie Bugle Boy" to a standard rock riff to Lee Greenwood singing "I'm Proud to be an American") establish a "commonsense" and highly sentimental history of Hollywood patriotism (or as Larry King put it while introducing the montage, "Over the years the beat of the music changes, but the heart beneath it never waivers"). This nostalgic display of stars with its thesis of unchanging Hollywood sentiment obscures the different historical contexts in which World War II, Korea, Vietnam, and the Gulf War were fought (and obviously also the very different levels of popular support these wars had).

The montage sequence ends with an overhead traveling shot picturing a vast audience of GIs applauding Bob Hope during the Gulf War. The sequence then dissolves back to an overhead traveling shot of the celebrity audience applauding in the Shubert Theatre. This dissolve from the GIs to the Emmy audience—and the fact that the shots are perfectly matched—establishes a visual rhetoric that asks viewers to imagine that soldiers and celebrities are contiguous publics, and perhaps even comparable public servants. Immediately after the dissolve, the show cuts back to Larry King (live) on stage where he speaks into the camera: "Once again we're in a time when America's armed forces are being sent to defend our freedom, and once again the entertainment industry is giving what it can." The entire segment legitimates future wars through a sentimental journey down Hollywood's wartime past.

The segment is capped off by yet another invocation of Hollywood's self-referential public sphere. Larry King speaks directly into the camera but not, as is usually the case, in order to address the home audience. Instead, he addresses an ailing Bob Hope at home: "We know that Bob Hope is watching at home tonight. And you should know, dear Robert, that we are thinking of you. . . . From all of us here, thanks for the memories." King's direct address to Hope—intercut with stars applauding in the studio audience—creates a completely enclosed universe of citizen celebrities, orchestrating a set of complex relays between popular memories of vintage Hollywood, military history since World War II, and the present-day meanings of nationalism and war. In this televised display of celebrity patriotism, public service and publicity find their ideal meeting ground.

Osama bin Laden Meets the *South Park* Kids

In the introductory pages to his essay "The Uncanny," Sigmund Freud discusses the intellectual uncertainty he faces during World War I when he finds it impossible to keep up with the flow of international publications.[44] In today's world of electronic "instant" histories, these problems of intellectual uncertainty are compounded in ways that Freud could never have imagined. The "uncanny" seems an especially appropriate trope for the current situation, as nothing seems to be what it was and everything is what it wasn't just minutes before it happened. In this context, the literate pursuit of history writing seems slow to the point of uselessness. This is, of course, compounded by the fact that the publishing industry is painfully behind the speed of both war and electronic media. So rather than partake in either historical "conclusions" or future "predictions," I want to open up some questions about television and nationalism vis á vis the changing economies of industrially produced culture.

Given the political divisions that have resurfaced since 2001, it seems likely that the grand narratives of national unity that sprang up after 9/11 were for most people more performative than sincere. In other words, it is likely that most viewers really did know that all the newfound patriotism was really just a public performance of belief in national myths of unity. And if you didn't perform this role, then somehow you were a bad American. In this respect, no matter what they thought of the situation, in the wake of 9/11 stars had to perform the role of "love it or leave it" citizen to remain popular (a lesson that Bill Maher learned with a vengeance when his TV show *Politically Incorrect* was cancelled).[45]

But did the performance really work? Just days after the attacks, the limits of performative nationalism were revealed in *America: A Tribute to Heroes* when, in the final sequence, everyone gathered 'round Willie Nelson to sing "America the Beautiful." Now, this was certainly a bad performance. Most of the celebrities were either too embarrassed to sing, or else they just didn't know the words to this show tune turned national anthem.[46] Some stars were visibly squinting at tele-prompters with consternation—hoping to sing a verse. Yet, because the telethon was foremost aimed at baby boom and post–baby boom generations, most audiences would have known the popular ballads that were directly aimed at these niche generations. Clearly, pop songs like John Lennon's "Imagine" (sung by Neil Young), Bob Marley's "Redemption Song" (sung by Wyclef Jean), or Paul Simon's "Bridge Over Troubled Waters" have more historical meaning to these taste publics than any national anthem does.

More generally, I think the post-9/11 performance of nationalism will fail because it really does not fit with the economic and cultural practices of twenty-first-century U.S. media society. The fact that there is no longer a three-network broadcast system means that citizens are not collected as aggregate audiences for national culture. As we all know, what we watch on TV no longer really is what other people watch—unless they happen to be in our demographic taste culture. The postnetwork system is precisely about fragmentation and narrowcasting. While the new multichannel cable systems may not provide true diversity in the sense of political or cultural pluralism, the postnetwork system does assume a culture that is deeply divided by taste—not one that is unified through national narratives.[47] In a multinational consumer culture it becomes difficult for media to do business without addressing the niche politics of style, taste, and especially youth subcultures that have become central to global capitalism. In the end, the new media environment does not lend itself to unifying narratives of patriotism, if only because these older forms of nationalism have nothing to with the "return to normalcy" and normal levels of consumption. While nationalist popular culture does, of course, exist (and obviously rose in popularity after 9/11), it appears more as another niche market (those people who hang flags off their cars), than as a unifying cultural dominant.[48]

The actual cultural styles in these new narrowcast media markets are increasingly based on irony, parody, skepticism, and "TV literate" critical reading protocols. For people who grew up watching *The Simpsons*'s hilarious parodies of mass culture and national politics, for people who fell asleep to Dave Letterman or Conan O'Brien, and for viewers who regularly watched *Saturday Night Live*, *In Living Color*, *The Daily Show*, and *Mad TV*'s political/news parodies—a sudden return to blind patriotism (and blind consumerism) is probably not really likely.

In the first week after the September 11 attacks, the cable operators and networks all did cover the same story—and for a moment the nation returned to something very much like the old three-network system.[49] Yet, the case of 9/11 also demonstrates that in the current media landscape, it is hard to sustain the fantasy of utopian collectivity that had been so central to previous media events. Comparing media coverage of 9/11 to the coverage of the Kennedy assassination, Fredric Jameson argues that back in 1963, a utopian fantasy of collectivity was in part constructed through news reporters' "clumsiness [and] the technological naiveté in which they sought to rise to the occasion." But, he claims, the media are now so full of orchestrated spectacle and public violence on a daily basis that many people had a hard time seeing media coverage of 9/11 as documents of anything sincere, no less as any kind of inter-subjective, utopian communication. As Jameson puts it, despite the many claims that America lost its innocence on 9/11, it was "not America, but rather its media [that had] . . . definitely lost its innocence."[50]

Certainly, for industry executives who work in the competitive environment of narrowcasting, sentiments of national belonging and utopian collectivity quickly gave way to the "bottom line." In fact, even in the "good will" climate of September 2001, the industry was still widely aware of the competitive realities of the postnetwork marketplace. CNN, which then had an exclusive deal with the Al Jazeera network, tried to block other news outlets from broadcasting its satellite transmissions of bin Laden's video address.[51] Even the celebrity telethon was a source of industry dispute. Worried that cable telecasts would undercut audience shares for broadcasters, some network affiliates and network-owned-and-operated stations tried to stop a number of cable channels from simulcasting *America: A Tribute to Heroes*. According to *Variety*, upon hearing of possible cable competition, "some of the vocal managers at the Big Four stations . . . went bananas and threatened to cancel the telethon and schedule their own local programming."[52] So much for humanitarianism in the postnetwork age!

Given this competitive media marketplace, it comes as no surprise that industry insiders quickly revised their initial predictions about the fate of American popular culture. By October 4, the front page of the *New York Times* proclaimed, "In Little Time Pop Culture is Back to Normal," stating that the industry was backtracking on its initial predictions that the events of September 11 would completely change culture. David Kissinger, president of the USA Television Production Group, told the *Times* that the industry's initial reaction to the attacks may have been overstated and that because most industry people were "terror stricken" on September 11, "We shouldn't be held accountable for much of what we said that week."[53]

In fact, within a month, even irony was back in vogue, especially on late-night TV, but increasingly also on other entertainment programs. By mid-November, Comedy Central's *South Park*—a cartoon famous for its irreverence—ran an episode in which the *South Park* kids visit Afghanistan. Once there, Cartman (*South Park*'s leading bad boy) meets bin Laden, and the two engage in an extended homage to Warner Brothers' cartoons. Bin Laden takes the roles of the wacky Daffy Duck, the dull-headed Elmer Fudd, and even the lovesick Pepé Lé Pew (he is shown romancing a camel much as Pepé romances a cat that he thinks is a skunk). Meanwhile, Cartman plays the ever-obnoxious Bugs Bunny (like Bugs, he even does a drag performance as a harem girl wooing a lovesick bin Laden, whose eyes, in classic Tex Avery cartoon style, pop out of his head).

Although the episode was the usual "libertarian" hodgepodge of mixed political messages (some seemingly critical of U.S. air strikes, others entirely Orientalist), its blank ironic sensibility did at least provide for some unexpected TV moments. In one scene, when the *South Park* kids meet Afghan children in a war-torn village, American claims of childish innocence (promoted, for example, in *West Wing*'s fictional classroom) are opened up for comic interrogation. Dodging a U.S. bomb attack, the Afghan children tell the *South Park* kids, "Over a third of the world hates America." "But why?" ask the *South Park* kids, "Why does a third of the world hate us?" And the Afghan kids reply, "Because you don't realize that a third of the world hates you." While the episode ends with an over-the-top cartoon killing of bin Laden, and an American flag waving to the tune of "America the Beautiful," the program establishes such a high degree of pastiche, blank irony, and recombinant images, that it would be difficult to say it encourages any particular "dominant" reading of the war. The laughter seems directed more at semiotic breakdowns, perhaps mimicking the way in which news coverage of the war seems to make people increasingly incapable of knowing what's going on—a point that one of the *South Park* characters underscores at the end of the show when he says, "I'm confused."

To be sure, programs like *South Park* and the niche cable channels on which they appear might not translate into the old enlightenment dream of "public service" TV with a moral imperative for its national public. Television Studies is, of course, riddled with debates over the question of whether these new forms of narrowcasting and multichannel media outlets will destroy what some critics call common culture. In response to the increasing commercialization and fragmentation of European electronic media, scholars like Jostein Gripsrud, Graham Murdock, and James Curran champion European public service broadcast models, and even while they do not advocate a simplistic return to paternalistic models of "cultivation" and taste, they seek a way to reformulate the ideal of an electronic democratic culture.[54] In the United States, the situation is somewhat different. The "public interest" policy rhetoric on which the national broadcast system was founded has been woefully underachieved; broadcasters did not engage a democratic culture of diverse interests, but rather for the most part catered to the cultural tastes of their target consumers (which for many years meant white middle-class audiences). Moreover, the networks often interpreted public service requirements within the context of public relations and the strengthening of their own oligopoly power.[55] Meanwhile, the underfunded Public Broadcasting System grew increasingly dependent on corporate funding. And, as Laurie Ouellette argues, by relying on paternalistic notions of "cultivation" and catering to narrowminded taste hierarchies, the network has alienated audiences.[56]

Still, I am not saying that the new multichannel and multiplatform system of niche culture is necessarily better. Instead, we need to ask exactly what the new fragmented niche networks, as well as the proliferation of Internet sites, provide. What do the new forms of multinational media outlets offer beyond the proliferation of products and styles? The question is even more complex when we consider the fact that cable and broadcast networks, Internet sites, search engines, television producers/distributors, movie studios, radio stations, newspapers, and publishing companies are increasingly part of global conglomerate media structures (Disney, Rupert Murdoch's News Corp., Viacom, Time-Warner, etc.).[57] As in other postindustrial modes of capitalism, in the media industries there is both fragmentation and centralization at the same time; any attempt to consider the political effects of the multiplication of channels (and fragmentation of audiences) still has to be considered within the overall patterns of consolidation at the level of ownership.[58]

Perhaps I am a bit overly optimistic, but I do want to end by suggesting some alternative possibilities within the highly consolidated, yet also fragmented, global mediasphere. As Daniel Dayan and Elihu Katz argue, although media events may be hegemonically sponsored and often function to restore consensual values, they always also "invite reexamination of the status quo." Following Victor Turner, Dayan and Katz claim that media events put audiences in a "liminal" context, outside the norms of the everyday. Even if media events do not institutionalize new norms, they do "provoke . . . mental appraisal of alternative possibilities."[59] In this sense, although I have focused primarily on media myths of reunification and nationalism, it is also true that 9/11 provoked counternarratives and political dialogues. In particular, 9/11 made people aware of new prospects for communication in a rapidly changing media environment.

Certainly, the Internet allowed for a collective interrogation of mainstream media and discussions among various marginalized groups. According to Bruce A. Williams, while "mainstream media reiterated themes of national unity, the chatrooms allowed different groups of Americans to debate what the impact of the attacks was for them specifically."[60] Internet sites like Salon.com—as well as access to a host of international news outlets—provided alternative views and global discussions. Convergence platforms opened up venues for expression. For example, after 9/11, the MTV chat room included criticisms of U.S. policy and the bombing of Afghanistan, while a chat room hosted by the Black Entertainment Television network included conversations on whether it was possible to reconcile black beliefs about racist police and fire departments with the heroic images of police and firefighters after 9/11. Resistance groups from around the globe used the Internet as a forum for antiwar e-mails, virtual marches, and group organizing. The Social Science Research Council's web site allowed scholars to weigh in on the events at Internet speed. The "low tech" medium of radio (especially National Public Radio) likewise provided alternative voices.

That said, my point here is not that "new" media or "alternative media" are categorically "better" than TV. Certainly, many Internet sites and talk radio stations were filled with right-wing war fever.

As Williams suggests, because the Internet allows for insular conversations, some message boards (such as "Crosstar") discussed
ways to draw clear ideological boundaries and to keep "dissident
voices" (i.e., liberals) off the board.[61] In this respect, we should not
embrace the Internet in some essentialist sense as a pure space
of pluralism that is always already more democratic than "old"
media. Instead, it seems more accurate to say that the presence of
multiple media platforms holds out hopeful possibilities for increased
expression, but what this will amount to in terms of democracy and
citizenship remains a complex historical question.

In addition to the Net, the presence of the Al Jazeera news network had a destabilizing effect on the status of information itself.
Al Jazeera officials defy the democratic legacy of the "free press"
that had been so crucial to U.S. Cold War politics. Whereas the
United States used to claim that its so-called free press was a reign-
ing example of "free world" democracy, Al Jazeera now has taken
up that same public pose, claiming that it will present all sides of
the story from a Middle Eastern vantage point. In their book on Al
Jazeera, Mohammed El-Nawawy and Adel Iskandar discuss how
the network's post-9/11 coverage—especially its coverage of the
U.S. bombings on Afghanistan and the circulation of bin Laden's
videotapes—quickly became a public relations crisis for the Bush
administration.[62] Troubled by the bad PR, the Bush administration
formed a Hollywood Summit to discuss the role the industry might
play in the war on terrorism. The military also met with Hollywood
talent at the University of Southern California's Institute for
Creative Technologies, a military/Hollywood alliance that Jonathan
Burston aptly terms, "militainment."[63] By late November 2001,
President Bush signed an initiative to start the Middle East Radio
Network (which strives to counterbalance anti-Americanism in the
Arab world and is aimed especially at youth audiences).[64] As such
federally sponsored efforts suggest, the proliferation of news outlets,
entertainment networks, and Internet sites, as well as the mounting
synergy between Hollywood and the military, has changed the
nature of semiotic warfare, and the United States is certainly keen
to play by the new rules of the game.[65]

Back to Normal?

On the one hand, as I have suggested above, much of the TV landscape looks like a continuation of the same kinds of programs that

aired prior to 9/11, and for this reason it is tempting to say that television's "return to normal" transcended the events of 9/11, and everything is as it was before. On the other hand, 9/11 haunts U.S. commercial television.[66] The memory of 9/11 now—in 2005— circulates in ways that disrupt the kind of historical narratives and nationalist logic that had been so central to the initial return to the normal TV schedule.

Since 2001 the history and memory of 9/11 has in fact become a national battleground—not only in the notorious fights over Ground Zero's reconstruction, but also on the electronic spaces of television. By March of 2002, major networks began to feature commemorative documentaries that told the story of 9/11.[67] By March of 2004, President Bush launched a presidential campaign with TV ads that showed historical footage of the firefighters, implicitly equating their heroism with his presidency. But whereas nationalist historical pedagogy initially served to solidify consent for the Bush administration, now the history and memory of 9/11 is not so simply marshaled. On March 5, 2004, just one day after the ads began to circulate, CNN interviewed a woman who had lost her husband on 9/11. Unlike the speechless pregnant widows on *Oprah* back in 2001, this woman had regained her voice and spoke quite articulately of her disgust for the president's use of 9/11 footage for political ends.

In the end, I suspect the current situation is ripe for new visions of apocalyptic techno-futures, with satellites, guided missiles, surveillance cameras, and communication media of all kinds at the core of an ongoing genre of techno-warfare criticism waged by the likes of Baudrillard, Virilio, and many others.[68] But, it seems to me that as forceful and perceptive as this kind of work has been, this is really just the easy way out. Instead of engaging in yet another stream of doom and gloom technological disaster criticism, it seems more useful to think about how cultural studies and media studies in particular might hold on to a politics of hope. What I have in mind is in no way the same as utopian claims to transcendence and unity (whether local, national, or global) through new media technologies. Rather, this politics of hope is situated in a confrontation with the actually existing historical divisions around us. This materialist politics of hope should embrace the new global media environment as an opportunity to listen to "the third of the world that hates us" rather than (to use Bush's formulation) clutter the globe with messages about "how good we are." The world has heard enough about America. Time now to tune in elsewhere.

Notes

Lynn, Spigel, "Entertainment Wars: Television Culture After 9/11," *American Quarterly* 56, no. 2 (2004): 235–270. © The American Studies Association. Reprinted with permission of The Johns Hopkins University Press.
Thank you to Marita Sturken, Jeffrey Sconce, Jan Olsson, Chris Berry, and four anonymous readers for their help with this essay.

1. "Disaster Programming," Variety.com, September 21, 2001, 1. For more on TV network cancellations of violent movies see John Dempsey, "Cable Nets Nix Violent Pix in Wake of Tragedy," Variety.com, September 16, 2001, 1–2; Joe Flint and John Lippman, "Hollywood Revisits Terrorism-Related Projects," *Wall Street Journal*, September 13, 2001, B2; Joe Flint, "TV Programmers Avoid All Allusions to Attacks," *Wall Street Journal*, September 28, 2001, B6.

2. For speculations on the "end of irony" see Jeff Gordinier, "How We Saw It," *Entertainment Weekly*, September 28, 2001, 12; Peter Bart, "Where's the Snap & Crackle of Pop Culture?" Variety.com, September 30, 2001, 1–2. Note, however, that a counterdiscourse popped up immediately in venues like the *Onion* and Salon.com, which used irony early on. In an online essay, James Der Derian noted some of the inconsistencies in what he called the "protected zones of language" after 9/11. For example, Der Derian notes that irony was in some venues under attack; "President Bush was given room to joke in a morale-boosting visit to the CIA, saying he's 'spending a lot of quality time lately' with George Tenet, the director of the CIA." Der Derian also took on *New York Times* reporter Edward Rothstein for taking an "opportunist shot at postmodernists and post-colonialists" by "claiming that their irony and relativism is 'ethnically perverse' and produces 'guilty passivity.' " See Der Derian's "9.11: Before, After, and In Between," in Social Science Research Council, After September 11 Archive, SSRC.org, 5. (The original posting date is no longer on the site.)

3. Jennifer Netherby, "Renters Flock to Video Stores," Videobusiness.com, September 21, 2001, 1–2. *Video On Line* reported, "Wall-mart stores asked the studios for a list of their titles that contain scenes of the World Trade Center, presumably to take some merchandising action on those movies." See VideoBusiness.com/news, September 13, 2001, 1.

4. "Domain Names Grow After Attacks," Variety.com, September 25, 2001, 1.

5. Even while cable outlets are not regulated by the Federal Communications Commission to the extent that the broadcast networks are, they are still widely perceived as "service" industries and arbiters of public safety in times of crisis (obviously, this is the platform of cable news outlets like CNN, which dramatically increased its viewership after 9/11).

6. I am borrowing Raymond Williams's term "a whole way of life," which he used to define culture. See his *Culture and Society: 1780–1950* (New York: Columbia University Press, 1958, 1983), 325.

7. More generally, 9/11 disrupted the familiar/consumer uses of a host of communication technologies from cell phones to television to satellites to video games, all of which now resonated in an uncanny sense with their militaristic/wartime uses for which their basic technology was developed.

8. Mary Anne Doane, "Information, Crisis, Catastrophe," in Patricia Mellencamp, ed., *Logics of Television: Essays in Cultural Criticism* (Bloomington: Indiana University Press, 1990), 222–239.

9. Vanessa O'Connell, "TV Networks Cut $320 Million of Ads in Crisis," *Wall Street Journal*, September 19, 2001, B5.

10. *Variety* reported that "commercial breaks were back across the board Monday [September 17]." Rick Kissell, "TV Getting Back to Biz and Blurbs," Variety.com, September 17, 2001, 1.

11. Jack Valenti, "Hollywood, and our Nation, Will Meet the Test," Variety.com, September 27, 2001, 1–2.

12. The president said this in a televised address he delivered at Chicago O'Hare Airport with the aim of convincing people to return to plane travel. Note, too, that in subsequent months, various advertisers linked their promotional discourses to 9/11 and the idea of patriotic consumption. (For example, ads for United and American airlines as well as financial corporations did this).

13. For examples of literature on TV news, 9/11, and Afghanistan, see *Television and New Media* 3, no. 2 (May 2002); Daya Kishnan Thussu and Des Freedman, eds., *War and the Media* (Thousand Oaks, Calif.: Sage, 2003); Stephen Hess and Marvin Kalb, eds., *The Media and the War on Terrorism* (Washington, D.C.: Brookings Institute, 2003); Barbie Zelizer and Stuart Allan, eds. *Journalism After September 11* (New York: Routledge, 2002).

14. As other scholars have argued, we should not accept at face value the information/ entertainment binary that underpins the ideological logics of mainstream media systems. This binary—and the related binaries of important/trivial; private/ public; masculine/feminine; and high/low—not only elides the fact that news is also narrative (and increasingly entertaining), but also fails to acknowledge that entertainment also serves to provide audiences with particular ways of knowing about and seeing the world. See, for example, Richard Dyer, *Only Entertainment* (New York: Routledge, 1992); John Fiske, "Popular News," in *Reading Popular Culture* (Boston: Unwyn and Hyman, 1989); James Freedman, ed., *Reality Squared: Televisual Discourse on the Real* (New Brunswick, N.J.: Rutgers University Press, 2002).

15. Der Derian, "9.11," 2.

16. For an interesting discussion of media references to Pearl Harbor and the rerelease of the film after 9/11, see Cynthia Weber, "The Media, The 'War on Terrorism' and the Circulation of Non-Knowledge," in Thussu and Freedman, *War and the Media*, 190–199.

17. This kind of coverage is, of course, symptomatic of the general rise of "info-tainment" in the climate of media conglomeration and a ratings-driven commercial ethos. For speculation on the social/political effects of the news coverage of 9/11 in terms of "infotainment," see Daya Kishan Thussu, "Live TV and Bloodless Deaths: War, Infotainment and 24/7 News," in Thussu and Freedman, *War and the Media*, 117–132. There is much additional literature on issues of infotainment. See, for example, Leonard Downie Jr. and Robert G. Kaiser, *The News About the News: American Journalism in Peril* (New York: Knopf, 2002); and Pierre Bourdieu, *On Television*, trans. Priscilla Parkhurst Ferguson (New York: New Press, 1998). For analysis of the effect that 'round-the-clock coverage of "real time" wars has on foreign policy, see Piers Robinson, *The CNN Effect—The Myth of News, Foreign Policy and Intervention* (New York: Routledge, 2002).

18. Claude Brodesser, "Feds Seek H'wood Help," Variety.com, October 7, 2001; Michael Schneider, "Fox Salutes Request by Bush for 'Wanted' Spec," Variety.com, October 10, 2001.

19. Michel de Certeau, "History: Science and Fiction," in *Heterologies: Discourse on the Other*, trans. Brian Massumi (Minneapolis: University of Minnesota Press, 1986), 199–221.

20. Roland Barthes, *Mythologies*, trans. A. Lavers (London, Cape, 1972); Marita Sturken *Tangled Memories: The Vietnam War, the AIDS Epidemic and the Politics of Remembering* (Berkeley: University of California Press, 1997). For more on the role of memory/nostalgia in film, television, and other popular media, see for example, Cahiers du Cinéma interview with Michel Foucault, reprinted in *Edinburgh Magazine* 2 (1977): 19–25; Patrick Bommes and Richard Wright, "Charms of Residence," in Richard Johnson et al., eds., *Making Histories: Studies in History Writing and Politics* (London: Hutchinson, 1982); George Lipsitz, *Time Passages: Collective Memory and American Popular Culture* (Minneapolis: University of Minnesota Press, 1989); Robert Rosenstone, *Visions of the Past: The Challenge of Film to Our Idea of History* (New York: Belknap Press, 1996); Robert Rosenstone, *Revisioning History: Film and the Construction of a New Past* (Princeton, N.J.: Princeton University Press, 1994); Marcia Landy, ed., *The Historical Film: History and Memory in Media* (New Brunswick, N.J.: Rutgers University Press, 2000); "Special Debate," *Screen* 42, no. 2 (Summer 2001): 188–216 (this is a series of short essays on trauma and cinema); David Morely and Kevin Robins, "No Place Like Heimet: Images of Homeland," chapter 5 in Morely and Robins, *Spaces of Identity: Global Media, Electronic Landscapes and Cultural Boundaries* (London: Routledge, 1995), 85–104. Purnima Mankekar, *Screening Culture, Viewing Politics: An Ethnography of Television, Womanhood, and Nation in Postcolonial India* (Durham, N.C.: Duke University Press, 1999).

21. Louis Chunovic, "Will TV News—Or its Audience—Finally Grow Up?" *TelevisionWeek*, September 24, 2001, 15. Note that news executives responded to such criticism. For example CBS's Mel Karmizan and Fox News Channel's Roger Ailes promised to upgrade news programs and to cover more international issues.

22. So, too, this ABC lineup followed the logic of what Daniel Dayan and Elihu Katz see as integral to media events more generally: namely, a "neo romantic desire for heroic action by great men followed by the spontaneity of mass action." See Dayan and Katz, *Media Events: The Live Broadcasting of History* (Cambridge, Mass.: Harvard University Press, 1992), 21.

23. Some people have told me that they found it a useful source of "modeling" for their own conversations with their children.

24. Several other series also created special episodes about the attacks or else planted references to 9/11 in preexisting episodes. NBC's *Third Watch* began its season on October 29 with a documentary in which real-life emergency workers recalled their experiences on 9/11. ABC's *NYPD Blue* added two scenes acknowledging the attack into its season opener on November 6. As *New York Times* critic Caryn James pointed out, "The creators of 'Third Watch' and 'N.Y.P.D. Blue' have said they felt a responsibility to deal with the events, but the decision was practical, too. Their supposedly realistic characters would have seemed utterly unbelievable if they had ignored such an all-consuming tragedy." See Caryn James, "Dramatic Events That Rewrite the Script," *New York Times*, October 29, 2001, E7.

25. Josh lists many of the same Taliban injustices that President Bush listed in his first televised speech to Congress after the attacks.

26. Edward W. Said, *Orientalism* (New York: Vintage Books, 1979), see especially 284–328.
27. Ibid., 291.
28. Lauren Berlant, *The Queen of America Goes to Washington City: Essays on Sex and Citizenship* (Durham, N.C.: Duke University Press, 1997).
29. As Slavoj Žižek wrote just days after the attacks, this sense of a pure "evil Outside" was the response of a public living in a fake Matrix-like existence, a public that had for so long considered itself immune to the suffering endured on a daily basis by other world populations, and in any case, in no way responsible for its own perpetuation of violence around the world. Slavoj Žižek, "Welcome to the Desert of the Real!" posted on Re: Constructions. mit.edu, September 24, 2001. The title is taken from a line in the film *The Matrix*. Žižek's short essay was later developed in a book. See his *Welcome to the Desert of the Real* (London: Verso, 2002). Der Derian, "9.11," 4–5, similarly evokes *The Matrix*.
30. Jack Lule, "Myth and Terror on the Editorial Page: The *New York Times* Responds to September 11, 2001," *Journalism and Mass Communication Quarterly* 29, no. 2 (2002): 275–293.
31. Yet, as Marita Sturken argues, this "end of innocence" theme is common to the stories spun around national disasters (for example, the same language was used after JFK's assassination). See Sturken, *Tangled Memories*, chap. 1.
32. Justin Lewis, "Speaking of Wars . . ." *Television and New Media* 3, no. 2 (May 2002): 170.
33. In this sense, it is interesting to note how television created a *continuous past*, particularly with regard to World War II and Vietnam. In place of the grave generational divides these wars had previously come to signify, television presented unifying narratives that bridged the gap between the self-sacrificing "Greatest Generation" and baby boomer draft dodgers. This was most vividly displayed when Vietnam POW/Senator John McCain met 1960s youth rebel Stephen Stills on the *Tonight Show*, reconciling their differences.
34. Jayne Rodgers, "Icons and Invisibility: Gender, Myth, and 9/11," in Thussu and Freedman, eds., *War and the Media*, 206, 207.
35. Linda Williams, *Playing the Race Card: Melodramas of Black and White: From Uncle Tom to O. J. Simpson* (Princeton, N.J.: Princeton University Press, 2001), 24.
36. One month after the attacks, *Variety* reported, "A rash of documentaries—some put together in a hurry—that aim to explain terrorism is a hot property." See Andrea R. Vaucher, "Arab, Terror Docus Heat Up the Market," Variety.com, October 10, 2001, 1.
37. U.S. and British air strikes on Afghanistan began on October 7, 2001, and American warplanes attacked the Taliban in the field on October 10, 2001.
38. Saira Shah cited in Janelle Brown, " 'Beneath the Veil' Redux," Salon.com, 1–2.
39. Rick Kissell, "Bush Speech, Telethon Both Draw Record Auds," Variety.com, September 23, 2001, 1–2.
40. As one of the readers for this article suggested, the telethon's aura of liveness might have also helped to stave of the fear that TV and commercial culture were themselves "dead." To be sure, live "call-in" donations to stars ensured that money was still circulating through the media wires (here, not through the crass commercialism of TV as usual, but through the exchange economies of charity).
41. He said this on the broadcast.
42. Gary Smith cited in Joseph Adalian, "Show Finally Goes On and TV Biz Takes Heart," Variety.com, November 4, 2001, 1.

43. Underscoring the show's global impact, later in the ceremony there is a video montage of leaders from around the globe offering their condolences to the American public.

44. Sigmund Freud, "The Uncanny," in *Studies in Parapsychology* (New York: Collier Books, 1919, 1963), 19–60. Freud discusses his lack of bibliographical references vis á vis the war in Europe on 20.

45. When I delivered this paper at a conference at the University of California, Berkeley, Ratiba Hadj-Moussa pointed out that this dynamic of national performance doesn't necessarily suggest that people don't in some way believe in the performance. I want to thank her for this observation. Clearly, through the act of national performance, it is possible to actually believe in the role you are playing—and even to believe in it more than ever!

46. Note, too, that "America the Beautiful" replaced the actual national anthem after 9/11 because no one seemed to be able to remember the words to the "Star Spangled Banner."

47. Even news is now a matter of taste and "branded" by networks in ways that appeal to consumer profiles. For example, the news on Fox (especially its markedly conservative talk-show hosts) attracts one of cable TV's most loyal publics, but many on the left mock its pretense of "Fair and Balanced" reporting. Al Franken's bestseller *Lies and the Lying Liars Who Tell Them: A Fair and Balanced Look at the Right* (New York: E.P. Dutton, 2003), and the ensuing lawsuit with Fox obviously drew on the more taste-associated taste publics that define themselves in distinction—in Bourdieu's sense—not only to Fox News, but to the viewers who (they imagine) watch it. For his discussion of taste as social distinction, see Pierre Bourdieu, *Distinction: A Social Critique of the Judgement of Taste*, trans. Richard Nice (Cambridge, Mass.: Harvard University Press, 1984).

48. Even before the attacks, patriotic symbols were reemerging as a fashion fad. Corporations such as Tommy Hilfinger, Polo Ralph Lauren, and the Gap Inc.'s Old Navy sported the flag trend, while European haute couture designer Catherine Malandrino unveiled her flag-motif fall collection in the summer of 2001 (which included a skirt that Madonna wore on her concert tour). See Teri Agins, "Flag Fashion's Surging Popularity Fits With Some Fall Collections," *Wall Street Journal*, September 19, 2001, B5. According to Agins, the post-9/11 flag fashions were an extension of this trend, not an invention of it.

49. In 1992 Dayan and Katz speculated on the fate of television, nationalism, and media events in what they saw to be an increasingly multichannel and segmented television system. They argued that while the old three-network or public broadcast systems "will disappear," television's previous functions of "national integration may devolve upon" media events. Their speculation now seems particularly apt. See Dayan and Katz, *Media Events*, 23. They also predicted that with new technologies and possible erosion of the nation-state, "media events may then create and integrate communities larger than nations," 23.

50. Fredric Jameson, "The Dialectics of Disaster," *South Atlantic Quarterly* 101, no. 2 (Spring 2002): 300.

51. According to *Variety*, news organizations were "furious that CNN wouldn't forego competition" and "rallied against exclusives, saying that they don't serve the public's interest during a time of national crisis." ABC News spokesperson Jeffrey Schneider disputed any exclusivity deal by arguing fair use. He said,

"There was no question in anybody's mind that these images from Al-Jazeera were of compelling national interest," and "We felt we had a duty to broadcast them to the American people which far outweighed whatever commercial agenda CNN was attempting to pursue in this time of war." Meanwhile, Walter Isaacson, CEO of CNN News Group, told *Variety* that CNN had a "reciprocal affiliate deal" with Al Jazeera and that "it's Al-Jazeera's material and we don't have a right to give it way." However Isaacson did admit, "in a time of war, we won't make a big deal about this sort of thing." See Paul Bernstein and Pamela McClintock, "Newsies Fight over bin Laden Interview," Variety.com, October 7, 2001, 1–2.

52. John Dempsey, "Invite to Cablers to Join Telethon Irks Affils," Variety.com, September 20, 2001, 1. The underlying reasons for the broadcasters' concern had to do with issues of East Coat–West Coast transmission times. The big four networks—ABC, CBS, NBC, and Fox—aired the telethon at 9 P.M. Eastern time, and because they wanted to make it seem like a simultaneous nationwide event, they also showed it taped via a dual feed at 9 P.M. on the West Coast. Some single-feed cable networks such as TBS and the National Geographic Channel, however, planned to show the telethon live at 6 P.M. on the West Coast, and thereby preempt the 9 P.M. taped West Coast network broadcast. Some network affiliates and owned-and-operated stations were simply unhappy that any cable networks were airing the telethon, even if cablers showed it simultaneously (at 9 P.M.) with the Big Four.

53. David Kessinger cited in Rick Lynman with Bill Carter, "In Little Time Pop Culture is Almost Back to Normal," *New York Times*, October 4, 2001, 1.

54. See, for example, Jostein Gripsrud, ed., *Television and Common Knowledge* (New York: Routledge, 1999), esp. Graham Murdock, "Rights and Representations," 7–17; James Curran, "Mass Media and Democracy Revisited," in James Curran and Michael Gurevitch, eds., *Mass Media and Society*, 2nd ed. (London: Arnold, 1996), 81–119.

55. See, for example, Vance Kepley, Jr., "The Weaver Years at NBC" *Wide Angle* 12, no. 2 (April 1990): 46–63, and "From 'Frontal Lobes' to the 'Bob-and-Bob Show': NBC Management and Programming Strategies, 1949–65," in Tino Balio, ed., *Hollywood in the Age of Television* (Boston: Unwin-Hyman, 1990), 41–62; Lynn Spigel, "The Making of a Television Literate Elite," in Christine Geraghty and David Lusted, eds., *The Television Studies Book* (London: Arnold, 1998), 63–85.

56. Laurie Ouellette, *Viewers Like You? How Public TV Failed the People* (New Brunswick, NJ: Rutgers University Press, 2002).

57. ABC is now owned by Disney (which owns, for example, the Disney theme parks, radio stations, cable networks like ESPN and Lifetime, retail outlets, feature film companies, newspapers, and magazines; the Multiple System Operator, Comcast, has recently bid for the now struggling Walt Disney Company; CBS is owned by Viacom (which also owns, for example, Paramount Studios as well as cable networks like MTV and Nickelodeon, theme parks, radio stations); NBC recently merged with Vivendi-Universal (GE owns 80 percent of NBC Universal; Vivendi owns 20 percent), it has a joint venture with Microsoft, and its holdings include, for example, cable channels like MSNBC and Bravo and film and television production houses; and Fox is owned by Rupert Murdoch's News Corp. (which owns, for example, Fox Broadcasting, Fox News Channel, Fox Sports Net, motion picture companies, magazines like *TV Guide*, *Elle* and *Seventeen*,

book publishers, numerous newspapers, and delivers entertainment and information to at least 75 percent of the globe). Meanwhile, media conglomerate Time-Warner owns a large number of cable channels, production companies, home video, magazines, music companies, and book publishers (for example, HBO, Cinemax, TNT, Comedy Central, E! Entertainment, Black Entertainment Network, Time-Life Video, Warner Brothers Television, Book of the Month Club, and its notorious deal with AOL). With telephone and cable operators like Comsat acquiring and partnering with media corporations and moving into content, the synergy among these sectors is even more pronounced. These ownership structures make these media organizations more like vertically integrated movie studios of the classic period, as they have controlling stakes in all sectors of their industry—production, distribution, and exhibition—in addition to obvious benefits of owning multiple and related companies that reduces risk and increases opportunities for synergy between different companies in the umbrella corporation. Note, however, that the great instability of the technologies market (including, of course, the fate of AOL and the AOL–Time Warner merger) begs us to ask new questions regarding the future of media conglomeration and convergence.

58. Media conglomerates often say that consolidation of ownership leads to more choice (for example, some media conglomerates claim that consolidation of business holdings allows them to use income from their mainstream media outlets to launch minority channels). However, a variety of media activists, industry executives, media scholars, and government officials have sharply attacked conglomeration and questioned the degree to which freedom of speech and diversity of representation can exist in a deregulated media system in which just a few major corporations own most of the media sources. See, for example, Patricia Aufderheide, *Communications Policy and the Public Interest: The Telecommunications Act of 1996* (New York: Guilford Press, 1999); Patricia Aufderheide, ed., *Conglomerates and the Media* (New York: New Press, 1997); Robert McChesney, *Corporate Media and the Threat to Democracy* (New York: Seven Stories Press, 1997); Ben H. Bagdikian, *The Media Monopoly*, 6th edition (Beacon Press, 2000); Dean Alger, *Megamedia: How Giant Corporations Dominate Mass Media, Distort Competition, and Endanger Democracy* (New York: Rowman and Littlefield, 1998).

59. Dayan and Katz, *Media Events*, 20.

60. Bruce A. Williams, "The New Media Environment, Internet Chatrooms, and Public Discourse After 9/11," in Thussu and Freedman, *War and the Media*, 183. It should be noted that the Pew Research Center found that nine out of ten Americans were getting their news primarily from television after the 9/11 attacks. See "Troubled Times for Network Evening News," *Washington Post*, March 10, A1. However, citing an ABC News poll, Bruce A. Williams claims "almost half of all Americans now get news over the Internet, and over a third of them increased their reliance on online sources after September 11." See Williams, "The New Media Environment," 176.

61. Williams, "New Media Environment," 182. Although Williams cites various online attempts to draw ideological boundaries, he doesn't necessarily view this as a bad thing. While he admits that some such attempts were disturbing, he also argues that "insular conversations that are not easily accessible to the wider public play a positive role by allowing marginalized groups to clarify their distinct

values in opposition to those of the society-at-large within the safety of a sympa-thetic and homogeneous group" (184). Despite his pointing to the insular nature of the web and the desire of some groups to draw ideological boundaries, Williams also argues that there was a general air of civility on the Net (188–189).

62. The administration viewed the presence of Al Jazeera's graphic war footage and bin Laden's videotapes (which were aired around the world) as a grave problem. On October 3, 2001 (a few days before the bombings began), Secretary of State Colin Powell asked the Qatari emir, Sheikh Hamad bin Khalifa, to "tone down" Al Jazeera's inflammatory rhetoric, and the Bush administration specifically requested that the tapes be taken off the network. The International Press Institute sent a letter to Colin Powell, stating Powell's tactics had "serious con-sequences for press freedom" (176–177). Al Jazeera journalists defended their coverage of graphic images by stating that they were trying to cover the war objectively, from both sides (Mohammed El-Nawawy and Adel Iskandar, *Al-Jazeera: The Story of the Network That is Rattling Governments and Redefining Modern Journalism*, updated ed. [Cambridge, Mass.: Westview Press, 2002], 176–81). See also El-Nawawy and Iskandar's discussion of Europe's and Al Jazeera's coverage of Afghanistan (ibid., 186–189).

63. Jonathan Burston, "War and the Entertainment Industries: New Research Priorities in an Era of Cyber-Patriotism," in Thussu and Freedman, *War and the Media*, 163–175. For more see James Der Derian, *Virtuous War: Mapping the Military-Industrial Media Entertainment Network* (Boulder, Colo.: Westview, 2001). At ICT, technologies—such as immersive simulation games—are being developed simultaneously as entertainment and military technologies.

64. A member of the Bush administration met with Hollywood studio chiefs and network executives in Beverly Hills on October 18 to discuss efforts to "enhance the perception of America around the world." See Peter Bart, "H'wood Enlists in War," Variety.com, October 17, 2001, 1–3. A few weeks later, they gathered in what was referred to as a "summit" to discuss more detailed plans for Hollywood's participation in the war effort. See Rick Lyman, "White House Sets Meeting with Film Executives to Discuss War on Terrorism," Variety.com, November 8, 2001, 1–3. See also Pamela McClintock, "Nets Rally Stars Around Flag," Variety.com, December 3, 2001, 1–2.

65. Meanwhile, in a connected fashion, Al Jazeera's presence also threatens the hegemony of Western global news sources. Driven by fierce competition for Arab audiences, in January 2002, CNN officially launched its Arabic web site, CNNArabic.com. See Noureddine Miladi, "Mapping the Al-Jazeera Phenomenon," in Thussu and Freedman, *War and the Media*, 159. Note that CNN launched the web site at the same time (January 2002) that Al Jazeera withdrew its exclusivity agreement with CNN because of the dispute over a tape CNN aired without Al Jazeera's approval.

66. In a provocative thesis, Bret Maxwell Dawson argues that while TV returned to much of its previous content, television's temporal and narrational forms were "traumatized" by 9/11. He argues that the effects of this trauma can be seen in the way that elements of catastrophe television (e.g., live broadcasts, an aura of authenticity, and an obsession with time) have appeared with increasing pop-ularity in reality TV and programs like Fox's *24*. See his "TV Since 9/11," unpublished Master's Thesis, University of South Wales, Sydney, Australia, 2003. While I would not posit such deterministic notions of trauma, it does

seem useful to think about how 9/11 relates to a particular historical conjuncture in aesthetic ideals of TV realism, and in particular TV's obsession with the reality genre and real time (which, as Dawson admits, began before 9/11).

67. This cycle of memorializing documentaries began with CBS's *9/11* (aired 3/10/02), which was followed by *Telling Nicholas* (HBO, 5/12/02), *In Memoriam: New York City, 9.11* (HBO, 5/26/02), and others. For a seminar I taught at UCLA, Sharon Sharp wrote a very interesting paper, "Remembering 9/11: Memory, History, and the American Family," which considers how these documentaries used sentimental images of the family in crisis to tell histories of 9/11.

68. Baudrillard and Virilio both have published monographs on 9/11. See Jean Baudrillard, *The Spirit of Terrorism: And Requiem for the Twin Towers*, trans. Chris Turner; Paul Virilio, *Ground Zero*, trans. Chris Turner (London: Verso, 2002).

Chapter 7

The Country Connection: Country Music, 9/11, and the War on Terrorism

William Hart

In the United States, country music has long served as a conveyer of values that go far beyond mere entertainment. Certainly, like any genre of popular music, country has a functional value as entertainment, just as a car has functional value as transportation. Also like the automobile, country music has exchange value. Toby Keith's new country CD costs $17.98; a BMW 5 Series 525i costs $40,000. But beyond this, country music—like other commodities—has sign value.[1] A BMW or a Jaguar can be used as a sign of social distinction or social status, just as the Mini Cooper—immortalized by Madonna in the pop song "American Life"—gained currency as a signifier of urban hip, progressive style, and understated consumer satisfaction.[2] As part of this process of social distinction, we do not buy just one product, but we typically buy into a whole system of products and develop a lifestyle around such commodities. The Madonna fan, driving along in his Mini Cooper, wears designer jeans, drinks double soy lattes, and attends Pilates classes. The Toby Keith fan drives a Ford truck, shops at Wal-Mart, drinks Bud Light, and attends church with her kids. Marketers assume this clustering of products, as do, undoubtedly, political campaigners and analysts.

The 2000 presidential election illustrates this well, as does the notoriously facile, yet ubiquitous division of the nation into "red states" and "blue states." As the story goes, the red states, which were won by George W. Bush, stretched along the Rockies into the Great Plains and into the South. Al Gore's blue states were found in the Northeast (e.g., New York and Massachusetts), along the West Coast (California and Washington) and in pockets of the Midwest. In the context of the 2000 elections many analysts commented on the red-states vs. blue-states division, correlating it with the cultural and social divisions that define the so-called two Americas.[3] According to this formula, working-class red-state people are "more likely to listen to country music or watch NASCAR," while blue-state people are "more likely to know who slept with whom in the latest episode of TV's *Sex and the City*."[4] According to Fox News conservative political analyst Cal Thomas, it is "country music and gun-owning America against Madonna and big-city liberalists."[5]

Why do people buy into the alleged substance of these divisions and the consumer practices and products associated with them? On an individual level, one reason would be to affirm a sense of social distinction. However, at a social level the reason for this clustering of products, subjectivities, and regionalisms is rooted in a history of relationships among political and economic institutions of power. In the context of 9/11 and the war on terrorism, these connections became especially prominent. In this chapter, I explore connections the country music industry has forged with presidential politics, conservative media industry executives, and the U.S. military.

They Don't Call It Country for Nothin'

The genre of country music has long shown a penchant for patriotic and prowar tunes. Commercial country music did not begin until the 1920s and thus did not comment in song about World War I. However, by the time of World War II, the country music industry was well established nationally. As commentary on World War II, country artists penned and sang such songs as Denver Darling's "Cowards Over Pearl Harbor," Carson Robinson's "We're Gonna Have to Slap the Dirty Little Jap," Ernest Tubbs's "Soldier's Last Letter," and Gene Autry's "At Mail Call Today." Anticommunism and American piety were common themes of country songs about the Korean War, songs that linked strong militarism and strong religious faith, for example, "They Locked God Outside the Iron Curtain" and "Let's Keep the Communists Out." While firmly supportive of the Korean War effort, country artists also recognized the sacrifices of the soldiers with songs like Tubbs's "Missing in Action" and "A Heartsick Soldier on Heartbreak Ridge."[6]

While popular rock music became increasingly associated with the anti–Vietnam War movement, country music for the most part held fast to a prowar stance. While a few songs like Loretta Lynn's "Dear Uncle Sam" and Johnny Cash's "What is Truth" questioned the war to some degree, others held firm to belief in the righteousness of the war (e.g., Tubbs's "It's for God, Country and You, Mom (That's Why I'm Fighting in Viet Nam")). Most country songs marched on with melodies extolling the heroism of the U.S. soldiers fighting in Vietnam, songs like Staff Sergeant Barry Sadler's "The Ballad of the Green Berets," Marty Robbins's "Private Wilson White," and, interestingly, "The Battle Hymn of Lt. Calley," a song that glorifies William Calley, who was court martialed for his actions during the My Lai Massacre. Protesters who questioned U.S. foreign policy regarding Vietnam became targets of criticism in country music. "Viet Nam Blues," written by Kris Kristofferson, and Merle Haggard's two popular anthems, "Okie From Muskogee" and "The Fightin' Side of Me," expressed disdain and contempt for antiwar protestors.

Out of the Iranian hostage crisis (1979–1981) came the Charlie Daniels Band's "In America," which proclaimed America's renewed strength after Ronald Reagan won the presidency and challenged other nations' doubts about America. "This lady may have stumbled but she ain't never fell. / And if the Russians don't believe that they can all go straight to hell." Building up to the Persian Gulf War of 1991, Hank Williams, Jr. warned Saddam Hussein with the song "Don't Give Us a Reason." Aaron Tippin's "You've Got to Stand for Something" reached the Top 10 on the charts and became a career-making single for him. Lee Greenwood's popular anthem "God Bless the USA," which originally went platinum in 1984, appeared on the charts again during the Persian Gulf War. In Greenwood's anthem he sings "I'd thank my lucky stars to be livin' here today. / Cause the flag still stands for freedom / . . . And they can't take that away. / And I'm proud to be an American / Where at least I know I'm free."

Presidents and Patriotic Country Music

In addition to being popular and perhaps because of it, Lee Greenwood and his song "God Bless the USA" became part of presidential campaign politics. The 1984 Reagan campaign adopted Greenwood's song, and in doing so continued a tradition that had already been established. According to country music scholar Curtis Ellison, the connections that presidents have forged with country music in shaping their political images can be traced back at least to Richard Nixon.[7] While in the midst of the Watergate scandal in 1974 Nixon dedicated a new Grand Ole Opry House in Nashville, Tennessee. He opened the new Opry by singing "God Bless America" and "Happy Birthday" to his wife, Pat. He praised country music, proclaiming that it was the "heart of America" and a kind of music that "makes America a better country."[8] The one exception to the presidential penchant for country music endorsements is possibly Bill Clinton, who distanced himself from country music, opting for rock and R&B, and even playing two rock/R&B songs on his saxophone on *The Arsenio Hall Show* during his first campaign.

While some past presidents may have endorsed and used country music in their campaigns, George H. W. Bush appears to have fully embraced country music and its values. During his first term as vice president, Bush wrote "I love country music. . . . I love the lyrics of country music, and the patriotism of the people. . . . It's a great mix of music, lyrics, barrooms, Mother, the flag and good-looking large women. There is something earthy and strong about it all. . . ."[9]

Coming into the 1988 presidential campaign Bush suffered an image problem. He was seen as an elite prepster from the East Coast who lacked the "earthy" qualities that would legitimate him as a man of the people. To gain this stature, key strategists and advisors in the campaign coordinated an image make-over. According to some critics, Mary Matalin, who ran the Bush campaign, along with people like Lee Atwater and Roger Ailes, Bush's "image adviser," transformed Bush from "an East Coast preppy into a country music-loving, pork rind-eating Texan who went down to J.C. Penney to buy himself socks."[10] Because of the abrupt and peculiar image transformation, critics questioned Bush's motives for stressing his fondness for country music, pork rinds, beer, and bass fishing.

At the televised Country Music Awards in Nashville, Tennessee, in 1991, several months after the Gulf War, Bush spoke of the personal influence country music had on him. "Country music gives us a window on the real world. And when I want to feel a surge of patriotism or turn nostalgic or even when I need a little free advice about Saddam Hussein, I turn to country music. . . ." He added: "Barbara and I will always be grateful for what the country music family did for our troops in the Gulf and for their families."[11] Bush felt so strongly that in 1994 he wrote an essay titled "My Country & Western 'tis of Thee" in *Forbes* magazine with the sole purpose of defending his love of country music. "A good country song is like a Norman Rockwell painting. It captures the essence of the American spirit. . . ."[12] More recently George H. W. Bush has continued to praise country music and country musicians. Bush declared on the televised 2002 Country Music Association Awards program that country music "embraces the values that make our nation strong."[13]

Like Father, Like Son, Like Country

According to a 2004 issue of *Country Weekly*, "President George W. Bush is the biggest country music fan to inhabit the Oval Office since . . . well, since his dad, the former President Bush."[14] George W. Bush was born in New Haven, Connecticut, and grew up in Midland, Texas, until high-school age. He then attended elite eastern prep schools, after which he went to Yale University. Like his father, his affection for country music seems genuine. In fact, his musical preferences defined him long before his political aspirations would. While working on an MBA at the Harvard Business School in the early 1970s, Bush enjoyed country music and beer with friends at a country music club, the Hillbilly Ranch, in Boston on the weekends. After a career in the oil industry and as managing general partner of the Texas Rangers baseball team, Bush was elected governor of Texas in 1994. The triumphant song following Bush's victory rally was "God Blessed Texas" by the country group Diamond Rio.

In Bush's run for president, country music was integrated prominently into the campaign. In January of 2000, his father joined his campaign in New Hampshire at a country music concert. County artists Lorrie Morgan and the group Brooks and Dunn were among the performers at the August 2000 Republican National Convention. Country stars Travis Tritt and Hank Williams Jr. helped the Bush campaign by appearing at rallies in Tennessee, the home state of Al Gore. Bush ended his campaigning in November with another rally in Tennessee, which included country stars Loretta Lynn, Lee Greenwood, and Billy Ray Cyrus. Cyrus performed his song "We the People," which was adopted as the official Bush campaign theme song. Country singers Lyle Lovett, Lee Ann Womack, and Asleep at the Wheel were featured performers at the January 20 inauguration. Long-time Bush family friend and country singer Larry Gatlin hosted the Florida ball celebrating the Bush victory and publicly defended the Supreme Court's controversial decision on the elections by saying, "It's not a perfect world; that's why we have laws."[15]

While in office, connections between George W. Bush and country music have continued to evolve, especially following the events of September 11 and the subsequent wars on terror in Afghanistan and Iraq. Country stars, like Toby Keith, echoed in song Bush's strong prowar stance. In December 2001 a columnist for the *Weekly Standard* wrote, "The world's war on terrorism may be colloquially called 'Bush's War,' but he has an army of soldiers in the music industry strumming to make September 11 come alive for us over and over. Bush never called them up. They rose to the occasion without being asked."[16] These musician soldiers came and continued to come mainly from the ranks of country music. In "This Ain't No Rag, it's a Flag," Charlie Daniels raises the nationalist pitch to a mockery of Islamic practice: "This ain't no rag it's a flag / And we don't wear it on our heads / It's a symbol of the land where the good guys live." In "America Can Survive," Hank Williams, Jr. affims the desire for vengeance, singing "A tooth for a tooth and an eye for an eye / That's an old slogan we're gonna' revive / Because America can survive." Comedian/country singer Ray Stevens sings in "Osama–Yo' Mama," "And I can just hear Dubyah sayin', / 'You in a heap 'o trouble boy / And I don't think you will enjoy / Our game of search and destroy / We got your terror right here, and we gon' run it up yo' rear.' " Echoing the threat of forcible sodomy as the nation's preferred method of payback, Toby Keith, in "Courtesy of the Red, White and Blue (Angry American)" sings "You'll be sorry that you messed with the US of A / 'Cause we'll put a boot in your ass / It's the American way."

According to a *Washington Times* article, Toby Keith's album "Unleashed," which included "Courtesy of the Red, White and Blue," became a favorite of President Bush in 2002.[17] Furthermore, at rallies on various U.S. military bases, country music was the theme music. At these rallies, top country music stars like Keith,

Mark Wills, and Darryl Worley were invited to open for Bush. In March 2003, at a rally held at MacDill Air Force Base in Florida, Bush thanked Keith and Worley for "coming and providing [their] talents today in support of—support of our efforts to make the world a more peaceful place."[18]

Clear Channel, Cumulus, and the Dixie Chicks

Although not as widely known as Disney, Time Warner, or News Corp, Clear Channel is one of the United States's top ten media conglomerates, with $8.4 billion in revenue. Clear Channel, with its home office in San Antonio, Texas, owns 1,239 radio stations, while its next closest competitor, Cumulus, owns 260.[19] On the company web site Clear Channel states that they can reach more than 100 million U.S. radio listeners each week. Clear Channel also promotes events, like concerts. In 2003, the company produced over 6,000 U.S. concerts and generated about 50 percent of the concert ticket revenue in the United States. Many of the concerts were produced in the 120 live entertainment venues that Clear Channel owns or operates exclusively. In addition, the company owns 155,000 advertising displays (billboards), which reach more than 50 percent of the adult U.S. population. Clear Channel also owns or operates 40 U.S. television stations. The company continues to grow internationally as well.[20]

In the buildup to the war with Iraq, Clear Channel was accused of banning songs and destroying CDs of the country group Dixie Chicks, after the lead singer for the group, Natalie Maines, said at a London concert that they were ashamed that President Bush was from Texas, the trio's home state. As one of the lone country music voices questioning the need for war in Iraq, the Dixie Chicks faced boycotts, threats of harm to themselves and their families, and strong criticism from country music fans, country music DJs, and fellow country artists. Contrary to accusations, Clear Channel management has stated that they did not ban Dixie Chicks songs or destroy their CDs. Clear Channel has issued statements claiming that they leave programming decisions to local program directors. According to John Hogan, CEO of Clear Channel Radio, program directors "do what they think is right for their own listeners."[21] The banning of Dixie Chicks songs and the much-publicized CD-crushing events that resulted from Maines's remarks at the London concert were not organized by Clear Channel, but by a competing media company, Cumulus. Cumulus banned Dixie Chicks songs on all of their 42 country stations. Also in a show of media power, Cumulus sent a memo to Sony Music Group, who owns the Dixie Chicks recording contract, asking for a public apology from Maines before Cumulus would lift the ban.[22]

While Clear Channel did not ban the Dixie Chicks as a mandate from upper management as did Cumulus, Clear Channel stations throughout the nation organized boycotts and prowar rallies. DJs and program directors at many country stations, including those owned by Clear Channel, did refuse to play Dixie Chicks songs because of the large numbers of listeners who called requesting that the group's music not be played. One Dallas program director expressed skepticism about these callers and e-mailers, however. "Are they really our listeners," he asked. "Or are they people who don't listen to our station and are being incited by media and talk radio?"[23]

Rallies for America

At the beginning of the Iraq War, conservative radio talk show host Glenn Beck organized "Rallies for America." According to some critics Beck organized the rallies in response to antiwar comments from film and music celebrities like the Dixie Chicks. Beck's show is syndicated by Premiere Radio Network, a Clear Channel subsidiary, which also syndicates the programs of conservative hosts Dr. Laura Schlessinger and Rush Limbaugh. Beck's attendance at the rallies began in Dallas in mid-May and proceeded onto other cities like Cleveland, Atlanta, Philadelphia, and San Antonio. Eventually over 100,000 people attended his Rallies for America. Critics saw these events as "pro-war" rallies that were being promoted by Clear Channel for political gain. John Hogan, CEO of Clear Channel Radio, countered the accusations and said the events were "rallies for the troops." Hogan added that Clear Channel is "completely and totally apolitical. . . . We are in the business of attracting listeners. We're not in the business of propagating a certain political agenda. It's just bad business."[24]

However, critics drew attention to the prowar nature of the rallies and the fact that Clear Channel provided financial support for the gatherings. Most of the rallies were organized and paid for, in part, by local Clear Channel stations.[25] Clear Channel also paid for advertising and the hire of musicians.[26] At the rally in Charleston, South Carolina, all six Clear Channel stations in the listening area promoted the event and most of the stations were in attendance. A web site for the Charleston event reads: "Thank you to all the Clear Channel Charleston listeners who came out to support our troops!"[27] At the San Antonio rally, U.S. Rep. Sheila Jackson Lee (D-Houston), who opposed military action in Iraq, was booed as she began her speech. Later, the representative and her party were led from the rally under protective police guard.[28] Beck ended the series of eight rallies that he lead with a large event in Huntington, West Virginia, which included appearances by members of Jessica Lynch's family. Also in attendance were country singers Darren Norwood, Tracy Byrd, and Lee Greenwood. Byrd's set included Merle Haggard's "Fightin' Side of Me." Lee Greenwood ended the rally with his performance of "God Bless the U.S.A." In a *New York Times* editorial, Clear Channel and Beck defended the "Rallies for America," arguing that the rallies were pro-troops and were grass-roots efforts organized by communities. However, a Clear Channel executive also said that Beck "encouraged listeners to call their stations to promote events to acknowledge US forces overseas and support their families at home."[29] For many, this begs the question: Which comes first, grassroots effort or listener encouragement?

"A lot of country music fans love Sean"

Like Glenn Beck, conservative talk show host Sean Hannity took issue with the Dixie Chicks and urged his listeners to avoid the group. Hannity faulted the Chicks for disrespecting President Bush in a time of war. He found their remark insulting and said he would not choose to listen to Dixie Chicks music, opting instead for other female country singers, such as Sarah Evans and Martina McBride. Hannity is known as the cohost of *Hannity & Colmes* on the Fox News Channel and as host of the nationally syndicated radio program *The Sean Hannity Show*, which is carried on nearly 400 ABC Radio Network stations, which reach over 10 million listeners from his home station WABC in New York. In addition to authoring the 2003 book *Let Freedom Ring*, he is also author of *Deliver Us from*

Evil: Defeating Terrorism, Despotism, and Liberalism. In 2003 Hannity received the Marconi Award for Network/Syndicated Personality of the Year. And in 2004 he was named National Talk Host of the Year at the annual Radio & Records Talk Radio Seminar. Hannity often reminds his audiences that he is a fan of country music. He said in a July 2004 airing of his radio show that if he came back in a second life he would like to be a country singer. In an interview with country singer Charlie Daniels, Hannity said that he's drawn to country music because of the values of faith, family, and country that he finds in it, values that he claimed were missing in other types of music like "rap music and some of the garbage that's out there."[30] Until just recently the theme song for Hannity's syndicated radio show was "Independence Day" by country artist Martina McBride.[31] The chorus of the song is: "Let freedom ring, let the white dove sing / let the whole world know that today / is a day of reckoning. / Let the weak be strong, let the right be wrong / roll the stone away, let the guilty pay / it's Independence Day." In a bizarre move that resembles the television industry's "repurposing" strategies after 9/11 (as Lynn Spigel in this volume describes), Hannity used this 1993 song about spousal abuse as a post-9/11 prowar anthem.

Country musicians were common guests on Fox News programs post 9/11. Hannity's colleague on Fox News, Bill O'Reilly, had several country artists appear. In 2003 Clint Black, Lee Greenwood, Merle Haggard, Dolly Parton, and Travis Tritt all appeared once. Charlie Daniels appeared on the *O'Reilly Factor* in June 2002 and September 2003. Between 9/11 and the end of 2003, *Hannity & Colmes*'s country star guest list included Charlie Daniels, Sarah Evans, Lee Greenwood, the Oakridge Boys, Randy Travis, Phil Vassar, Mark Wills, and Darryl Worley. Some of the stars performed on the program, an unusual occurrence on this type of talk show. Equally unusual is the frequency of appearances: Evans, Greenwood, and Worley appeared twice each on the program and Charlie Daniels appeared five times. On July 5, 2004, Greenwood appeared on *Hannity and Colmes* to promote a new CD called *Patriotic Country*, which includes Greenwood's "God Bless the U.S.A," Toby Keith's "Courtesy of the Red, White and Blue," Darryl Worley's "Have You Forgotten?" and Martina McBride's version of "God Bless America."

In addition to the many appearances by country stars on his radio and television programs, Hannity's 2003 and 2004 "Stadium of Fire" concert events prominently featured country artists. In 2003 Hannity headlined the patriotic event with country star Martina McBride and in 2004 he headlined with country star Reba McEntire. The Stadium of Fire event is part of the annual American's Freedom Festival in Provo, Utah, an Independence Day celebration, which draws hundreds of thousands of spectators annually. The organizers of the festival promote it as nonpolitical, however, the 2004 Stadium of Fire event was criticized for turning into a Republican convention, with Hannity promoting conservative views. Some took offense at the tribute to the late Ronald Reagan and to the appearance of Oliver North, a conservative radio personality who had a key role in the 1987 Iran-Contra scandal.

On July 8, 2004, Hannity also sponsored and hosted an event called the "2nd Annual 770 WABC AM Hannity Freedom Concert" at the Six Flags amusement park in New Jersey. The concert featured performances by McBride, Worley, Evans, Daniels, and lone rocker, Ted Nuggent. Hannity even sang part of "The Devil Went Down to Georgia" with Daniels. Oliver North and conservative columnist and author Ann Coulter were also in attendance. Hannity broadcasted his radio and TV show from the concert at Six Flags. During his afternoon radio program from Six Flags, Hannity received a fax from George W. Bush, which North read to the audience. Bush sent greetings to all those gathered for the Freedom Concert and expressed his gratitude to the troops abroad.

"What is the Pentagon Doing in the Music Biz?"

Along with Toby Keith and Darryl Worley, a little-known musician from Minneapolis, Dean Justin, added his song "Carry the Flag" to the collection of post-9/11 patriotic country music. "We won't give in to terror, we won't give in to fear / 'Cuz I like grandma's apple pie and my mama's smile." While the song did not reach Billboard's top singles charts, it did make Billboard's Top 10 singles sales charts for 11 consecutive weeks from July 2003 to September 2003, indicating that while the song did not get much airplay, it sold well. The alleged origins of the song may be equally telling. According to an article in Minneapolis's *Star Tribune*, the Pentagon in September 2002 "solicited" an owner of a small Minneapolis production studio to "deliver a new song to help boost troops' morale." Justin was asked to record a pop/R&B version and a country version of "Carry the Flag" that was sent to military outposts. Radio personality Rick Dees first played the song on his station, KISS-FM, in October 2002, which led to the song's airing on hundreds of other stations. (Dees's famous program the "Weekly Top 40" is syndicated by the Premiere Radio Network, a subsidiary of Clear Channel. KISS-FM in Los Angeles is a Clear Channel station.) Eventually Justin made the Billboard charts and received thank you letters from two generals and an admiral for his song. The question that arises from this interesting partnership of the U.S. military and music industries was voiced by the author of the *Star Tribune* article, who asked, "what is the Pentagon doing in the music biz?"[32]

The question overlooks the fact that this is not the first instance of the state's involvement in music promotion. The Pentagon also played an important role in the release of Toby Keith's song "Courtesy." Keith originally wrote his song shortly after 9/11 to play for people in the military during United Service Organizations (USO) tours. According to a *60 Minutes* interview, Keith never intended to release the song on a CD. However, after Keith played his song for Pentagon leaders in Washington, the Commandant of the Marine Corp, Gen. James L. Jones, persuaded Keith to release the song. In the *60 Minutes* interview Keith said that the commandant told him "you have to release it. You can serve your country in other ways besides suiting up in combat. We will go kick their butts, but we survive on morale. . . . I highly recommend that you put that song out."[33] Keith followed the general's recommendation and released the song, later recording a live version for military personal at the Pentagon. The single was released late May 2002. A live version provides the soundtrack for the video, which hit the Billboard video charts in early July 2002.

The U.S. military is also tied to a relatively new country artist, Darryl Worley, and his 9/11 song "Have You Forgotten?" in a variety of ways. First, Worley was inspired to write the song after returning from a USO tour in Afghanistan in December 2002. By March 2003 the song was on the Billboard charts. At the end of March Worley was invited, along with Toby Keith, to perform at a rally with President Bush at MacDill Air Force Base. At the rally General Michael DeLong told the audience, "If Darryl Worley, Toby Keith and the Star-Spangled Banner can't get your blood boiling, you're at the wrong place."[34] Early in April 2002, at a concert in Alabama, Army Lieutenant General Richard Cody awarded Worley an

American flag that had flown at the Pentagon during the first 9/11 anniversary. And on April 11, 2003, at a ceremony in Washington, D.C., Worley received the USO Merit Award, past winners of which include Elizabeth Taylor, Bob Hope, and Steven Spielberg, artists with much longer and more illustrious careers than Worley's. As the single reached No. 1 on the country charts, Defense Secretary Donald Rumsfeld hosted Worley at the Pentagon for a concert that was broadcast worldwide on American Forces Radio and Television (see figure 7.1).

According to a Marine press release, the song brought tears to Rumsfeld's eyes. And as Worley sang "Hear people say, we don't need this war, / but I say there's some things worth fighting for. / What about our freedom, this piece of ground? / We didn't get to keep 'em, by backing down," Rumsfeld shook his fist in the air. Worley told the audience, "Now, it's been called a pro-war song. If that means that I support my president and the conflict that we just took care of over there, then I guess that's what it is if that's what it has to be. But it's a whole lot more to me. It's a pro-America song. It's a pro-military song."[35]

Some post-9/11 country music videos have been set on military bases with off-duty troops playing performing roles in the videos. The video for Gary Allan's song "Tough Little Boys" was shot on an Army and Air National Guard base in Tennessee. The video shows actual soldiers holding pictures of their daughters and ends with the daughters and soldiers running toward and embracing each other on the base. In a CMT interview Allan said he enjoyed doing the video since the crew "got to tell them where to fly the helicopters and put them in shots . . . it was a lot of fun. It was like getting to play with a whole lot of toys."[36] John Michael Montgomery's "Letters from Home" video was also shot on a Nashville-area National Guard base and featured mostly reservists who had recently returned from Iraq. The video for Toby Keith's "Courtesy" is a collage of live concerts in front of troops. Some scenes in the video for Keith's 2004 song "American Soldier" were shot at California's Edwards Air Force Base. The video includes scenes of Keith singing among fighter jets and some off-duty soldiers and their families. In a reciprocal exchange, Keith got to use the base for his video, and the military used "American Soldier" as the soundtrack for two National Guard promotional videos.

The preference the U.S. military has for country music starts at the top. Recently Commander of U.S. Armed Forces in Iraq,

Figure 7.1. Secretary of Defense Donald H. Rumsfeld and country singer Daryl Worley at Worley's April 2003 concert at the U.S. Pentagon. DoD photo by Helene C. Stikkel.

Source: www.dod.mil/photos/Apr2003/030416-D-2987S-098.html.

Gen. Tommy Franks "has been inviting his country music pals to CentCom to help boost morale."[37] The list of recent performers includes Phil Vassar, Jo Dee Messina, Randy Travis, Charlie Daniels, Ricky Skaggs, and Neal McCoy. According to one newspaper article, CentCom staff joke that the base is becoming "ol' Nashville." During a March 2003 concert Franks got on stage and sang country favorites "Convoy" and "Is Anybody Going to San Antone." In June 2003 Franks appeared on stage again at the CentCom "Freedom Concert" with Florida Governor Jeb Bush and country artists Charlie Daniels, Kenny Rogers, Darryl Worley, and Chris Cagle. The concert was carried live on country music stations across the nation and on Armed Forces Radio worldwide.

Franks's preference for country music is rooted in his childhood growing up in Midland, Texas. Franks is a long-time fan of country. Musically, he draws the line at rap, a judgment his wife Cathy explains as follows, "Let's just say that's not his generation."[38] Franks's personal preferences in music may explain why a disproportionate number of USO musical performers are from the country music industry. According to a *Billboard* article, Franks personally requested the 2003 tour lineup of performers. Consequently, in the USO, hip-hop and rap performers have been "noticeably under-represented, even though about 27% of the troops are African-American and hip-hop has a big following among white fans."[39] There is a long history of political influence behind the choice of USO entertainers. The Nixon administration avoided rock acts during the Vietnam War, whereas during the Clinton administration more rock acts went on USO tours. According to a veteran USO source, if more country music acts are appearing in USO tours it may be because the "country music community is traditionally patriotic, with deep ties to the military. . . . It's that 'good old boy' thing. And many musicians in the urban black community have long been distrustful of the military."[40]

The USO's preference for country is also reflected in the fact that it is actively promoting the "Patriotic Country" CD mentioned earlier, which includes Greenwood's "God Bless the U.S.A," Keith's "Courtesy of the Red, White and Blue," and Worley's "Have You Forgotten?" The CD will be used to raise funds for the USO and visitors to the web site sendacdtoasoldier.com can send copies of the CD, with a choice of messages including "Good luck. Come Home Safely!" to U.S. soldiers as part of a USO care package. According to the site, "Thoughtful gifts, reminders of home, and inspirational patriotic music are sure to lift the spirits of active-duty troops." Indeed, lifting the spirits of troops has been the main function of the USO since its inception during World War II when General Eisenhower announced that he was facing a problem with troop morale. As a result the USO was founded in 1941 by a Hollywood talent agent and by Prescott Bush, George W. Bush's grandfather.

Country Coda

Country radio reaches more adults than any other format. Each week nearly 42 million adults tune to country radio in the U.S.[41] Country music is also the most popular format for radio stations. There are 2,318 country music stations, followed by 1,863 adult contemporary, 1,208 oldies, and 1,199 news/talk stations.[42] And the trend is growing: over the past three years Country Music Television (CMT) has nearly doubled their household penetration (from 39 million to 75 million).[43] In a 2002 country music poll 65 percent of those polled indicated that they liked country music.[44] Recognizing the widespread popularity of country artists, many companies have used country stars to promote a growing list of consumer goods and products including Bud Light, Dr. Pepper, Ford trucks, and Mr. Coffee.

Country artists are well aware of the increasing popularity and power of country music to mobilize social identities, consumer practices, and political commitments. In his 1989 hit "What This World Needs Is A Few More Rednecks," Charlie Daniels observes: "Now you intellectuals may not like it / But there ain't nothin' that you can do / Cause there's a whole lot more of us common-folks / Than there ever will be of you." A sense of pride is taken in the "redneck" social identity label. Country music has a long history of using the label in popular songs like "Rednecks, White Socks, and Blue Ribbon Beer" and "High-Tech Redneck." More recently, in "Redneck Woman," Gretchen Wilson sings "Victoria's Secret, well, their stuff's real nice. / Oh, but I can buy the same damn thing, on a Wal-Mart shelf, half price." Wilson brings us back full force to the clustering of consumer products, the consolidation of social identities, and disagreements over the soul of America—a sense of national division effected through pronouncements of consumer allegiance. Another recent country song and music video makes this division explicitly clear, in the manner of an agreement to disagree, which is where this discussion ends. Montgomery Gentry's video for "You Do Your Thing" from late summer 2004 contains a segment in which protestors at peace rallies carry "Wage Peace" placards while the country artist sings, "I'll pray to God any place, any time / And you can bet I'll pick up the phone if Uncle Sam calls me up / You do your thing, I'll do mine."

Notes

1. Jean Baudrillard, *For a Critique of the Political Economy of the Sign*, trans. Charles Levin (St. Louis, Mo.: Telos Press, 1981).
2. The lyrics further link the automobile with American military determination: "I drive my Mini Cooper/And I'm feeling super-dooper/Yo they tell me I'm a trooper/And you know I'm satisfied." Madonna and Mirwais Ahmadzai, "American Life," Warner Brothers Records Inc., 2003.
3. The phrase two Americas was coined by vice-presidential hopeful John Edwards, in a stump speech delivered in Des Moines, Iowa, on December 29, 2003, in

criticizing Bush administration policies that Edwards believed had effected a division of the country into "haves" and "have nots."

4. David Aikman, *A Man of Faith: The Spiritual Journey of George W. Bush* (Nashville, Tenn.: W Pub. Group, 2004), 176–177.
5. *The O'Reilly Factor*, first broadcast November 7, 2000; transcript available from Lexis/Nexus.
6. Melton A. McLaurin, "Proud to Be an American: Patriotism in Country Music," in *America's Musical Pulse: Popular Music in Twentieth-Century Society*, ed. K. J. Bindas (Westport, Conn.: Praeger, 1992).
7. Curtis W. Ellison, *Country Music Culture: From Hard Times to Heaven* (Jackson: University Press of Mississippi, 1995).
8. Barbara Ching, *Wrong's What I Do Best: Hard Country Music and Contemporary Culture* (New York: Oxford University Press, 2001), 5.
9. George H. W. Bush, *All the Best, George Bush: My Life in Letters and Other Writings* (New York: Scribner, 1999), 326–327.
10. Joe Eszterhas, *American Rhapsody* (New York: Knopf, 2000), 296.
11. George H. W. Bush, *Remarks at the 25th Anniversary of the Country Music Awards in Nashville, Tennessee* (George Bush Presidential Library); available at bushlibrary.tamu.edu/research/papers/1991/91100308.html.
12. George H. W. Bush, "My Country & Western 'tis of Thee," *Forbes*, May 9, 1994, 153 (magazine online); available from InfoTrac.
13. Quoted in Nigel Williamson, "Land of Hope and Ol' Glory," *The Times* (London), November 8, 2002 (online newspaper); available from Lexis/Nexus.
14. Bob, Paxman, "Mr. Strait Goes to Washington" *Country Weekly*, April 13, 2004, 30.
15. Andrea Billups, Christian Toto, and Joseph Curl, "Politics Take a Back Seat to Revelry," *Washington Times*, January 21, 2001 (online newspaper); available from Questia.com.
16. Beth Henary, "And the Band Played On," 12/11/2001, *Weekly Standard*, December 11, 2001 (online magazine); available at weeklystandard.com
17. Tom Gray, "Toby Keith Delivers Drama, Favorite Songs," *Washington Times*, October 11, 2003 (online newspaper); available from Questia.com.
18. Office of the White House Press Secretary, "President Rallies Troops at MacDill Air Force Base in Tampa," MacDill Air Force Base, March 26, 2003, for immediate release at www.whitehouse.gov/news/releases/2003/03/20030326-4.html.
19. Maria Figueroa, Damone Richardson, and Pam Whitefield, *The Clear Picture on Clear Channel Communications, Inc.* (Ithaca, NY: Labor and Industry Research, Cornell University, 2004) (online report); available at www.dpeaflcio.org/pdf/Clear%20Channel%20_Final%20Report%201-28-04.pdf.
20. Clear Channel, "Press Room," available at www.clearchannel.com.
21. Clear Channel, "Know the Facts," available at www.clearchanel.com.
22. Bill Friskics-Warren, "There's Your Trouble," *Country Music*, July 2003.
23. Chris Neal and Bob Paxman, "Tarred and Feathered," *Country Weekly*, April 29, 2003, 35.
24. Eric Boehlert and John Hogan, interview by Terry Gross, *Fresh Air*, July 23, 2003; transcript available on Factiva(quoted in Boehlert,19xx).
25. Tara Godvin, "Thousands Gather in W.Va. for Final Stop of Rally for America," *Associated Press*, May 24, 2003 (online); available at Factiva.com.

26. Oliver Burkeman, "Bush Backer Sponsoring Pro-War Rallies," *The Guardian*, March 26, 2003 (online newspaper); available at www.guardian.co.uk.
27. Newsradio 730 WSC, "Let Freedom Ring Rally for America," available at www.730wsc.com/rallyrecap.html.
28. Lisa Sandberg, "Showing Their Colors," MySA.com, March 2, 2003 (online newspaper); available at www.mysanantonio.com.
29. Clear Channel, "Know the Facts," available at www.clearchanel.com.
30. *Hannity & Colmes*, first broadcast April 2, 2002; transcript available from Lexis/Nexus.
31. *Hannity & Colmes*, first broadcast July 5, 2004; transcript available from Lexis/Nexus.
32. Chris Riemenschneider, "Troops Carry Justin to Charts," *Star Tribune*, September 12, 2003 (online newspaper); available at www. startribune.com.
33. *Toby Keith Uncut: 60 Minutes II Special*, broadcasted on CMT, February 1, 2004.
34. William MacDougall, "The Song Remains the Same: Georgie on My Mind," CounterPunch, April 5, 2003 (online magazine); available at www. counterpunch.org.
35. Linda D. Kozaryn, "A Singer, A Song and America's Armed Forces," American Forces Press Service, April 16, 2003 (online); available at www.defenselink.mil/news/Apr2003/n04162003_2003041610.html.
36. CMT.com, "Gary Allan enlists soldiers for 'Tough Little Boys,'" October 9, 2003 (video online); available at CMT.com.
37. Paul de La Garza, "A Command of Country Music," *St. Petersburg Times*, March 15, 2003 (online newspaper); available from Factiva.com.
38. Ibid.
39. Bill Holland, "Rap, Hip-Hop AWOL in Iraq," *Billboard*, May 24, 2003 (online magazine); available from Factiva.com.
40. Ibid.
41. *MRI Country Listener Analysis: 2002 Analysis Highlights* (Country Music Association, 2002) (report online); available at www.countrymusic.org/marketing/industry_statistics_listener_analysis2000.asp.
42. "U.S. Radio Formats by State and Possession," in *Broadcasting & Cable Yearbook 2002–2003* (Broadcasting & Cable, 2002), D–644.
43. Phyllis Stark, "We Need Diversity in the Music and Styles That Are Accepted," *Billboard*, July 10, 2004 (magazine online); available from Lexis/Nexus.
44. Angela King, Sean Ross and Phyllis Stark, "Clear Channel's Influence Raises CRS Attendees' Concerns," *Billboard*, March 16, 2002 (magazine online); available from InfoTrac.

Discography

The Charlie Daniels Band. "In America," *A Decade of Hits*, © 1983 Sony Music Entertainment.
The Charlie Daniels Band. "This Ain't No Rag, It's a Flag," *Freedom and Justice For All*, © 2003 Audium Entertainment.
Greenwood, Lee. "God Bless the U.S.A." *Greatest Hits, Vol. 2*, © 1988 MCA.

Keith, Toby. "Courtesy of the Red, White and Blue (Angry American)," *Unleashed*, © 2002 SKG Music Nashville.

Stevens, Ray. "Osama–Yo' Mama," *Osama–Yo' Mama*, © 2002 Curb Records.

Williams Jr., Hank. "America Will Survive," *Almeria Club Recordings*, © 2002 Curb Records.

Worley, Darryl. "Have You Forgotten?" *Have You Forgotten*? © 2003 SKG Music Nashville.

Chapter 8

"Your Flag Decal Won't Get You Into Heaven Anymore": U.S. Consumers, Wal-Mart, and the Commodification of Patriotism

Jennifer Scanlon

In the immediate post-9/11 world, it appeared that the retail sector might rank second to the airline industry on the list of economic casualties. Pollsters depicted the post-9/11 American as a survivalist, sealed hermetically or at least with duct tape in a home loaded down with canned goods, connected to the world primarily through the television cable. Locked into news channels, their remotes seemingly incapable of processing connections to the shopping network, television viewers appeared unable to respond positively to the invitations of advertisers on any channel. "There are very few events that can actually scare some consumers from spending, [but] the events of [September 11] fall into that category," stated Diane Swonk, chief economist at Bank One in Chicago.[1] The attacks on the World Trade Center and Pentagon threatened to undermine not only the nation's infrastructure and reputation but also its equation of spending with citizenship. "There is a risk of a sudden attack of prudence," noted David Wyss of Standard and Poor's, in a particularly apt turn of phrase. "If people stop living beyond their means, this could turn into a recession."[2] Fortunately for the economy, however, and in keeping with a historical tradition of spending, the dual afflictions of "affluenza" and "mall-aria" came out of remission, patriotism was recast as consumerism, and people quickly resumed their customary practices.[3] This article explores the performance of patriotism through consumerism on the part of both the American public and its largest supplier of retail goods and corporately generated American identity, Wal-Mart. Arguably, Wal-Mart and the American public bond in a way that ensures that contemporary patriotism is marked and measured by little more than consumer performance, and that contemporary globalization, in many of its forms, is developed and brought to us by Wal-Mart.[4]

Fostering Consumerism in the Post-9/11 United States

Encouraging consumerism, which is vital to the nation's economy, while simultaneously respecting people's shock and grief in the aftermath of the terrorist attacks, provided retailers with a number of dilemmas. The vital signs did not look promising. Mall traffic fell 6.8 percent in September and October of 2001, and a further downward spiral seemed likely.[5] Retailers needed a strong argument, a plea to those who clung too tightly to their consumer dollars. The dilemma retailers faced was the risk of appearing crass and opportunistic, anti-American rather than patriotic, in linking the future of the nation to consumer spending. Fortunately for retailers, they didn't have to wait long for an eager, outside spokesperson to emerge and speak on their behalf, in this case straight from the Oval Office. President George W. Bush cheered consumers on in the tragedy's aftermath: "We cannot let the terrorists achieve the objective of frightening our nation to the point where we don't—where we don't conduct business, where people don't shop," he implored.[6] Stingy consumers surrendered to the enemy; real Americans sacrificed, paradoxically, by shopping. "I was struck by this," the president told the nation, "that in many cities, when Christian and Jewish women learned that Muslim women—women of cover—were afraid of going out of their homes alone, that they went shopping with them, that they showed true friendship and support—an act that shows the world the true nature of America."[7] With this tribute to "white" American women's benevolence, and this bizarre appellation, "women of cover," the president simultaneously veiled all Muslim women, relegated them to a place both within and outside the mainstream of American culture, and made shopping an act of significant political and cultural solidarity.[8]

Some consumers were more than happy to take the president's words as direct orders from the Commander in Chief. A condominium manager in St. Petersburg, Florida, spent $7,000 on new furniture in October 2001, then ordered a new roof; her husband began looking for a new car. "We were saving to do it next year," she stated, "but we bought now because we don't want the terrorists to think they won."[9] In a query that, like many others, turned the events of September 11 into a proper noun, a California television station asked its viewers, "Are you reluctant to spend money after the Attack On America?" The vast majority of respondents indicated they had no intention of cutting down on spending. "Let's not give in to the terrorists at all," wrote one viewer. "Shop till you drop. We in America are free, we don't want to end up like Afghanistan . . . what a screwed up country that is." Another made clear that spending money was a next step in the response to terrorism: "We've grieved, prayed, memorialized and now are retaliating. We can all do our part by spending money as usual for the common everyday things." One of the few voices to disagree put little stock in the president's message: "My gosh have you heard and seen all the layoffs since. I understand why the President wants us to spend, but I depend on my income to survive. If I was to get laid off where would I be—homeless and President Bush will not help keep the roof over my head if that happens."[10]

Wal-Mart At the Ready on September 11

Wal-Mart, the nation's largest retailer and now, not incidentally, also the world's largest company, had long promoted itself as small-town America writ large, and as a potent symbol of getting and spending. As a result, the big-box retailer was well poised to sell consumer spending as civic duty, shopping as patriotism, on and after September 11. One of Wal-Mart's many mottos, "Our Pledge . . . To Save You More," as well as its red-white-and-blue displays and frequent use of the terms "America" and "American," linked the store to the American flag and purchasing to patriotism well before the events of September 11. Wal-Mart's other slogans have included "Buy American," "Bring It Home to the USA," "Bring It Back to the USA," "We Buy American Whenever We Can. So You Can Too. Together We Can Do It," "Support American Made," and "Made Right Here."[11] The store's frequent use of "we" in its advertising is purportedly inclusive: the corporation and the consuming public are a team. There's no "us" and "them" in Wal-Mart; we're all family, American-style. Wal-Mart anthropomorphizes the corporation by linking the company, its founder, Sam Walton, and the venerable Uncle Sam of patriotic lore through products like Sam Walton's "Sam's Choice" brand of soft drinks.

Americans may have secured themselves indoors after September 11, but not before they ran to Wal-Mart for the two things the store offers: community and consumption. "The day of the attacks," stated a Wal-Mart store manager in Pennsylvania, "we had many people who were alone come into the store because they wanted to be around other people and have someone to talk to." Despite its bright lights, massive indoor setting, and cold white walls, Wal-Mart stood in for the town square, the neighborhood gathering place, a place for human connection on a day that shook many people to the core. The store manager finished with a statement that offers several available readings: "We want them to know that we are still here for them."[12] Wal-Mart positions itself as a support system for citizens, arguably outside of the realm of consumerism: Wal-Mart remains standing, remains open, on September 11. It simultaneously offers itself as necessary link between Americans and their need to keep consumer identity intact: even when the world is turned upside down, we can right it. The retailer sold 116,000 American flags on September 11, 2001, an increase of roughly 110,000 over the same day a year earlier. It subsequently sold out of the almost half a million flags it had in stock nationally.[13] When people thought of purchasing symbols of American identity and perseverance, they turned to Wal-Mart.

Because of its global positioning, Wal-Mart also served as a 9/11 gathering place outside of the United States. People living abroad went to Wal-Mart stores to connect with home; foreigners went to Wal-Mart to express solidarity. In this sense Wal-Mart's big box served as a visual symbol of American identity, perhaps an even more potent or compelling site than the nation's many embassies worldwide. Managers at a Wal-Mart store in Argentina invited in a priest to lead the store's workers, or "associates," in prayer, and a store in Brazil invited people in to sing for peace. Consumers responded to the invitations. "Although Brazil is so distant," one participant in the sing-along stated, in what sounds like a rousing endorsement of contemporary globalization, "Wal-Mart just makes us feel as one global family that does come together in times like this."[14]

Post-9/11 Purchasing as Active Patriotism

The media picked up on, repeated, and celebrated Wal-Mart's impressive flag sales statistics, thereby furthering the link between patriotism and purchasing and keeping consumer participation in the minds of the citizenry. In the weeks that followed September 11, the public's determination to fly the stars and stripes in the face of terrorism was offered as perhaps the strongest symbol of our collective identity and determination to fight the ubiquitous yet elusive enemy. The accompanying notion of patriotic purchasing emerged quickly and with full force, in the voices of media, advertisers, politicians, and of course, consumers. This national initiative, patriotic purchasing, included the generalized spending to show loyalty to the nation and its economy as well as the particular consumption of patriotic symbols such as flags, banners, and bumper stickers. Advertisements for red-white-and-blue paraphernalia in the newspapers, on television, on radio, and perhaps most insistently, on the Internet, lured customers in. "Do you love the United States of America?" the USA Patriotism web site asked. "Is it a fervent love? Do you have allegiance to its government and institutions regardless of your political beliefs? Are you angry/upset about what happened on September 11, 2001? If you said yes, then you can proudly state that you are patriotic!" Patriots, by definition, adorned themselves in symbols. "So welcome fellow patriot to USA Patriotism! Where it is all about being patriotic and showing it!" Eager to include potential global customers as well, the site welcomed people not only of all political stripes but of all nationalities: ". . . And that includes friends and supporters of the USA, who are patriots of their countries."[15] Another site encouraged consumer participation with these words: "There's more than one way to show your patriotism. You can display it on your heart or you can display it in your home."[16] Feeling it in the heart but stopping short of displaying it sartorially or domestically proved woefully inadequate in the patriotic marketplace.

In what could be called, in the post-9/11 penchant for mercenary metaphors, a bloodless coup, advertisers and merchandisers won the battle against a sluggish spending trend by linking patriotism, American prosperity, and consumerism. The best deal available to Americans was that they could fight the evil forces from outside by even more fully embracing the existing "American way of life." Unlike the days and wars of old, when people sacrificed by having less, by stretching the dollar, contemporary Americans could sacrifice by filling the stores, increasing credit card debt, and displaying material goods as symbols of morality and civic duty. Patriotism became most clearly manifest in purchasing, in shopping the country back to its rightful place in the world order. It was a newly cast yet familiar, comforting performance.

Performing Patriotism: The Flag as Prop

In and outside of Wal-Mart, flag-inspired clothing, decorative goods, and collectibles served as props for the performance of patriotism. From the typical T-shirts, ties, and paperweights to the more creative suspenders, golf balls, Frisbees, hair scrunchies, jewelry, teddy bears, and playing cards, the flag was ubiquitous. T-shirt designs ranged from small American flags embroidered on the pocket and slogans like "Never Forget September 11" to more militant flag-accompanied statements, including "Been Loadin' for Bin Laden," and "It's Personal Now."[17] Celebrities quickly joined in; even Madonna donned a flag-patterned kilt onstage at a Los Angeles performance.[18] The public responded with particular enthusiasm to the invitation to adorn their vehicles with symbols of patriotism. Flag-related automotive items included window banners and flags, air fresheners, antenna balls, vinyl decals, license plates, bumper stickers, seat covers, and key chains (see figure 8.1). "People who ordinarily couldn't tell Flag Day from flag football suddenly felt compelled to display the stars and stripes," wrote Dr. America, aka Jim Farrell.[19] Some flag vendors envisioned and capitalized on quick returns on their advertising investments; others launched new businesses or conducted significant 9/11-related "charity work" by giving away free flags. Americas & Americas designed a World Trade Center flag, in which the World Trade Center serves as a backdrop for the stars, and won the 2002 Outstanding Business Award for the State of Florida. The company's charity-related flag enterprise, Flags on Cars, came into being post 9/11 and subsequently gave away thousands of free flags in anticipation of the war in Iraq.[20]

In addition to cars, people decorated their homes with flags. Newspapers included paper flag inserts that could be hung in windows. Many people displayed one or more flags in or outside their homes. "Most houses already have a flagpole," argued one observer in an interesting if unintentional commentary on the depth of many people's patriotism: "One week it might display a frog or 'Happy Halloween,' but it makes it easy to wave an American flag as well."[21] A couple in Erie, Michigan, turned their house into a flag: "We went outside the day after the attacks because we decided to hang the flag up. But it looked so small. It didn't seem enough. So we said, 'Let's just paint the house like the flag.' "[22]

Although many of the flag-related items seem fairly kitsch, in keeping with what one might expect to encounter on the racks of, say, Wal-Mart, the link between consumer spending and patriotic sentiment was not restricted to the working or middle classes.

Figure 8.1. After 9/11 automobiles became the most visible sign of Americans' performance of patriotism. Photograph by Jennifer Scanlon.

People of all classes embraced the visual in their displays of patriotism. Sales of upscale flag items increased tremendously. Art and antique consultant Susan Kleckner assessed the high-end market: "Anything that has a flag, an eagle or red, white and blue is selling. This has been a kick upward for American folk art."[23] A hand-sewn American Grand Union or Continental flag sold at auction for $163,500, breaking previous records for any flag sale. American furniture and folk art that had remained unsold at Christie's sold at unexpectedly high prices on October 12, the company's first sale date after the attacks.

Not everyone embraced the flurry of flags. Some, of course, called for a concurrent reexamination of the place of the United States in the world and recognition that flag-waving had limited long-term value. Cultural critic Tom Farrell put it succinctly: ". . . if the flags of our current grief and solidarity aren't matched by our continuing, active citizenship, they'll just be a colorful betrayal of what the flag itself really stands for."[24] As the flag became ever more present, however, it framed a discourse of patriotism in which solidarity demanded conformity of values rather than vigorous discussion of issues. Media conformity as well as consumer commitment to defining patriotism through goods rather than actions ensured that decorative statements effectively replaced community debate. As James Howard Kunstler argued, the ensuing insularity "put the kibosh on any criticism of the 'American way of life.' "[25] It subsequently mandated the equation between patriotism and war. Patriots, who flew flags, also supported "our troops"; those opposed to the war, according to this definition, did not support the troops and simply were not patriots.[26]

In previous times of national crisis, people could feel a part of things by actively doing something to participate in the war effort. During the Second World War, for example, people understood their own personal sacrifices as tied to a larger effort. In the post-9/11 setting, Robert Thompson argues, people have felt helpless and engage in spending because it provides something concrete to do.[27] Arguably, however, the link to spending was more than an anxiety reliever; it was simultaneously understood as a concrete way to act out national solidarity. Consumers, who wouldn't tolerate being taxed $1 a gallon on gasoline to pay for the war, ironically displayed their patriotism by marking as patriotic the possession that many argue most closely ties us to war in the Middle East: the automobile (see figure 8.2). Interestingly, the automobile industry led the way in the post-9/11 television world with commercials that directly made

Figure 8.2. This spare tire cover remains popular and demonstrates the ways in which messages of patriotism can also demand specific forms of unity. Photograph by Abigail Daley, reprinted with permission.

the connection between purchasing and patriotism. Before the end of September 2001, General Motors had launched "Keep America Rolling," while Ford introduced "Ford Drives America." In both cases, 0 percent financing was equated with getting the country back on its feet more than with giving consumers a break.[28]

Wal-Mart, too, had a lot to gain by keeping the flag and other symbols of American identity front and center. In an ingenious post-9/11 service effort that marked the company again as truly, deeply American, Wal-Mart invited citizens-consumers to the store to dispose of their worn American flags, arguing that the company's centrality in communities made it a convenient place for people to part with worn flags in appropriate, respectful ways (see figure 8.3).[29] Perhaps flag disposers also proved themselves good customers of new flags and other consumer goods. Lest we find this behavior un-American, however, the words of a reporter for the *St. Louis Post-Dispatch* remind us of the quintessentially American nature of the flag-as-performance process: "The explanation is as American as apple pie," he wrote. "Ms. Fei's factory sells flags to wholesalers for about $1 each. They retail for around $25."[30]

Figure 8.3. Wal-Mart continues to promote its own patriotism and respect for the flag through its flag retirement program. Photograph by Abigail Daley, reprinted with permission.

Wal-Mart's Place in American Retailing

Founded over 40 years ago in rural Arkansas by Sam Walton, Wal-Mart now brings in annual revenues of $250 billion and hosts a computer network that reportedly holds three times the data of the Internal Revenue Service system. It is the largest retailer in Canada and Mexico and, globally, serves 100 million customers a week.[31] Wal-Mart does have the humble roots it repeatedly harkens back to: Sam Walton started out with one store in a small town, goods stacked on tables or hung on racks, three checkouts, and a staff of 25.[32] The company now spends over $400 million a year in advertising to keep that small-town image alive and well.[33] This investment has paid off. Wal-Mart is widely admired by the American public as well as by the corporate and finance communities: *Fortune* magazine named Wal-Mart the most admired company in the United States in 2003 and 2004, up from the second spot in the rankings in 2002 and the third spot in 2001.[34] Considering its many blemishes, its well-publicized lawsuits, and other scandals, this is a significant accomplishment.

From the start Wal-Mart founder Sam Walton, frugal himself, knew that Americans respond to the bottom line and determined to offer them low prices. He did so by pursuing a unique strategy. He offered store "guests," as he called them, name-brand health and beauty products at cost. Responding to the all-time-low prices on these goods, consumers flocked to the store and stocked up as well on the many other items that resulted in enormous profit margins, many as high as 30 percent.[35] A second strategy, from the start, was to underpay employees, or associates. The wage rate at the opening store in Arkansas was $.50 to $.60 an hour, well below the federal minimum wage of $1.15 an hour.[36] Forty years later, associates remain grossly underpaid. The majority of today's associates are women, the average wage a little over $8.00 an hour, representing a pay rate that puts a family of four well below the poverty line and eligible for food stamps. Employees must pay for the major share of the cost of health insurance, which only 2 in 5 opt to do.[37]

Low wages form one component of the Wal-Mart strategy; another is the gendered targeting of employees and customers. Women form the majority of Wal-Mart employees at the associate level but few are found in management. In 1985, not one woman stood among the company's 42 top officers.[38] Currently, women make up 72 percent of the Wal-Mart workforce but only 33 percent of management.[39] The National Organization for Women (NOW) named Wal-Mart a "Merchant of Shame" in June 2002, largely because of its discriminatory policies in relation to women employees.[40] The company has faced and continues to face numerous lawsuits from women who charge gender and racial discrimination.[41] In a recent development, a federal judge, following a nine-month review of the case, approved class-action status for a suit filed against the company. Alleging that Wal-Mart pays women less than their male coworkers, and that the company overlooks women when it comes time for promotions, the suit could represent as many as 1.6 million current and former employees, making it the largest private civil rights case in United States history.[42]

No women currently serve on Wal-Mart's board of directors. Interestingly, Hillary Clinton was the first female Wal-Mart board member. At an annual meeting in 1987, Sam Walton addressed the issue of women in Wal-Mart management by drawing attention to Clinton's presence: "We haven't gotten as far as we would like . . . [but we have] a strong willed young lady on the board now who has already told the board it should do more to ensure advancement for women."[43] Clinton resigned in 1992 during her husband's presidential campaign, before she or anyone else had a significant impact on the culture of gender at Wal-Mart.[44] Nevertheless, women remain Wal-Mart's strongest customers. As retail consultant Wendy Liebmann puts it, Wal-Mart has become "the benchmark by which American women rate all shopping."[45] Women shoppers appreciate one-stop shopping and low prices and seem disinclined to view shopping as an act with political significance. In fact, four of ten American women visit Wal-Mart weekly. "Through shoppers and 'associates' alike," writes Liza Featherstone, "Wal-Mart is making billions from female poverty."[46]

Patriotism: Wal-Mart's Greatest Defense

One of the ways in which Wal-Mart has battled a reputation for discrimination and other "anti-American" activity is, again, through its performance of patriotism, its continual celebration of American identity in product displays, advertising, and related programs.

The link between patriotism and purchasing attracts customers, quells dissent, and has become part and parcel of the Wal-Mart corporate agenda. In a Securities and Exchange Commission filing in 1998, Wal-Mart identified patriotic appeals among the items that made the company so successful. "The company's competitive position within the industry is largely determined by its ability to offer value and service to its customers," the filing reads. "The company has many programs designed to meet the competitive needs of its industry. These include 'Everyday Low Price,' 'Item Merchandising,' 'Store Within a

Store,' and 'Buy America' programs."[47] The "Buy America" program provides an excellent case study of the ways in which contemporary claims of patriotism require little more than flag-waving. Wal-Mart launched its "Buy America" program in the mid-1980s. A *Washington Post* illustration of the program features Sam Walton as a bald eagle, wings spread in a gesture of protection (see figure 8.4).[48] All of the stores hung red-white-and-blue banners that read "KEEP AMERICA WORKING AND STRONG." In combination with decorated trucks and decorated stores, the real or simply implied patriotic link to store products made Wal-Mart appear American both in identity and production. U.S. consumers, who at least state that American-made means something to them, took the company at its word.[49] It did not take long for the critics of Wal-Mart to expose the giant retailer. Complaints surfaced over the years and culminated in a 1992 NBC *Dateline* expose of Wal-Mart. It was the most-watched *Dateline* program in the series' history, detailing offenses such as adorning clothing racks with "Buy America" signs when the clothing featured on the racks was produced outside the United States.[50] As *Dateline* repeatedly demonstrated, "Made in the USA" signs, patriotic labels, and misleading banners suggested that goods made in Bangladesh, Korea, and China were produced within the United States. As it turned out, a significant percentage of Wal-Mart products are produced outside the United States, contrary to the image and contrary to the publicity. What irked people most in the exposé was the juxtaposition of the image and the reality of Wal-Mart. "Most, if not all, major U.S. retailers import much of what they sell," writes Wal-Mart watchdog Bob Ortega. "They just don't wrap themselves in the flag while they're doing it."[51]

The company's response has been, by and large, to avoid the issue rather than make significant changes. Since the *Dateline* episode, Wal-Mart has faced numerous allegations of selling products produced with sweatshop and child labor and of falsely implying that products made outside the United States are U.S.-made. In one legal case, after the Federal Trade Commission charged Wal-Mart with not identifying the country of origin on Internet-advertised products, the company simply removed the products from its site.[52] In another case, after a National Labor Committee team entered a Wal-Mart store and recorded the place of production of over 100,000 items, they found that 83 percent of the goods were imported. Wal-Mart's response, that the company itself didn't know the numbers so they doubted the veracity of the National

Figure 8.4. In 1985, *The Washington Post* depicted Sam Walton as an eagle protecting the United States economy through his Buy-American campaign.

Labor Committee's calculations, appeared problematic in light of the company's impressive computer network.[53]

Globalization Means Walmartization

Wal-Mart's strategy of patriotic self-promotion, in combination with underpaying employees, initially afforded it a curious and effective niche; now, however, it serves as a menacing model for the future of the U.S. and global workforces. One longstanding element of Wal-Mart's local and global formula is a rabid anti-union stance. As Bob Ortega puts it, the company uniformly "walmartizes" its employees with a manual declaring, "There is no need for a union at Wal-Mart!"[54] Anti-union from the start, the retailer hired a professional union buster early on when union organizing efforts emerged at a store in Missouri. Although this attorney had little impact at the Missouri site, because the "agitator," Connie Kreyling, had already been fired and other employees had been sufficiently silenced, he set up a series of anti-union practices for Sam Walton. Kreyling, who successfully took her case to the National Labor Relations Board, would be one of many who took on Wal-Mart and won—won the right not to unionize but to retain her position. But Wal-Mart's union-busting approach has featured the carrot as much as the stick: its fairly successful strategy has included profit-sharing, a company cheer, employee picnics, incorporating employee suggestions into store culture, and, importantly, promoting Wal-Mart as quintessentially American in culture and practice.[55]

"At Wal-Mart we respect the individual rights of our associates and encourage them to express their ideas, comments and concerns. Because we believe in maintaining an environment of open communications, we do not believe there is a need for third-party representation," Wal-Mart explains to employees in a phrase that avoids the word "union" altogether. To supplement the written and spoken word, mandatory employee trainings and meetings include anti-union videos. In the only Wal-Mart–related union organizing success story to date, butchers in the meat department at a Wal-Mart in Jacksonville, Texas, voted to unionize. Wal-Mart's swift response included phasing out butchers and selling only prepackaged meat at that branch and at almost 200 others.[56] A 56-page managers' guide, "The Manager's Toolbox to Remaining Union Free," puts it bluntly: "It is important that you be constantly alert for efforts by a union to organize your associates."[57] In what may have a significant impact on employee organizing efforts, however, a 2003 decision by the National Labor Relations Board determined that Wal-Mart must change existing benefits information to indicate that employees who are represented by unions will remain eligible for benefits during collective bargaining efforts. The company must also post notices in every store stating that they will not discriminate against unionized workers.[58]

Wal-Mart's anti-union efforts allow it to underpay associates and reap enormous profits. According to *Forbes* magazine, five of the eleven richest Americans and twenty richest individuals globally in 2004 are members of the Walton family, reportedly worth over $20 billion each.[59] These financial successes have not trickled down to employees, and unionization may be employees' only hope.

As the company well knows, the implications of unionizing at Wal-Mart are enormous. Erik Gordon explains: "Unionizing a giant, New Economy employer like Wal-Mart would be as big of a coup as unionizing Ford was to the United Auto Workers. Failing to unionize it is frustrating to the unions and damages their assertion that they are needed by today's workers."[60] In the 1970s, according to another union executive, because of the U.A.W.'s contract with General Motors, the nation's largest employer at the time, worker standards across the United States improved overall. Wal-Mart's practices rapidly lower worker standards overall, and the union issue is the most visible manifestation of the process. As Featherstone argues, "there's substantial evidence that many of the problems suffered by Wal-Mart's female employees would be alleviated by a union."[61] According to one study, two-thirds of women in union-ized retail jobs had health insurance, while only one-third of their nonunionized counterparts had the coverage. Women workers in unions also faced smaller gender and racial wage gaps.[62] These issues cross gender lines and, increasingly, cross national lines as well. Given Wal-Mart's power and reach in the global economy, its anti-union and other related policies have enormous implications for the world workforce. One economist puts it bluntly: "I joke we're all going to be working for Wal-Mart someday."[63]

The Wal-Mart grocery business provides a good example of the "Walmartization" process at work. As of 1995, Wal-Mart sold no food; now it is the country's largest grocery retailer. Many super-market employees in the United States are unionized, so when Wal-Mart moves into a community with a Supercenter, which sells food as well as innumerable other products, employees of grocery chains have a great deal to lose. With wages of up to $25 an hour, as well as a host of benefit programs that result from union agreements, particularly with the United Food and Commercial Workers, many supermarket workers have maintained a healthy standard of living. With the advances of Wal-Mart, two things tend to happen. First, some supermarkets close, leaving employees the option of a roughly 50 percent reduction in pay if they move to Wal-Mart. Second, other supermarkets, trying to stay open and compete with Wal-Mart, cut salaries.[64] The battle is on in California, where Wal-Mart was slated to open as many as forty Supercenters in 2004. Community resis-tance stalled the process temporarily, but as the first of these opened in California, supermarket employees outside of Wal-Mart signed, for the first time and in a move heralded as the end of the livable wage for supermarket employees, a two-tiered labor contract.[65] Under this arrangement, new hires will be paid on a differential wage scale than current employees. This move, employees note, is contradictory to union principles of solidarity but necessary in the Wal-Mart world. As the *New York Times* describes the struggle, "It is, at bottom, about the ability of retail workers to earn wages that keep their families out of poverty."[66]

In one of the many ironies of the post-9/11 United States, Wal-Mart and the nation's valorization of the "working-class heroes" fails to extend to any concerted commitment to their improved or even adequately maintained standard of living. In fact, the more than $1 billion Wal-Mart has received in economic development subsidies from states, while the company netted nearly $9 billion in profits in 2003, is not just arguably linked to state tax cuts in publicly funded health insurance, child care, education, and other important programs aimed at the working class: a report by the Democratic staff of the House Education and Workforce Committee states that because wages and benefits are so poor, a Wal-Mart store with 200 employees costs taxpayers roughly $420,000 per year in social service costs.[67]

Wal-Mart's most recent scandal suggests the very real ways in which the company, with its highly influential form of globalization, seeks further to undermine workers and families in and outside the United States. An October 2003 federal raid of 60 Wal-Mart stores, in 21 states, resulted in the arrest of over 250 undocumented workers. "Operation Rollback," as it was dubbed in terminology that suggests both the "roll back prices" of Wal-Mart and the nation's understanding of "wetback" illegal aliens, busted janitors employed by subcontractors that clean Wal-Mart stores. In what could amount to an enormous class action suit against Wal-Mart, some of these workers, who are now facing deportation, describe working sixty-hour weeks and being denied overtime pay, days off, or sick days. Wal-Mart, of course, denies knowledge that the workers who cleaned the stores were illegal employees. "The Wal-Mart culture is based on respect for other people, and we would never condone treating anyone poorly, legal or otherwise," argues company spokesperson Mona Williams. "We want to get to the bottom of this and are as eager as anyone to see whatever evidence federal officials might have."[68]

Wal-Mart company officials state further that they require cleaning contractors to hire only legal workers. However, according to the lawsuit, and to federal officials, Wal-Mart knew or ought to have known how many hours were needed to clean its stores and how much it paid those contractors. Further, federal officials allege that recorded meetings among Wal-Mart executives, managers, and contractors reveal that Wal-Mart had direct knowledge of the violations.[69] One employee arrested in the raid argues that the store manager at the Wal-Mart in Lexington, Virginia, knew that illegal immigrants were cleaning the floors: "It's obvious," he states. "They knew the whole crew consists of foreigners who don't speak English."[70] Ironically, again, and in another interesting manifestation, Wal-Mart's practice forms a powerful counterpoint to claims of patriotism. The post-9/11 national consciousness includes a commitment to security, to policing the borders, to staking a clear identity claim on who is and who is not American. Wal-Mart, in furthering the use of undocumented workers in the United States, makes clear the degree to which its global growth necessitates disrespect for borders. Low, low prices, rather than an all-American identity, rely on discrepant relationships in the global economy. "No American wants to do this job," argues the detained employee. "If they hired Americans, it would take ten of them to do the work done by five Czechs. This helps Wal-Mart keep its prices low."[71] And low prices seem enough for the consuming public, who seem largely disinclined to hold Wal-Mart accountable for anything more. The events of September 11 and the culture of consumerism have formed a curious bond that furthers American ignorance about real world conditions. As Slavoj Žižek argues, ". . . on September 11, the USA was given the opportunity to realize what kind of world it was part of. It might have taken this opportunity— but it did not; instead it opted to reassert its traditional ideological commitments: out with feelings of responsibility and guilt towards the impoverished Third World, *we* are the victims now!"[72] Victimization, consumerism, patriotism, and disregard for female and immigrant employees go hand in hand.

Wal-Mart's critics have long called for truth in advertising. The list of demands has grown to include the following: that Wal-Mart actually buy American-made products, allow independent monitoring of overseas factories, terminate any contracts that include child and/or sweatshop labor, treat employees fairly, and consider community issues when planning store openings. However widely admired, the company faces a veritable slew of lawsuits. Among these, The National Labor Relations Board has heard twenty-eight complaints against Wal-Mart since November 2001, in charges of anti-union activities including threats, interrogations, and disciplining.[73]

Other critics of Wal-Mart have organized protests at the stores, with slogans like "On the first day of shopping, my true love bought for me, all gifts made in sweat shops overseas." Another: "Always in court, always Wal-Mart."[74] The Maquila Solidarity Network, which monitors sweatshop abuses, gave Wal-Mart the "People's Choice Award" in 2002 for its bad treatment of employees in and outside of the United States. Others try to reify the mythical or real Sam Walton to call the company back to its alleged moral center: "Wal-Mart must restore the integrity and respect for the individual that were the hallmarks of Sam Walton," argues the United Food and Commercial Workers union.[75] The company continues to grow at exponential rates, however, and seems unlikely to slow down enough to revisit either real or apocryphal former values or practices.

U.S. Citizen-Consumers and Political Insularity

One can argue that several things keep Wal-Mart at the top of the game. The corporate structure of low pay and sales of cheap goods often produced outside the United States works, for one. In addition, Wal-Mart has mastered the technology game, easing operations through sophisticated computer networks. The company also has friends in high places. Senator Tim Hutchinson of Wal-Mart's home state of Arkansas used the post-9/11 atmosphere to introduce two amendments to the 2001 Labor House and Human Services budget in order to cut $25.5 million from the National Labor Relations Board. Ostensibly to secure funding for community health centers, the cut in the NLRB budget would effectively have prohibited the agency from going after Wal-Mart on a number of issues.[76] Even his party could not back Hutchinson on a move so clearly biased, however, and the amendments did not pass. Not surprisingly, in the NLRB cases that have been resolved, eighteen in all, the company was found guilty in ten and settled out of court in the other eight.

In addition to friends in high places, however, the biggest supporters of Wal-Mart, regardless of its employment practices or questionable solidarity with this nation and its people, are our friends, our neighbors, ourselves. The company may have recently been pulled from the Domini 400 Social Index, a list of socially responsible firms, but it remains an incredibly admired—and of course, frequented—store in and outside of the United States.[77] Its critics must understand its appeal. For one thing, as Wal-Mart recognizes and appeals to women, so must its critics. Those who lament the demise of the department store must recognize that the big-box retailer has a similar appeal in at least one important regard: one-stop shopping. As women in and outside the United States have assumed additional responsibilities in the public world, they have not, either by custom or by pleasure, abandoned their roles as shoppers. Their harried lives and multiple responsibilities, as much as Wal-Mart's "low, low" prices, make Wal-Mart shopping appealing.

Critics can also do well by further studying this connection between consumer identity and patriotic identity, particularly as it is put forth by Wal-Mart. Ironically, of course, but quite deliberately, the largest and most profitable retailer in the United States presents itself using images of simpler, bygone days in which "American values" informed daily life. The mythology of family values, quite present in store displays, banners, Wal-Mart branded products, store flyers, and television includes the value of patriotism and clearly appeals to American consumers.[78] Wal-Mart advertising purposely features, rather than models, real Americans: Wal-Mart employees, their children, even their pets. This myth of Wal-Mart as everyday life, as the marketplace of American life, sits well with the self-perceptions of many Americans, who see little if any contradiction between continual consumption, a bottom-line approach to spending, a lessening of rights for workers, and the well-being of a nation and its people. Wal-Mart effectively taps into, furthers, and remains largely unchallenged by contemporary American cultural performances of patriotism outside of that big box.

Measuring Patriotism Beyond the Flag

In fairness to Americans, and perhaps to Wal-Mart, it makes sense to look for other, noncommercial measures of patriotism in the post-9/11 context. In other words, are there alternative, credible, non-market-driven ways in which U. S. citizens have performed patriotism since 9/11? Has the citizenry truly made a renewed commitment to civic duty following the attacks on America? One of the most salient measures, arguably, would be voter registration.

A comparison between voter turnout for 2002 and 1998, the previous non-Presidential election year, reveals only a very slight increase in voter participation, from 45 percent of eligible citizens voting in 1998 to 46 percent in 2002.[79] Another measurable indicator suggests that Americans quickly resumed a less than stellar civic performance of patriotism in the aftermath of the flag-waving frenzy. According to the *New England Journal of Medicine*, the country's blood centers collected 167,000 more units of blood in the week following 9/11 than they had in the same period the previous year (this statistic is eerily similar to Wal-Mart's flag sales statistic).[80] However, within months, the American Red Cross warned that supplies were dwindling, and the situation has grown increasingly worse since then. Telephone calls to 800–blood center numbers escalated astronomically in September 2001, from 1,555 in August to 290,661 in September. However, October's rates dipped down to 5,938, November's to 1,105, and December's to 673.[81] The situation currently is at crisis level. The Red Cross has had an enormously difficult time of turning 9/11 donors into regular donors, but it still includes a reference to September 11 in the first sentence of its web site appeal, hoping to capitalize on the supposed link between patriotism and blood donation.[82]

The flags continue, albeit in smaller numbers, to fly from houses and bob from automobile antennas, but the public's resumption of its old habits speaks louder than domestic, automotive, or sartorial displays. Scholars may debate the differences between sacrificing and spending, patriotism and nationalism, Wal-Mart practices and "the American way." But as long as the pursuit of goods remains the American way, in and outside of the "big box," any national commitment, relative to September 11, that "the only way to ensure that it will not happen here is to prevent it from happening anywhere else," is trampled under this mix of corporate hypocrisy and exploitation, American insularity, globalization, nationalism, and now war.[83]

Historian William Leach argued that, "Whoever has the power to project a vision of the good life and make it prevail, has the most decisive power of all."[84] In their all-to-cozily shared vision of the good life, Wal-Mart and the American public have formed a curious bond, enacting a ritual in which consumer participation stands in for patriotism, values are voiced but then lost in an overarching commitment to commodity culture. A Wal-Mart associate in Culpepper, Virginia, may have hit on the ways in which Americans weave together seemingly contradictory identities and make contemporary

Figure 8.5. Consumerism, combining faith and acts, provides stiff competition for other activities. Photograph by Jennifer Scanlon.

life workable for us—and for Wal-Mart. Traffic is light in her store on Sunday mornings, she reports, but "right after church, we get really busy."[85] Consumer participation has been reinvested with meaning in the wake of 9/11, heightened to the level of the sacred (see figure 8.5).[86] For the American performance of patriotism, a faith in a better life through the pursuit of goods, Wal-Mart is here for us, every day, right now, with low, low prices but decidedly high costs.

Notes

The chapter's title comes from the title of a song by John Prine, "Your Flag Decal Won't Get You Into Heaven Anymore," 1971, Atlantic Records compact disc 8296.

1. Jim Farrell, "Patriotic Consumption," *Dr. America Archives*, www.classical89.3online.org/archives/dramerica/america_patrioticconsumption.html (February 2, 2003).
2. Ibid.
3. John DeGraaf, et al., eds., *Affluenza: The All-Consuming Epidemic* (San Francisco: Berrett-Koehler, 2002); Farrell, "Mallaria," *Dr. America Archives*, www.wcal.org/archives/dramerica/america_mallanniv.html (March 10, 2003).

4. Recent publications that consider September 11 and its local and global impacts include: Stanley Hauerwas and Frank Lentricchia, eds., *Dissent from the Homeland: Essays After September 11* (Durham, N.C.: Duke University Press, 2003); Steven Chermak, Frankie Y. Bailey, and Michelle Brown, eds., *Media Representations of September 11* (Westport, Connecticut: Praeger, 2003); Eric Hershberg and Kevin W. Moore, eds., *Critical Views of September 11: Analyses from Around the World* (New York: The New Press, 2002); Slavoj Žižek, *Welcome to the Desert of the Real! Five Essays on September 11 and Related Events* (London: Verso, 2002); Craig J. Calhoun, Paul Price, and Ashley Timmer, eds., *Understanding September 11* (New York: The New Press, 2002).

5. Nancy B. Fair, et al., "Impact of September 11, 2001 on Consumer Spending: A Look at Holiday Spending," *Journal of Textile and Apparel, Technology and Management* 2, no. 1 (Fall 2001): 1.

6. Embassy of the United States, Dublin, Ireland, *President Bush Holds Prime Time News Conference*, October 11, 2001, www.dublin.usembassy.gov (July 9, 2003).

7. Ibid.

8. The federal government assisted consumption by granting roughly $200 million in 2003 to merchandisers developing antiterrorist merchandise. See Peter Stiglin, "Shopping for Terror: The Nation 'Gears Up,' " *Orion Online Magazine*, September/October 2003, www.oriononline.org/pages/oo/sidebars/absurd/index_absurd.html.

9. Mark Albright, "Uncertainty Quieting U.S. Cash Registers," *St. Petersburg Times*, October 6, 2001, sec. 1A.

10. KOVR-TV 12 News, Sacramento, California, "Are You Reluctant to Spend Money After the Attack on America?" *Question of the Day*, September 26, 2001, wwwkovr13.com.html (July 9, 2003).

11. For a full analysis of the business practices that accompanied Wal-Mart's sales slogans, see Bob Ortega, *In Sam We Trust: The Untold Story of Sam Walton and Wal-Mart, the World's Most Powerful Retailer* (New York: Random House, 2000).

12. Bridgette Shade, "Retailers Say Providing Comfort, Means to Express Patriotism are Part of Their Role," *Pittsburgh Post-Gazette*, September 11, 2002, sec. W4.

13. When Wal-Mart reported $220 billion in sales in March 2002, it became the world's largest company. See Richard Ernsberger, "Wal-Mart World," *Newsweek*, May 20, 2002, 50; *St. Louis Post-Dispatch*, "Oh Say Can You See," October 3, 2001, sec. F1; Alison Beard, "Collectors Rush in to Fly the American Flag," *Financial Times*, June 7, 2002, 30.

14. Wal-Mart Online, "Wal-Mart Associates Around the World Grieve, Pray and Support the U.S. Relief Effort," *Wal-Mart News*, September 18, 2001, www.walmartstores.com (March 10, 2003).

15. USA Patriotism!, *USA Patriotism!*, www.usa-patriotism.com (September 26, 2003).

16. Gocollect, Inc, *Gocollect*, www.gocollect.com/patriotic/index.html (March 11, 2003).

17. Olivia Barker, "Flags Will Be in Style for a While," *USA Today*, September 25, 2001, sec. 1D.

18. Ibid.

19. Farrell, "American Flag 2001," *Dr. America Archives*, www.wcal.org/archives/dramerica/america_americanflag2001.html (March 10, 2003).

20. Americas & Americas Inc., *FlagsonCars*, www.flagsoncars.com.html (September 26, 2003).

21. Shade, *Pittsburgh Post-Gazette*, sec. W4.
22. *USA Today*, "Everywhere, Every Day is a Flag Day," October 17, 2001, sec. 8D.
23. Beard, *Financial Times*, 30.
24. Farrell, "American Flag 2001," *Dr. America Archives*.
25. James Howard Kunstler, "Maul of America," *Orion Online Magazine*, 2001, www.oriononline.org/pages/oo/curmedgeon/index.html.
26. For one example of this, see Victor Davis Hanson's collection of essays on September 11, Victor David Hanson, ed., *An Autumn of War: What America Learned from September 11 and the War on Terrorism* (New York: Anchor Books, 2002).
27. Robert Thompson quoted in Damien Cave, "The Spam Spoils of War," in *Signs of Life in the U.S.A.: Readings on Popular Culture for Writers* (Boston: Bedford/St. Martin's, 2003), 124.
28. Christopher P. Campbell, "Commodifying September 11: Advertising, Myth, and Hegemony," *Media Representations of September 11*, ed. Chermak, Bailey, and Brown (Westport, Connecticut: Praeger, 2003), 47–65.
29. Wal-Mart Online, "VFW, Wal-Mart, SAM'S CLUB Team to Respectfully Retire Worn American Flags," *Wal-Mart News*, July 1, 2002, www.walmartstores.com.html (March 10, 2003).
30. *St. Louis Post-Dispatch*, "Wholesale Patriotism," September 25, 2001, sec. B6.
31. Richard Ernsberger, *Newsweek*, 50.
32. Ortega, *In Sam We Trust*, 55.
33. Ibid., xii.
34. Wal-Mart Online, "Recent Awards and Recognition," *Wal-Mart News*, March, 11, 2003, www.walmartstores.com.html (March 11, 2003). In 2003, Wal-Mart displaced General Electric, which had held the top spot for five years. For the 2004 rankings, see Ann Harrington, "America's Most Admired Companies," *Fortune*, March 8, 2004, 80–82, 109–116.
35. Ortega, *In Sam We Trust*, 58–59.
36. Ibid., 55.
37. Liza Featherstone, "Wal-Mart Values: Selling Women Short," *The Nation*, December 16, 2002, 11. In Featherstone's writing, the average Wal-Mart wage was $7.50; as of 2004 it has gone up to over $8.00, according to Paul Waldman, "Cheney Sings Wal-Mart's Praises," *Gadflyer*, May 14, 2004, www.gadflyer.com.html (May 17, 2004).
38. Ortega, *In Sam We Trust*, 211.
39. Featherstone, *The Nation*, 13.
40. Cristina Bull, "NOW Declares Wal-Mart a Merchant of Shame," *National NOW Times*, Fall 2002, 1.
41. For information about pending lawsuits, see the web site *Wal-Mart Watch*, www.walmartwatch.com.html (March 11, 2003).
42. Ann Zimmerman, "Wal-Mart Suit Has Class Status; Ruling in U.S. Makes Case Largest Civil-Rights Action Against a Private Employer," *Asian Wall Street Journal*, June 23, 2004, sec. A4.
43. Sam Walton quoted in Ortega, *In Sam We Trust*, 214.
44. Ibid., 214.
45. Wendy Liebmann quoted in Featherstone, *The Nation*, 11.
46. Ibid., 14.
47. UFCW Online, "Wal-Mart 10 (K), April 23, 1998," quoted in *Buy American Campaign*, www.ufcw.org.html (March 23, 2003).

48. Caroline Mayer, "Wal-Mart Flys the Flag in Import Battle," *Washington Post*, April 21, 1985, sec. E1.
49. UFCW Online, *Buy American Campaign*, www.ufcw.org.html. In a report cited from the International Mass Retail Association in 1994, 84 percent of Americans "strongly or moderately" preferred goods produced in the United States. Additionally, 64 percent "strongly or moderately" indicated that they would be willing to pay more for such goods.
50. A subsequent article in *Time* magazine reported that, although Wal-Mart denied *Dateline's* charges, company president David Glass "just looked like a deer caught in the headlights." *Time*, "Nailed," January 14, 1993, 16.
51. Ortega, *In Sam We Trust*, xiii.
52. "Top 10 Wal-Mart Worst Actions," *Wal-Mart Watch*, www.walmartwatch. com.html (March 2, 2003). On the complex history of "Buy American" campaigns and other forms of economic nationalism, see Dana Frank, *Buy American: The Untold Story of Economic Nationalism* (Boston: Beacon Press, 1999).
53. Ortega, *In Sam We Trust*, xii.
54. Ibid., 210.
55. Ibid., 86.
56. Geoff Schumacher, "Viva Las Vegas: UFCW Launches National Drive to Unionize Wal-Mart," *In These Times*, March 15, 2001, 10.
57. Steven Greenhouse, "Trying to Overcome Embarrassment, Labor Opens a Drive to Organize Wal-Mart," *New York Times*, November 8, 2002, 28.
58. UFCW Online, "Wal-Mart Ordered to Remove Anti-Union Language from Benefits Material," www.ufcw.org.html (March 11, 2003).
59. David Armstrong, "World's Richest People: The Top 20," *Forbes*, February 2004, www.forbes.com/maserati/billionaires2004/cz_top20bill04.html.
60. Stephanie Armour, "Wal-Mart Takes Hits on Worker Treatment," *USA Today*, February 10, 2003, sec. 1B.
61. Featherstone, *The Nation*, 14.
62. Ibid.
63. Jim Hopkins, "Wal-Mart's Influence Grows," *USA Today*, January 29, 2003, sec. 1B.
64. Frank Green, "Food Fight," *San Diego Union-Tribune*, August 18, 2002, sec. H1.
65. Cheryl Glaser, "So-Cal Grocery Workers Sign a Two-Tiered Labor Contract," *Marketplace*, Minnesota Public Radio, March 3, 2004, www.marketplace. public.org.html.
66. *New York Times*, "The Wal-Martization of America," November 15, 2003, sec. A12.
67. David Sirota, Christy Harvey and Judd Legum, "Wal-Mart Welfare," *The Progress Report*, May 28, 2004, www.alternet.org/story.html?StoryID=18816 (June 1, 2004). On social service costs see Waldman.
68. Jeffrey Gold, "Suit Says Wal-Mart Conspired to Harm Workers," *The Record*, November 12, 2003, sec. A3.
69. Chuck Bartels, "More Than 300 Illegal Immigrants Seized in Raids on Wal-Mart Stores," *Associated Press*, October 24, 2003, www.mindfully.org/ Industry/2003/Wal-Mar-IllegalImmigrants24oct03.html.
70. Steven Greenhouse, "Illegally in U.S., and Never a Day Off at Wal-Mart," *New York Times*, November 5, 2003, sec. A1.
71. Ibid.

72. Slavoj Žižek, *Welcome to the Desert of the Real! Five Essays on September 11 and Related Events* (London: Verso, 2002), 47.
73. Armour, *USA Today*, sec. 1B.
74. Bull, *National NOW Times*, 2.
75. UFCW Online, "Worker Demands of Wal-Mart," *People's Campaign*, www.walmartdayofaction.com.html (March 11, 2003). The United Food and Commercial Workers Union argues that Wal-Mart must "restore the Wal-Mart spirit of company founder Sam Walton, of being a decent neighbor and good employer. Today's Wal-Mart is not the Wal-Mart of Sam Walton."
76. UFCW Online, "Senate Rejects Shameful Wal-Mart Ploy to Keep Workers from Union Information," *WalmaRTyrs*, November 2001, www.walmartyrs.com (March 11, 2003). This web site provides a voice for disgruntled current and former employees of Wal-Mart.
77. Russell Mokhiber and Robert Weissman, "Corporations Behaving Badly: The Ten Worst Corporations of 2001," *Multinational Monitor* 22, no. 12 (2001).
78. Stephen J. Arnold, et al., "Hometown Ideology and Retailer Legitimation: The Institutional Semiotics of Wal-Mart Flyers," *Journal of Retailing* 77 (2001): 243–271.
79. U.S. Census Bureau. *Voting and Registration in the Election of November 2002*. U.S. Department of Commerce, July 2004, 1.
80. Paul Schmidt, "Blood and Disaster—Supply and Demand," *New England Journal of Medicine* 346, no. 8 (2002): 618.
81. Cinda Becker, "Blood Rhetoric Exceeds Supply," *Modern Healthcare* 32, no. 27 (2002).
82. American Red Cross, *American Red Cross Website Blood Appeal*, www.redcross.org/donate/give/html (June 9, 2004).
83. Žižek, 49.
84. William Leach, *Land of Desire* (New York: Vintage Books, 1994), xiii.
85. *The Economist*, "My Wal-Mart 'Tis of Thee," November 1996, 27.
86. On the relationship between consumer culture and religion, see Tom Beaudoin, *Consuming Faith: Integrating Who We Are With What We Buy* (Chicago: Sheed and Ward, 2004); Vincent J. Miller, *Consuming Religion: Christian Faith and Practice in a Consumer Culture* (New York: Continuum, 2003); Rodney Clapp, ed., *The Consuming Passion: Christianity and the Consumer Culture* (Downers Grove, Ill.: Intervarsity Press, 1998).

Chapter 9

Mourning, Monomyth and Memorabilia: Consumer Logics of Collecting 9/11

Mick Broderick and Mark Gibson

It is not easy to find a line on the mass of cultural contradictions that is the sale of September 11 memorabilia on eBay.com. It is tempting to fasten on the religiosity, the heavy moral seriousness, that pass without reflection in reference to the event. "God bless America," "the memory of those lost," "this day of infamy": these compressed verbal formulae appear everywhere in the eBay material and are as ripe for ideological analysis as they would be in any other context. What kinds of closure do they exert over our memory of the event? How do they work to stitch the disasters of the World Trade Center and the Pentagon into narratives of American history and destiny? What function do they play in America's engagement—or lack thereof—with the rest of the world?

Figure 9.1

Figure 9.2. Awesome 911 2002 dollar bill, on one side it has USA*FDNY New York City, this non-negotiable note honors FDNY and USA firefighters everywhere, George W. Bush, Rudy Giuliani and on the other side it has the World Trade Centers 1970–2001 and the Pentagon with God Bless America dedicated to the memory of those lost on this day of infamy—September 11, 2001 . . . FDNT . . . NYPD . . . Flight 11 . . . Flight 93 . . . Flight 77 . . . Flight 175 . . . World Trade Center The Pentagon in Memory. Buyer pays 2.00 shipping and 1.30 for insurance.

But what to make of "2.00 shipping and 1.30 for insurance" in this advertisement? It is important to remember that we are looking here at an *auction* site. From a purely textual perspective, eBay is an extraordinary archive, offering examples of everything from nose cones of decommissioned nuclear weapons to neon pink macramé pot-holders from Iowa. Yet the form and style of entries are ultimately those of the huckster. Any serious engagement with the material must start from the obvious function of the site—to sell. This function presents a problem for critical analysis, for it proclaims in advance what the analyst might want to say: that for all their poignancy and tragedy, the figures and discourses produced by an event such as September 11 do not float free of material interests; that behind the religiosity, the moral seriousness, remains the dollar.

Money is one of the purest of abstract signs. It is pure representation; a signifier of something that stands in for its deemed exchange value (e.g., hours of labor, a commodity for purchase). But currency also informs national identity and legitimacy (legal tender) in its self-conscious deployment of, occasionally arcane, iconography and symbolism (the U.S. greenback's pyramid, omniscient eye, and text, "In God we trust"). Where commodities become fetishes, according to Marx, is in the ideological process that detaches consumers from the material labor required to produce the goods, creating a "false consciousness" and "idols of the mind," terms Marx invoked to suggest the displacement and denial involved in commodity fetishism. Mieke Bal has recognized that far from demystifying commodity fetishism from a transcendental position outside history, Marx turns commodities themselves into figurative, allegorical entities, "possessed of a mysterious life and aura,"[1] terms later adopted by Walter Benjamin to describe the age of mechanical reproduction. Such an associative detachment is already present in the "filthy lucre" of currency. So how should we interpret the commemorative coins, faux dollar bills, and casino chips commemorating 9/11 as attacks against the center of capitalism and the U.S. military–industrial complex (see figures 9.1, 9.2 and 9.4)?

The unabashed obviousness of material interests on eBay has made it an object of some controversy. In February 2002, New York City chief attorney Michael Cardozo went so far as to issue a "cease and desist" letter in an attempt to prevent the trade in September 11 items. The legal basis of the charge was focused on the sale of logos and insignia for private profit, but the moral case went wider. The sales, for Cardozo, were "blatant attempts to profit from mass murder . . . it's obvious that much of what is on [the] website is morally repugnant."[2] The charge echoed criticisms of street vendors selling 9/11 merchandise close to Ground Zero, including highly popular CD-ROMs full of copyrighted photographic material (see figure 9.3). Many complained that:

> Whether illegal, unethical or both, hawking the horrors of 9/11 so close to where so many firefighters died [. . .] betrays the memory of their lost colleagues. Tom Cleary, Firefighter: "It is beyond insulting to this department, to this city, to this nation to allow that to go on so close to such a sacred site. It's not going to become a mall. It's not a place to go shopping."[3]

The problem with these responses is that they fail to recognize how perceptions of commerce and capital were integral to the whole event. Had Cardozo and other critics missed that the chosen target of Osama bin Laden and Al Qaeda was the World *Trade* Center? Few commentators seem to have appreciated the irony of anticommercial sentiments being expressed at the very site of such massive commerce, free trade, and profit. EBay seemed in some ways to have recognized more clearly the stakes involved and had positioned itself, even before the criticisms emerged, to claim the

Figure 9.3. WTC World Trade Center September 11 Tribute CD. Memorabilia, collector's edition. Over 2,840 files on this tribute CD • World Trade Center Before 9/11/01 • World Trade Center After 9/11/01 • World Trade Center Audio Files 9/11/01 • World Trade Center Video 9/11/01 • World Trade Center Illustrations 9/11/01 • Pentagon Images 9/11/01 • Pentagon Audio 9/11/01. Buy the 911 Memorial CD NOW— Only $19.95.

moral high ground through an absolute fusion of commerce and patriotic respect. Within a week of the terrorist attacks it established an "Auction for America," donating the auction fee to charity in a bid to raise $100 million in 100 days.[4]

It misses the point to isolate Internet auctions as exceptional, and it is here perhaps that we can begin to come to grips with the phenomenon. If eBay confounds distinctions between reverence and commerce, then so too does the larger culture of which it is part. What better example of this than the "awesome" 9/11 dollar bill itself? Perhaps only a commemorative casino chip—"a nice addition to a chip collection"—also available through the site.

The choice of these items to memorialize a national tragedy and momentous world event—a choice, of course, quite independent of the auction sites through which they might be sold—is as curious as

Figure 9.4. This chip was manufactured to honor our heroes for the bravery and the lost of their lives. It has no casino affiliation. It was manufactured by the Paulson Gaming Supply Co. it is the hat and cane mold. It has very detailed art work. The American Eagle is on the front of the chip with the words September 11, 2001 In Honor Of Our American Heroes. The reverse side has The Twin Towers in New York and The Pentagon In Washington and Flight #93 in Shanksville, PA. This is one chip that is a tribute to all. [. . .] It makes a nice addition to a chip collection. Buyer pays $2.00 S&H It is in mint condition.

the conjunction of solemnity and sales promotion in the object descriptions. Like the choice of the New York Stock Exchange, in the days after the terrorist attacks, as the site for rallying the nation through "God Bless America," it raises questions about the peculiar conjunction of quasi-religious nationalism and capitalism only possible in the United States. Internet auction sites such as eBay open a window on this phenomenon, and a window that is more than accidental; in their own embeddedness within a field of commercial relations, they take us close to its heart.

A promising place to start in establishing a wider cultural context for the September 11 merchandise on Internet auction sites is to trace that most potent of themes in American mythology—the frontier. Any study of the discourses around these sites suggests that the connection is a significant one. The imaginative landscape of the frontier is routinely worked as a source of metaphors in thinking and writing about electronic commerce. In a typical narrative of the business success of the Internet entrepreneurs, for example, Christopher Price attributes the success of eBay to its capturing of "the pioneering spirit of the internet."[5] Earlier in the same book,

Price quotes a line from Bob Davis, head of Lycos, which makes the cultural reference further explicit: "When you're a pioneer sometimes you claim new territory and sometimes you take some arrows."[6] The Internet entrepreneurs here become rugged frontiersmen and the whole cultural repertoire of the American West is activated as a symbolic resource.

If such a use of the frontier metaphor ("pioneer," "new territory," "take some arrows") by Internet auction CEOs might be dismissed as playful, designed only to add color, other examples can be pointed to where it has been more systematically and assertively developed. Perhaps the best known is the manifesto "Cyberspace and the American Dream: A Magna Carta for the Knowledge Age," coauthored by Esther Dyson, George Gilder, George Keyworth, and Alvin Toffler, and published by the Progress and Freedom Foundation, associated in the mid-1990s with Newt Gingrich's vision for the Republican Party. The "bioelectronic frontier," write Dyson et al., "is an appropriate metaphor for what is happening in cyberspace, calling to mind as it does the spirit of invention and discovery that led ancient mariners to explore the world, generations of pioneers to tame the American continent and, more recently, to man's first exploration of outer space."[7] The opening up of the electronic frontier presents an occasion for rearticulating the American dream.

The potential in this that has been most emphasized in discourses around eBay is the association between the frontier and *democracy*. For Pierre Omidyar, the company's founder, its original aim was to keep alive the early promise of the World Wide Web: "The web had grown up very much as an individual and democratic thing . . . and what I wanted to do was bring the web to benefit individuals."[8] There are some ironies in this, given the near monopoly position that eBay has since achieved. The company is estimated to host over 90 percent of online auctions in the United States and is expanding aggressively into Canada, Germany, Australia, the United Kingdom, France, and Italy.[9] With a market capitalization at one time of over US$30 billion, it has traveled a long way from Omidyar's early amateur enthusiasm. It is true, nevertheless, that eBay has transformed the auction form, expanding it way beyond the small circle of connoisseurs and dealers who have monopolized it in the past, and changing the very definition of what can be thought of as "collectible."

At this level, the trade in September 11 memorabilia on eBay could be seen to merge with other democratizing movements following the event. In a provocative essay on collecting responses in New York, Barbara Kirschenblatt-Gimblett observes an almost countercultural quality in displays and exhibitions after the attacks on the World Trade Center.[10] Beginning with the intensely personal tributes of photographs and other objects laid around the site itself, it could also be found in more institutional settings. A striking example was the photographic exhibition "Here is New York: Images from the Frontline of History: A Democracy of Photographs," which opened in a Soho shopfront within weeks of the attacks:

> More like the Soho of the pioneering seventies than the Soho of the affluent nineties, the small, brightly lit white space of *Here Is New York* is covered with photographs. Identified only by a tiny number, the images are clipped to wires strung along the walls and across the space, like laundry on a line or wet negatives and prints in a darkroom. There are no frames, no labels, no names, and no uniformed guards.[11]

There are a number of similarities between such exhibitions and the eBay material: the anonymity of encounters, the absence of regulation, the informality, the openness to all. We should certainly allow that eBay may have enabled thousands, perhaps hundreds of thousands, literally to bring the event home, to weave it into the fabric of their everyday lives.

Such collecting behavior has a particular importance at times of crisis. Mary Ann Doane has suggested that catastrophe can be defined as "unexpected discontinuity in an otherwise continuous system" with sudden, unexpected events disrupting the temporal order.[12] In response to this discontinuity, artifacts can provide a spatial and tactile *permanence* that serves to remind, both physically and iconographically. Mementos have their place within the banality of the everyday and provide a parallel focus of the catastrophe long after, which may disrupt the routine or enable its continued function, paradoxically through displacement onto an object of remembrance that can be comfortably "forgotten."

In her analysis of "spontaneous shrines" erected at the time/place of tragedy, Sylvia Grider argues that these shrines act as communal performances of grief that enable individuals to "work out a personal connection to an otherwise numbing catastrophe," bringing comfort to thousands during a disaster.[13] For an international audience shocked by the incessant coverage of 9/11, personal access to New York's "Ground Zero" site and the Pentagon was problematic due to security restrictions; hence potential well-wishers were denied access to these locations. In this way Internet shoppers/auction bidders can be considered online pilgrims, just as Grider suggests those who visit spontaneous shrines come to "leave a ritual offering," or visit "a pilgrimage site to come to and see what others have left." It may be that the conspicuous consumption of 9/11 Internet auction merchandise is better understood as "paying respects online" by buying a small item as a token, like lighting a candle or leaving some small offering/prayer at a physical site.

According to Grider, these spontaneous shrines are a "widespread phenomenon," and increasingly include Internet "cybershrines," online photos of material shrines, memorial web pages, online condolence message boards, and virtual candles: "The shrines reduce the overwhelming enormity of the catastrophe to a more manageable human scale, thus helping to make the event more comprehensible, especially when the emotions evoked are new and raw . . . shrines are a metaphoric threshold which represents the end of numbness and the beginning of the ability to take action."[14] Such a transformative function associated with material culture may greatly inform the desire to purchase kitsch memorabilia, as a private means of owning and preserving a monument of the 9/11 disaster in the home as a personal shrine. As Grider says, most spontaneous public shrines are "temporary" and this transient and ephemeral nature can further explain the online bidder's drive to obtain more robust, permanent 9/11 mementos as commodities that will last (and possibly outlast their corporeal owners).

In relation to material culture more generally, Jean Baudrillard has asserted that: "collecting simply abolishes time. Or rather: by establishing a fixed repertory of temporal references that can be replayed at will, in reverse order if need be, collecting represents the perpetual fresh beginning of a controlled cycle, thanks to which, starting out from any term he chooses and confident of returning to it, man can engage in the great game of birth and death."[15] In this way mementos and commemorative souvenirs "control" time, recollection, grief, and trauma. According to John Elsner and Roger Cardinal, the Western compulsion to collect artifacts demonstrates an age-old reflection of "the triumph of remembrance over oblivion, to the permanence of Being over Nothingness."[16] Ordered collections contain "desires for suppression and ownership, fears of death and oblivion, hopes of commemoration and eternity."[17]

According to material cultural theorist Milhaly Cziksentmihaly, objects fundamentally serve to stabilize and order the mind, clearly a desirable function at a time of crisis and chaos.[18]

For Baudrillard it is in the symbolic realm of games and playing, where an object vanishes temporarily only to reappear, that invests our early attitudes toward loss and ownership. He suggests:

> *the object is that through which we mourn for ourselves*, in the sense that, in so far as we truly possess it, the object stands for our own death, symbolically transcended . . . we reach an accommodation with the anguish-laden fact of lack, of literal death. Henceforth, in our daily lives, we will continue to enact this mourning for our own person through the intercession of objects, and this allows us, albeit regressively, to live out our lives.[19]

Mieke Bal concurs, stressing that the "gendered anxiety" identified by Freud, and one that is classically seen to inform fetishism, can be displaced by another affect—such as time and death: "In accordance with Freud's concept of the death instinct, subjects constantly work their way through the difficulty of constituting themselves by re-enacting a primal scenario of separation, of loss and recovery, in order to defer death. Collecting can be attractive as a gesture of endless deferral of death in this way."[20]

So, if as the impressive weight of diverse scholarship implies (Czikentsmihalyi, Baudrillard, Elsner and Cardinal, Bal, and Pierce), these motivations underscore the cultural and psychic processes around collecting *in general*, what does it mean to purchase and collect mementos, souvenirs, and kitsch specifically concerned with cataclysm and death? Can we consider disaster merchandising as a further compounding of the impulse to mediate and negotiate national tragedy and personal survival? These objects certainly enable their owners to (re)create narratives of a remembered event more or less at will by looking at and/or containing that memory now projected or displaced onto a material object. The permanent display of a disaster artifact, such as a 9/11 collectible or memento (e.g., an item placed on a wall, table, or bookcase) evokes this recollection by its random intervention in daily life through its continuous presence, unlike a stored specimen that is returned to briefly on occasion through a conscious act of selective choice.

Similar collecting behaviors can be observed in relation to earlier events. 9/11 has its precedents in American history and it is worth

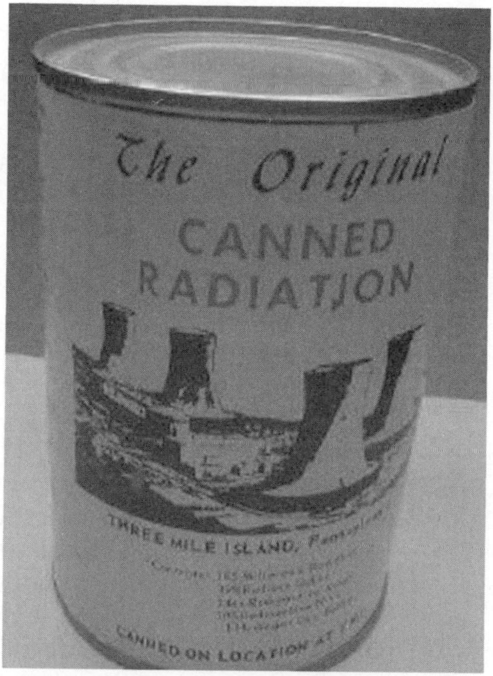

Figure 9.5.

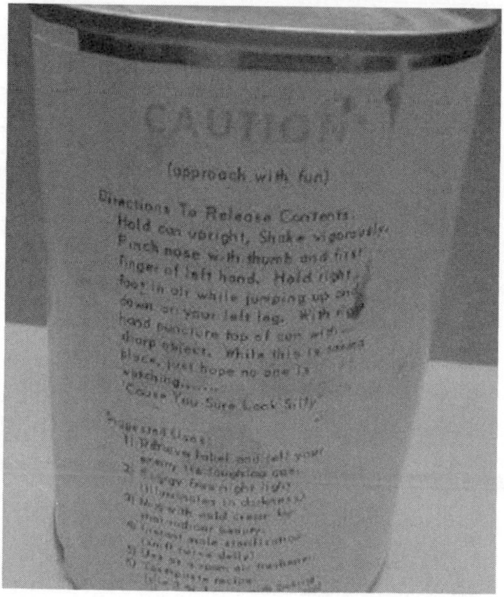

Figure 9.6.

recalling these antecedents and how they have been mediated. As in all such traumatic and unexpected tragedy, the public and political response is ultimately defined as a period of "crisis," a test of national resolve and commitment. Given this, we can consider "disaster" and "catastrophe" as synonyms equated with either man-made or natural devastation and tragedy, respectively, whereas "crisis" is concerned with the *process* of decision making when facing either past, current, or potential "disaster/catastrophes."

Twentieth-century U.S. tragedies of such significance can be considered in two distinct categories: premeditated attack and accidental disaster. In the first category sits Pearl Harbor (1941), the Oklahoma bombing (1995), the first fire-bombing of the World Trade Center (1993), and, in this century, the 9/11 attacks (2001). The second category comprises the NASA Apollo 1 fire (1967), the Three Mile Island partial meltdown (1979), and the Challenger (1986) and Columbia (2003) Space Shuttle explosions. All of these disasters have witnessed varying degrees in the commercialization of their horrors, ranging from institutionalized public memorials (*U.S.S. Arizona*) to novelty commemorative items such as joke cans of "radiation" for sale from Three Mile Island (see figures 9.5 and 9.6).

This last example marks a point of difference from the 9/11 material, as heavy moral pressure and self-censorship, in view of the gravity of the event, have suppressed humorous responses. Otherwise, however, there are strong continuities in the forms of

Figure 9.7. CHALLENGER—On the front is a full color picture of all the crew members. To the right of the picture is the name of each of the crew. On the back is a full color picture of the lift off of the last flight. This makes a great gift for anyone. Everybody that I show these to want one. This is a great memorial to those who are no longer with us.

memorializing. Two that bear particular mention are faux dollar bills and commemorative knives and other objects with frontier associations (see figures 9.7 and 9.8).

This Columbia Shuttle example incongruously deploys Native American iconography—the "stylish silver indian feather mold." Here material culture, to be bid for and purchased as mementos of national catastrophe, demonstrates the latency of what Fredric Jameson has termed "the political unconscious" (the layers of interpretation and historical contexts already embedded in such material);[21] namely the unacknowledged colonialism and evocation of pioneer conquest and territorial dispossession.

Following Susan Sontag's meditation on the "Imagination of Disaster,"[22] Patricia Mellencamp considers the Challenger disaster as having "exploded the modernist myth of technology (and also the Western frontier myth of the necessity of humans for space exploration) as unifying a dispersed audience."[23] Similarly Mary Ann Doane regards national "catastrophe" as an antidote to

Figure 9.8. SPACE SHUTTLE COLUMBIA COMMEMORATIVE POCKET KNIFE. The 440 Stainless Steel lock back blade measures 4 inches with an overall dimension of 7 inches. The handle has a stoic picture of the space shuttle crew smiling and approaching the shuttle for take off with the profiles of the president on one side and flag-carrying servicemen on the other. The handle is very heavy and has a polished gold steel finish. The knife has a stylish silver indian feather mold bearing cover.

modernity's technological "evolution," where utopian/progressive teleology is disrupted by these events.[24] This failure paradoxically confirms the risk of pioneer ventures while recognizing the appeal to frontier ideology.

Much of the cultural association surrounding these events is dependent upon the historical context of each disaster. 9/11 is unique in being branded as frozen in time by its temporal specificity. No other calamity is identified primarily by date as its nomenclature. The U.S. calendar is forever marked with this association, just as "July 4" commemorates American Independence and is symbolic of freedom and self-determination. But there are also a number of unifying themes. The loss of human life and the size and nature of that loss greatly influences how the dead will be mourned and/or memorialized. The failure of technology and the legitimating narrative of human progress through applied science and free-market capital (space exploration and nuclear power) is another. And in all cases trade in objects associated with the events, greatly facilitated by online auctions, have enabled broad-based participation in working through the questions they raise.

It would be too simple, however, to leave the analysis there. It is not enough to draw attention to the fact that online auctions allow the event to be brought home. It is important also to consider *how* the event is brought home, in *what ways* it is woven into everyday lives. Susan Willis makes the point in an essay on the meanings invested, following September 11, in the American flag. One of the most interesting examples is the flag that was raised Iwo Jima–style by New York firefighters at Ground Zero—an image, incidentally, that appears frequently among the eBay items (see figure 9.9).

The flag itself was later shipped to Afghanistan to be raised at Kandahar airport as confirmation of American victory over the Taliban (and still has currency via the "9/11 Pentagon flag," now revealed as bogus, that was draped over the felled statue of Saddam Hussein, and then quickly replaced with the Iraqi national flag, before an international TV audience). Writes Willis:

> One can imagine that the firefighter's flag will continue to circulate, following the antiterrorist special forces brigade to all the world's hot spots. With each unfurling, the flag will consecrate yet another site crucial to America's efforts to secure the global production and distribution of oil. The existence of this flag will finally bestow meaning on all the flags we purchase at Wal-Mart or on eBay.[25]

Figure 9.9. American Spirit Lighter WITH Pocket Knife NEW, Show your support the American way with this collection NICE Father's Day gift or give it as a thank you gift to the hero in your life. It is truly a wonderful patriotic statement and wonderful tribute to all the 9/11 heros.

It is not necessary to go all the way with Willis in her analysis of American foreign policy to recognize that a flag bought through eBay is part of a cultural–political–military complex some of whose effects may be a very long way from the democratic charm that Kirschenblatt-Gimblett discerns in collecting practices in New York.

Another aspect of the phenomenon is crucial here: the dominance, in the discourses and iconography of September 11 memorabilia, of the theme of *heroism* (see figure 9.10). As John Shelton Lawrence and Robert Jewett argue in their recently updated study of the American monomyth, the hero is a crucial point of tension between democratic and antidemocratic tendencies in American culture. Where the classical monomyth (Ulysses, St. George and the dragon, Hansel and Gretel) reflected rites of initiation, in which the hero returns from adventure to share the fruits of his exploits among his fellows, the American monomyth "derives from tales of redemption" in which the hero must always remain alienated from the community.[26]

The hero appears, in the latter, at the point where normal social institutions are revealed as incapable of responding to evil. While *opposing* evil, he must go outside the law to do so, and on completion of his mission he recedes into the obscurity from which he came. As Lawrence and Jewett point out, the form of the myth is odd, to say the least, in a country that proclaims itself as the global beacon of democracy. From D. W. Griffiths' *Birth of a Nation* to *The Matrix*, American popular fiction has presented us with countless narratives of the impotence of democratic institutions and the necessity of resorting to extralegal means.

A major point of reference for this mythology is, again, the frontier. Lawrence and Jewett trace its early-twentieth-century formulation to texts such as Owen Wister's Western novel *The Virginian*, first published in 1902.[27] A major line of development then runs through the Lone Ranger, Buffalo Bill, and John Wayne before it is transposed onto other backdrops such as the city (Superman, Dirty Harry) and space (*Star Trek, Star Wars*). And again, the frontier reference activates a connection not just with the content, but also with the *form* of the Internet auction. The subtitle of Christopher Price's book on the Internet entrepreneurs cited earlier is *Business Rules are Good: Break Them*. Like the frontiersman, the Internet entrepreneur inhabits a space in which the established social order cannot be relied upon. His aura derives from his independence; his willingness, where necessary, to take things into his own hands.

In the example of the World Trade Center and Pentagon "Let's Roll" pin, both the eagle and *Ol' Glory* overpower the smaller yet associated images of the WTC (in the background) and Pentagon (foreground) (see figure 9.11). Semiotically, we see capital literally backing the military, with the bellicose invocation "Let's Roll" connoting both an impatience for "pay-back" and a call to arms. This lapel pin is designed to be worn as an everyday reminder/incantation for America to act promptly and decisively, a pure signifier of what Meaghan Morris has identified nonpejoratively as the etymological origins of "banality," which either means "to issue an edict or summons (usually to war)," or "to obediently voice a rhythmic applause. . . ." This, Morris argues, is "the 'banal' enunciative duty of the common people, the popular chorus."[28] Such resonances are implicit in much of overtly patriotic, if not chauvinistic, online merchandising post-9/11, at once reflecting the clarion call to war of President Bush ("Bring it on!," he defiantly and provocatively greeted news of sustained attacks on coalition forces in Iraq after announcing

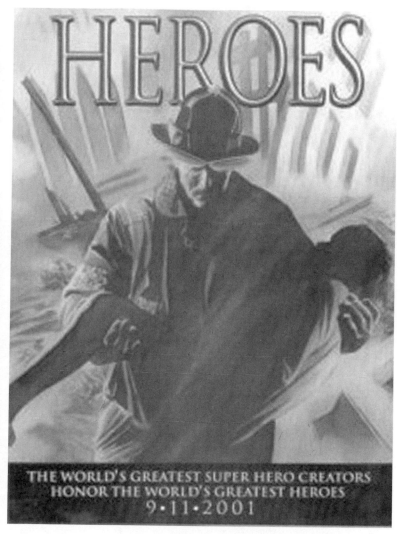

Figure 9.10. I have a copy of Heroes vol. 1 #1, I wish to sell. published by marvel in Dec. 2001. The first of the Sept. 11 tribute issues. magazine sized pin-up comic-book. full page, full color pin-ups related to Sept. 11, 2001. 1st print.

"major hostilities" had ceased), and the popular culture display of commemorative banality.

There are many resonances here with the neoconservative arguments that gained influence over White House policy after

Figure 9.11.

September 11, arguments in which frontier allusions also featured prominently. Robert Kagan, for example, in his influential analysis of increasing political differences between the United States and Europe, asks us to imagine ourselves in a forest in which life is put at risk by a rogue bear:

> The psychology of weakness is easy enough to understand. A man armed only with a knife may decide that a bear prowling the forest is a tolerable danger, inasmuch as the alternative—hunting the bear armed only with a knife—is actually riskier than lying low and hoping the bear never attacks. The same man armed with a rifle, however, will likely make a different calculation of what constitutes a tolerable risk. Why should he risk being mauled to death if he doesn't need to?"[29]

In the context in which they were offered, the allegorical references are clear: the bear is Saddam Hussein, the impotent knife-wielder Europe, the gun-slinging savior the United States. While they do not figure here directly, the United Nations and other international bodies are the temporizing "community" whose lack of resolve must be put aside for the common good. The terms of the monomyth, as identified by Lawrence and Jewett, could hardly be translated more perfectly to a geopolitical vision.

Yet there is an interesting twist in the monomyth in some of the 9/11 material. Traditional American mythology has intersected with the iconography of 9/11 disaster commemoration in such a way as to validate the everyday, the institutional, and the effective agency of liberal-democratic collective service. The buttons, plates, T-shirts, comic books, statuettes, faux coins, and banknotes depicting heroic emergency services and others who perished in the "line of duty" are often juxtaposed against existing icons of American pop culture (Superman, Mickey Mouse), now greatly diminished in stature. The ordinary police, firefighters, and paramedics become giants, literally dwarfing the previously emblematic U.S. representations of heroism, ingenuity, and innocence (see figure 9.12).

In this movement we witness a possible shift in the American monomyth via its renegotiation of heroic iconography, which previously embraced the paradoxical rejection (for a society that holds democracy as a core value) of democratic institutions by promoting superhuman or supernatural agency and/or the intercession of individual patriarchs whose might equates to right(eousness).

It is difficult to know which of the tendencies we have suggested above will emerge as dominant—the democratic "claiming" of the event, the authorization of heroic redemption outside normal political processes and the law, or the revaluation of the figure of the hero in such a way as to elevate the ordinary. What "9/11" ultimately comes to signify for America and the world will be left to future generations. As Foucault argues in *The Archaeology of Knowledge*,[30] we cannot expect resolute insight into such cultural perspectives while still within the contemporary "episteme"—we remain too close, in other words, to the event while conflicting modes of interpretation are still in flux and undergoing negotiation.

What should be clear, however, is that the online trade in objects associated with 9/11 provides a unique site for investigating the terms in which the history of the event is being made. Auction sites such as eBay offer an extraordinary window on the material culture through which, in countless and often quite unexpected ways, the memory of 9/11 is being institutionalized in everyday life. The television images of the hijacked airplanes plowing into the World Trade Center may be seared into the minds of millions, but they were also in many ways *zones of ambiguity*, ready to take on a multitude of meanings. In understanding these meanings, it is important to turn our attention to less spectacular phenomena: the lapel pin, the commemorative pocket knife, the kitsch collectable, the

Figure 9.12. You are bidding on Disney 9–11 Commemorative Fireman and Mickey. A grateful Mickey Mouse shakes hands with one of America's heroes. Throughout our national history many men have risked their lives to save those of others while fighting and helping with rescue operations. We salute and applaud their brave and self-sacrificing devotion to their calling in this tribute to America's firefighters.

faux dollar bill. If studies of material culture have established the importance of these, online auction sites have provided access for the researcher that could previously only have been dreamed.

But beyond this, online auction sites provoke us to consider the inherent commercial nature and the processes of transaction that emerged in response to the event. They are, above all, sites of capital where market forces are impossible to ignore. We cannot deceive ourselves, in considering a site such as eBay, that the event is somehow insulated from the field of commerce that otherwise informs our everyday lives. The electronic extension of this field is a particularly potent force in disembedding objects, meanings, and social interactions from established regimes of regulation and control. There are rich traditions in America of cultural response to such disembedding, organized, we have argued, around the trope of frontier. If they are traditions that have contradictory potentials—some democratic, some antidemocratic; some tending to zealous assertion of the law, some to indifference or contempt for legal process—they nonetheless provide quite a precise matrix for cultural invention and exchange. It is within this matrix that the memory of 9/11 is being forged.

Notes

1. Mieke Bal, "Telling Objects: A Narrative Perspective on Collecting," in *The Cultures of Collecting*, eds. John Elsner and Roger Cardinal (Carlton, Aus.: Melbourne University Press, 1994), 109.
2. Reuters, "NYC Warns EBay About 9/11 Item Sales," February 21, 2002. Posted at: www.techtv.com/news/internet/story/0,24195,3373165,00.html (November 5, 2003).
3. Jim Hoffer, "9/11 Profiteering At Ground Zero Called Immoral, Illegal," *Eyewitness News Extra*, New York, WABC, February 26, 2002.
4. Ina Steiner, "eBay Announces Fundraiser for Families of 9–11 Attack Victims," Auctionbytes-NewsFlash, Number 163, September 18, 2001, ISSN 1539–5065, posted at: www.auctionbytes.com/cab/abn/y01/m09/i18/s01 (November 5, 2003).
5. Christopher Price, *The Internet Entrepreneurs: Business Rules are Good: Break Them* (London: FT.com, 2000), 179.
6. Price, 3.
7. Esther Dyson, George Gilder, George Keyworth, and Alvin Toffler, *Cyberspace and the American Dream: A Magna Carta for the Knowledge Age*, 1994, www.hartford-hwp.com/archives/45/062.html (November 4, 2003).
8. Cited in Price, 180.
9. Garth Saloner and A. Michael Spence, *Creating and Capturing Value: Perspectives and Cases on Electronic Commerce* (New York: Wiley, 2002), 561.

10. "Kodak Moments, Flashbulb Memories: Reflections on 9/11."*Tactical Media Virtual Casebook: 9/11 and After*. Eds. Barbara Abrash and Faye Ginsburg. New York: New York University, 2002. www.nyu.edu/fas/projects/vcb.

11. Kirschenblatt-Gimblett, 11.

12. Mary Ann Doane, "Information, Crisis, Catastrophe," in *Logics of Television: Essays in Cultural Criticism*, ed. Patricia Mellencamp (Bloomington: Indiana University Press, 1990), 228.

13. Sylvia Grider, "Spontaneous Shrines: A Modern Response to Tragedy and Disaster (Preliminary Observations Regarding the Spontaneous Shrines Following the Terrorist Attacks of September 11, 2001)," *New Directions in Folklore 5* (October 2001), www.temple.edu/isllc/newfolk/journal_archive.html (October 12, 2003).

14. Grider.

15. Jean Baudrillard, "The System of Collecting," in *The Cultures of Collecting*, eds. John Elsner and Roger Cardinal (Carlton, Aus.: Melbourne University Press. 1994), 16.

16. John Elsner and Roger Cardinal, "Introduction," in *The Cultures of Collecting*, eds. John Elsner and Roger Cardinal (Carlton, Aus.: Melbourne University Press, 1994), 4.

17. Elsner and Cardinal, 5.

18. Milhaly Cziksentmihalyi, "Why We Need things," in *History from Things: Essays on Material Culture*, eds. Steven Lubar and W. David Kingery (Washington, D.C.: Smithsonian institution Press, 1993), 20–29.

19. Baudrillard, 17.

20. Bal, 112–13.

21. Fredric Jameson, *The Political Unconscious: Narrative as a Socially Symbolic Act* (London: Methuen, 1981).

22. Susan Sontag, *Against Interpretation* (New York: Farrar, Straus & Giroux, Inc., 1965).

23. Patricia Mellencamp, *High Anxiety: Catastrophe, Scandal, Age and Comedy* (Bloomington: Indiana University Press, 1992), 103.

24. Doane, 231.

25. Susan Willis, "Old Glory," *South Atlantic Quarterly* 101/2 (2002) (Special Issue: Dissent from the Homeland: Essays after September 11, ed. Stanley Hauerwas and Frank Lentricchia): 377.

26. John Shelton Lawrence and Robert Jewett, *The Myth of the American Superhero* (Grand Rapids, Mich.: William B. Eerdmans, 2002), 6.

27. Lawrence and Jewett, 31ff.

28. Meaghan Morris, "Banality in Cultural Studies," in *Logics of Television: Essays in Cultural Criticism*, ed. Patricia Mellencamp (Bloomington: Indiana University Press, 1990), 41.

29. Robert Kagan, "Power and Weakness," *Policy Review* (June/July 2002): 13.

30. Michel Foucault, *The Archaeology of Knowledge*, trans. A. M. Sheridan Smith (London: Tavistock, 1972).

Chapter 10
Social Fear and the
Terrorism Survival Guide

Joe Lockard[1]

Don't Worry, Keep Rolling!

The post–September 11 economy of the United States is a fear-infested and sober landscape. National security and security-related corporations, together with firms operating in support of the occupation of Iraq, have provided a major visible source of economic growth. Corporate sectors without any discernable claim on security products nonetheless work to integrate a national security consciousness into their corporate images. Grim, determined, and upbeat patriotism is being used to sell any product that needs selling.

Ad campaigns experiment on how to function within these times of economic sobriety, as evidenced in those successful "Keep America Rolling" ads that General Motors rolled out in the months following September 11. When George W. Bush told the country "Let's roll!" and revoiced the words of an airline passenger who fought back against the terrorist hijackers, he echoed, at the same time, a General Motors logo.[2] National security fears and durable goods, statesmanship and salesmanship, became woven together by a go-get-'em consumption-oriented manner of speaking. To be behind the wheel was to control national fate in the face of international terrorism.

Two years later such corporate patriotism has metamorphosed into Lockheed-Martin's "What We Believe" and "Liberty" television advertising campaigns adducing freedom as identical with its weapons products. Under the terms of merged interests of state and corporation, the "Liberty" ad informs audiences, where once there was a necessary choice to "work for a company or serve a nation—we do both." With Halliburton, Bechtel, MCI, DynCorp, ChevronTexaco, ExxonMobil, Fluor, and other multinational corporations in Iraq implementing U.S. foreign policy, as Devin Nordberg observes, "the Bush Administration's foreign policy, like domestic policy, often seems to come directly from corporate board-rooms."[3] Fear and its manufacture have become simultaneously social enterprise and corporate profit center.

But how is it possible to speak of the American manufacture of fear? Let's begin with the fear of corporate collapse. Which is to say that corporations with central positions in the U.S. economy, like the airlines, dealt with the depressed post–September 11 economic environment by lining up for billions in federal support and by tem-porarily moving rhetorical claims of "free market—no government interference" to the back burners. Obviously, the function of capi-talism is to protect capital, not labor, so unemployed workers do not get generous Congressional handouts. Social expenditures have been dedicated to alleviating corporate fears, but the fears of private citizens remain private business.

Our fear-intensive economy elides a central truth of economic life: social fears are a constant source of profit. Without fear and insecu-rity, capitalism would not have the economic sanctions that make it profitable. Progressive politics since the nineteenth century have undertaken the task of alleviating social insecurity and replacing fear with social security, either with or without first-letter capitalization. Post-60s Western capitalism has continued to pursue the basic intel-lectual outline of Friedmanian economics, which emphasizes the mar-ket utility of holding down social expenditures and imposing on labor a disciplinary fear of impoverishment.[4] A "liberalizing" IMF-oriented economy, as with those in Eastern Europe and other regions, cuts back on preexisting social protections in the name of economic effi-ciency and competition, thus raising the prevalence of social fear. Such expansion of social fear's prevalence occurs in a global, postmodern economic environment governed by the communication of symbolic power, one where fear constitutes awareness of and reaction to sym-bolic information as much or even more than immediate or remotely discernable risk. This is an economic environment, as Leonard Wilcox argues, characterized by "strategic efforts on the part of corporations to simulate profitability (here the Enron debacle is instructive)" and by "an economy in which money itself is an object of circulation that has only a screen-and-networked existence rather than a 'material' one."[5] Yet the susceptibility to catastrophic damage that Wilcox identifies in an economy of signs and symbols is more than a strategic vulnerability available for exploitation by terrorists. Nor did it appear, as the French writer Jean Baudrillard famously suggested, primarily via the interrelated functions of a "virtual" capitalism, a globalized media, and hyperreality—a society of copies that have no origins—within an economy motored by signs and visual images. Rather, this vulnerability is the cumulative result of a historic process involving the cultivation and transplantation, via global reorganizations of capital and trade, of fear itself as a discipline and as our chief motivation for labor. The broad crossnational trend toward diminution of labor's political power throughout the late twentieth century, accompanied by the intensifying strength of capital formations and their dominant political philosophies, has spread fear (via non-living wages, unemployment, absence of health insurance and pensions, homelessness) through daily economic and social life far more effectively than any single spectacular act of public terror. Susceptibility to social fear manifests an economic system that accumulates fear, in the diverse and multifold forms of social insecurity, as efficiently as capital.

If on one hand economic fear is a persuasive style of social coercion, it functions simultaneously as a style of consumption. What we might call "preventative consumption" is a fear response that seeks to avoid the consequences of unpreparedness or inaction. Consumption itself becomes insurance against fears, rational or irrational. Not only does the post–September 11 specter of Islamic terrorism generate a market for products that are located within this framework of preventative consumption (e.g., duct tape), but— a critical point—a product's actual relation to the political phenomenon turns out to be irrelevant (e.g., duct tape). The point is that success in a fear-linked market relies on associative links, since product value rises in correlation with its security value. Risk, ever-present in the economic calculus, suddenly has a face, even if invisible. As a critically elevated factor in the market, social fear not only motivates acts of consumption, it penetrates commodities thoroughly. Karl Marx made this point emphatically in *Capital* when he argued, "The mysterious character of the commodity-form consists therefore simply in the fact that the commodity reflects the social characteristics of men's own labour as objective characteristics of the products of labour themselves, as the socio-natural properties of these things."[6] In other words, commodity fetishism, which effectively attributes human characteristics to objects, flourishes in the post–September 11 economy by the infusion of fear as a natural property into goods-and-services production.

When people shop in response to fear, their actions transform the social risks caused by foreign, alien hatreds, thus reducing hatreds into the manageable features of known, familiar products, which may or may not bear any relation to legitimate causes of social fear. And in an interesting parallel development, this civil market environment based on fear, in its response to individual consumers, mirrors the expanding military market that translates a global fear-economy into military services and products. But perhaps this is not really so surprising, as the pervasiveness of social fear eliminates clear distinctions between civil and military markets. That same diffusion within alarm-ridden societies generates demands for massively increased security services and goods that can be linked to ideologies of security. During a period of globalization when "free trade" market economics focus on reducing labor costs in less-developed countries in order to expand profitability in developed countries, the intensification of economic fear in impoverished labor forces finds its reverse image in the intensification of existential fear in developed consumer economies. Existential fear circulates liberally throughout popular and mass culture in post–September 11 America, as Bianca Nielson's essay in this volume wonderfully demonstrates, encouraging consumers to purchase not only goods and services, but entertainment as well.

Fear itself thus has become a consumption item, and fear-dependent corporations feed off public paranoia created by terror attacks. From health insurance to financial services ads that emphasize "security," the post–September 11 media is filled with appeals to prevent what is almost impossible to prevent, and it invites us to do so through product consumption. Islamic terrorism has become an invisible yet ubiquitous brand name that joins disparate products anew. The fear of Allah-bonded men with death wishes and distant mullahs has become the covert unmentionable that enables insurance companies and Florsheim Shoes to employ the Statue of Liberty as their new-old advertising flack, or Ralph Lauren to merge Polo shirts with the flag as easily as Lockheed-Martin does to sell F-16 Fighting Falcons. All reaffirm freedom as consumer freedom. Images of American shrines and commercial invocations of "E Pluribus Unum" nationalize consumer purchasing power. To buy American is to meet the enemy. As we buy on, we roll on.

Entrepreneurship of Fear

It is the small-time profiteers of fear who speak messages that more socially restrained and polite major corporate advertising cannot voice directly. These are not the predictable Internet fraudsters hawking multivitamins against anthrax. Rather, outside the world of brand-name privilege and close to populist political roots, an entrepreneurship of fear has emerged to calm and consolidate fear as a socially useful consumer activity. The small-time contractors who built backyard fallout shelters fifty years ago have their contemporary followers in biowar rubber suit suppliers and survival school instructors.

For the most part, these are opportunists who are out to promote a product or service more than an ideological agenda. For that deeper level, the expensive and glossy *Terrorism Survival Guide* is a magazine that suits the times like the *Whole Earth Catalog* suited the '60s. Stocked with Ruger ads and shooting school addresses, it is available from magazine racks alongside *National Enquirer* and similar titles.[7] The cover features a crowd of subtitles, ranging from the informative "The Common Sense Guide to Staying Safe" to the alarming "Dangers We Face Now! What You Can Do to Meet the Threats!" It is a home-front magazine, with men in white rubber suits and another subtitle reading "Anthrax and Bio-Terror: Facts vs. Fear! Reality vs. Rumor!" Indeed, it would seem that *Better Homes and Gardens* has gone to biowar. The *Terrorism Survival Guide* reformulates economic activity as motivated survival; its pages spell out for us how to consume to survive. Homeland security and household security have merged into one; home investment and prevention of home invasion have become conjoined social discussions.[8] This is old-new territory, in that while domestic defense of the home from alien threat can be readily identified in nineteenth-century American popular literature and its log-cabin imagery, the threat horizon is now both globally diverse and locally specific. This home-protectionist discourse has altered considerably from the terrain of mid-twentieth-century neighborhood racial conflict—racist blockbusting and black-white civil rights contests over housing segregation—that Sinclair Lewis examines in *Kingsblood Royal* (1947), but rather the American Home of the twenty-first century resides in an ugly global neighborhood that requires defensive readiness against bioterrorists and similar mortal threats.

The *Terrorism Survival Guide* testifies eloquently to the fact that fear, in itself, is a domestic commodity. Its extensive gun promotions and survival book advertising rely on reader fear of social threats and general social chaos to promote sales. These are home safety products that can render home as a place impregnable against the fear of terrorism. In a couple of photographs, a middle-aged blonde woman demonstrates home defense techniques. In one vivid example of the new suburban hospitality, this well-prepared matron crouches to open the front door while holding a pistol at the ready for any unexpected guest. Another posed photo shows the same woman peering off a second-floor balcony, demonstrating how to cover the front driveway with a sniper rifle. An article on post–September 11 child psychology features the graphic accompaniment of a full-page photo of a toothy little girl in a clear plastic gas mask with face mike, carrying a Barbie doll decked out in her own gas mask (accessories sold separately, one presumes). Other essays identify proliferating sources of fear; the advertising provides home-front solutions. The magazine's obscure publisher, Pantheon International, specializes in glossy one-off mass market theme issues sold on shelf space where readers will likely find hunting, gun, and kindred magazines; the issue editor, Michael Bane, identifies himself as a security and survival expert.[9]

In this magazine, if the home is a prime target that must be rendered defensible, the neighborhood is an equally vulnerable target. In this world of fresh domestic threat, explains one writer, the local infrastructure is a prime target. "For example, before all this craziness, you may not have noticed that vehicle parked inappropriately near the county electric station. Make note of it now and report it. Before September 11 you might not have thought twice about people acting strangely around the local reservoir. You had better think twice now." George W. Bush made these same sentiments sound presidential when he asked terror-alert citizens to watch public activity for "something that is suspicious, something out of the norm that looks suspicious."[10]

Because sources of supply are at risk, homeowners need to prepare their regional lines of defense. There is an emphatic demand for explanation of the unknown, together with suspicion of those outside the norm or those who ask questions about the world. "Beware of anyone asking untoward questions regarding schedules, conveyance methods, social gatherings," advises Basic Anti-Terrorism Tip #3, followed by Tip #5's caution, "Be wary of individuals whose movements and actions are not logically motivated." Discrepant cultural logics, according to this hometown antiterrorism philosophy, demand fear, investigation, and action.

According to every essay and advertisement in this journal, the answer to these insecurities is the same: buy a gun! Although a gun would be useless in the face of the chemical, biological, and nuclear threats that the *Terrorism Survival Guide* details, such lapses in logic never seem to burden the magazine's editors. Rather, a firearm becomes a palpable defense even if it offers no protection. Buying a gun is simply the opposite of submission. Michael Bane frames this as a moral choice. "Like many Americans, I reached a moral and ethical crossroads after The Attack. I believe that although, in the real world, there are times when we must submit, as a culture and a nation, we have come to see submission as the preferred option."

In the *Guide*, any refusal to acknowledge the need to own personal weapons equates with capitulation and an acceptance of victimization. The notion that other means of self-defense may be more appropriate and effective never arises in this journal. Like so much else that passes for antiterrorism self-defense here, personal firearms ownership represents no more than symbolic consumerism. That need for a physical symbol of resistance, a new Remington stashed under the bed as a defense against inchoate foreign threats, is the same functional social motor that moves consumers who buy durable goods as a response to terrorism. Panic buying is a crisis response to violence, a means of managing excess social fear. Social fear never lacks for profit opportunities.

Homeland Insecurity

Since consumerism underwrites the conditions of national identity, the articles contained in the *Terrorism Survival Guide* establish an ideology that redirects readers' consumer energies into security-oriented myths of being and belonging in the United States. Bane provides an article entitled "Ten Ways Our Lives Have Changed" that posits a new sense of American national connectedness. The purpose of this new social interconnection, he suggests, lies in a national rediscovery of the American warrior self. The antigun lobby has led those who adopted a defeatist embrace of submission that swept the country in recent decades. Bravery and honor are emerging from a broad popular rejection of submission, and the nation now takes its bearings from a new social compass based on absolute virtues. "We bury our dead with the sure and certain knowledge that great good, and great evil, do, in fact, exist, and that our measure as individuals and as a people will be where we stand in that epic battle." To fine words like these, Jack London once answered, "[T]he magic of your phrases leads you to believe that you are patriotic. Your desire for profits, which is sheer self-ishness, you metamorphose into altruistic solicitude for suffering humanity."[11]

In this New America, which wakes each morning full of renewed patriotism, moral absolutism has disposed of relativism and self-questioning in a distant and dishonorable grave. What has triumphed is a national unity where social problems are no more than minor family problems, where the heterosexual nuclear family is firmly enthroned (and possibly enshrined in our constitution, as a safeguard against the encroaching threat of same-sex families), where invading aliens receive sound rebuff at the nation's borders, and where a vigilant home-guard military can project its high-tech force around the globe. Deep-rooted historical social differences disappear in such a scenario; instead, these differences are no more than an exuberant individualism that all share. In the end, according to Bane, "We are the warrior tribe who did the impossible—create an enduring government that celebrated, and continues to celebrate, our very contentious individualism."

This is the classic delusion of nationalism, the belief that a mystical nation-tribe has gathered its spirits to rise. In this delusion, racial, gender, and class divisions happen only "occasionally," fairly ignoring the contradiction of Bane's simultaneous argument that the divisions created by submission have prevailed for years. So history-writing serves to mythify and unite, not to document, analyze, and explain. The function of the nation-state is to translate the warrior-spirit into an operations plan. Yet what Bane provides is a classic marketing strategy: make consumers feel happy about what you suggest they are becoming. Here is resurgent America, a nation-product worth fighting for—and here too are the tools with which to fight and partake of the warrior-spirit. This is a call to a revived faith in tribalism, one where a sharing of warrior-kin replaces petty social in-fighting.

Fear operates both as obstacle and enabler in this ideological scheme. The *Terrorism Survival Guide* frames fear as another tactical tool, as an emotion whose correct management produces continuous situation evaluation reports and fluid responses. To qualify as fear, there must be a specific and immediately identifiable stimulus; a "formless" fear is mere intuition, he argues, forgetting the logic of inference. There has been a cultural over-use of fear and its language, Bane asserts, which detracts from threat-readiness and leads to an inability to distinguish real warning signals. The proliferation of fears, however, is endemic to a well-functioning capitalist economy. Fear is the marketing device for goods and services, and, at a social level, for the nation itself as product. The greatest fear and best marketing device is, at one and the same time, an assault on the American collectivity itself.

Toward Unlearning Fear

In 1927, in the context of the *Whitney* free-speech case, Louis Brandeis wrote, "Those who won our independence . . . [knew] fear breeds repression; that repression breeds hate; that hate menaces stable government; that the path of safety lies in the opportunity to discuss freely supposed grievances and proposed remedies. . . ."[12] What Brandeis distinguishes is the social cycle that the spread of public fear initiates, a cycle where oppressive government and violent opposition boil together in the same pot. Brandeis voices the classic Enlightenment fear of a state gone wrong, of government illiberality giving rise to hatred and street riots. Civil liberties were thus a venting mechanism, and a means of ensuring that repression did not metamorphose into much worse consequences.

John Ashcroft's illiberality and vitiation of civil liberties, however, created no street riots. Like the worst attorney general in U.S. history, A. Mitchell Palmer, Ashcroft emerged from a narrow-minded fear of the world's variety, a McGuffy-esque provincialism of neat picket fences and nineteenth-century American virtues. The mentalities of Palmer's 1920 Red Scare and Ashcroft's Moslem Scare are similar: Palmer's justification of warrantless arrest of aliens on grounds that "detention does not constitute imprisonment, nor even deprivation of liberty without due process of law"[13] sounds as though it were lifted from recent Justice Department briefs—yet the political landscape of the intervening eighty years has been revolutionized through the mass media and a global visual culture. Unlike the early twentieth century, where fears might inform state policy or market products, under late capitalism fear has become a streamlined public-private commodity. What the government announces, television news anchors interpret and expostulate.

In this media-driven economic regime, the consequences of social fear no longer lie primarily in an assault on civil liberties. The commodification and marketing of fear, fear-products, and nation-products has far outstripped the creation and defense of civil rights. America consumes its civil liberties, and consumption is its leading civil liberty. Challenges to such disastrous forms of national consumption, the consumptions fostered by present U.S. domestic and foreign policy, constitute the current heartland of oppositional politics within the United States. In order to formulate such political challenges, it needs to be recognized that an insidious politics lies within the marketing and consumption of social fear, one that arises from a xenophobic variant of national identity politics. In this paranoia of threat-belief, all manifestations of difference become sources of risk. A nation turns inward, into its fears, and shelters itself behind the luxurious walls of the U.S. economy, weapons pointed outward. Foreign policy has become a defense of this triumphal hegemonic identity and a demand for other nations to manifest their allegiance to such U.S. global primacy. An identity of national self-preservation emerges, one whose economic existence becomes preoccupied with hunting down existential threats and affixing "Wanted Dead or Alive" to threat sources. Ethnic identity politics goes onto a national war footing, one where all ethnicity is stripped down to visible good and invisible evil. American self-identification with prosperity is the only good identity, and the only one that counts.

Walter Benn Michaels argues that capitalism supplies objects of both fear and desire only to the extent that it simultaneously produces subjects—consumers—to consume them.[14] Today American subjectivity characterizes itself through fear, and the objects of desire are those that call consumers into being by granting them protection against fear. The *Terrorism Survival Guide*, as an emblematic document of our time, represents a stark synthesis of this transformation of fear into a simultaneous commodity and national identity; it constitutes a synthesis whose underlying system of values and beliefs is more easily visible for the magazine's extremism, which masquerades as plain and simple commonsense, or commonsense as self-defense. Such Manichean extremism in the putative defense of freedom requires an over-the-horizon evil. It wants a ubiquitous evil that resists critical thought. It demands and retains an irreducible evil that needs no explanation and finally invites a deep-seated cultural paranoia. In this sense, the *Terrorism Survival Guide* can be read simultaneously as a mapping of fear and as a national policy guide. Its narrative is a restatement of the cultural paranoia resulting from the transformative processes of fear commodification.

Commodifications of fear ultimately rely on manipulation through nostrums and ignorance. There is, though, a real frontline of homeland defense: teachers who refuse to mouth official dichotomies of good and evil, students who refuse to accept an uncritical perspective, and parents who refuse to barricade their homes against foreign ideas and people. A radical rejection of social aliens is at the heart of this homeland defense. It is an expanded concept of homeland defense that recognizes that contemporary American social fear derives ultimately from fear of the global poor and dispossessed, those with causes for anger. Western economies have privileged capital over labor, and have exported the social fears of capitalism—unemployment, impoverishment, inadequate health care and education—to purchase an indefatigable Western prosperity.

A homeland defense that refuses to recognize global fears and anger is no defense at all. Fear neither begins nor ends at the U.S. national borders: it was globalized long ago. In another world, as the Civil War was just beginning and national fears were rampant, the Transcendentalist poet Jones Very, moved by his antislavery convictions, wrote "[T]hough no human help the righteous know, / They fear not in the last, the trying hour."[15] Couched in Very's religious language was a very different cultural understanding of fear as a beginning of resistance, and not of fear as a pervasive means of commodity fetishism. To unlearn the commodification of fear will be to relearn resistance to fears of the world. *Chazak ve 'ematz.*[16]

Notes

1. Acknowledgements to Joel Schalit and *Bad Subjects* editors for comment on this chapter, and with thanks to my son David Raphael Lockard for promises kept.
2. "President Discusses War on Terrorism in Address to Nation, World Congress Center, Atlanta, Georgia," White House press release, November 8, 2001.
3. Devin Nordberg, "Corporations are the Only Victors in Iraq," *Detroit Free Press*, September 15, 2003.
4. See "Social Welfare Measures" chapter, 177–189 in Milton Friedman (with Rose Friedman), *Capitalism and Freedom* (Chicago: University of Chicago Press, 1962).

5. Leonard Wilcox, "Baudrillard, September 11, and the Haunting Abyss of Reversal," *Postmodern Culture* (Fall 2003) 14:1 at www.jefferson.village. virginia.edu/pmc/current.issue/14.1wilcox.html.

6. Karl Marx, *Capital*, vol. 1 (New York: Penguin, 1990), 164–165.

7. *Terrorism Survival Guide*, Operation Enduring Freedom series #2 (New York: Pantheon International, 2002). Similar post–September 11 titles in this new survivalist literature include Juval Aviv, *The Complete Terrorism Survival Guide: How to Travel, Work and Live in Safety* (Huntington, NY: Juris Publishing, 2003); *Terrorism Survival Guide: How Your Family Can Survive a Terrorist Attack in America* (Torrance, CA: Nonstop Internet, 2003); Rainer Stahlberg, *Surviving Terrorism: How to Understand, Anticipate, and Respond to Terrorist Attacks* (Fort Lee, NJ: Barricade Books, 2003); Angelo Acquista, *The Survival Guide: What to Do in a Biological, Chemical, or Nuclear Emergency* (New York: Random House, 2003); Charles Stewart and Robert G. Nixon, *Surviving Weapons of Mass Destruction* (Boston, MA: Jones and Bartlett, 2003); Elizabeth Terry and J. Paul Oxer, *Survival Handbook for Chemical, Biological and Radiological Terrorism* (Philadelphia, PA: Xlibris, 2003); Ken Cubbin, *Survival Tactics for Airline Passengers* (Leesburg, VA: Avionics Communications, 2002); and others.

8. For further discussion of this thematic correlation, see Bianca Nielsen, "Home Invasion and Hollywood Cinema: David Fincher's *Panic Room*," in this volume.

9. At present, Michael Bane hosts "Shooting Gallery," a firearms program on the Outdoor Channel. The general tenor of his post–September 11 political advocacy holds, "We've heard a lot lately about supposed wartime threats to civil liberties. But one constitutional right—the right to keep and bear arms—is likely to become more secure in the wake of Sept. 11," *Wall Street Journal*, December 11, 2001. Also see Bane's "Targeting the Media's Anti-Gun Bias," *American Journalism Review*, July/August 2001. Bane has directed the National Shooting Sports Foundation's media education program and is the author of over twenty books, most recently on extreme sports and outdoor survivalism.

10. "President Holds Prime Time News Conference," White House Press Office transcript release, October 11, 2001.

11. Jack London, *The Iron Heel* (Chicago: Lawrence Hill Books, 1980), 84.

12. *Whitney v. People of State of California*, 274 U.S. 357, 376.

13. Stanley Coban, *A. Mitchell Palmer: Politician* (New York: Columbia University Press, 1963), 240.

14. Walter Benn Michaels, *The Gold Standard and the Logic of Naturalism: American Literature at the Turn of the Century* (Berkeley and Los Angeles: University of California Press, 1987), 20.

15. "Fear not: for they are with us are more than they that are with them. 2 Kings 6:16," in Helen R. Deese, *Jones Very: The Complete Poems* (Athens: University of Georgia Press, 1993), 335.

16. Hebrew slogan, "Strength and Courage, " Joshua 1: 6.

Chapter 11

Home Invasion and Hollywood Cinema: David Fincher's *Panic Room*

Bianca Nielsen

> Panic is part of American political discourse . . . both mainstream parties think they can best persuade us by scaring us.
> —Jonathan Sterne and Zack Furness, "Panic: State of Mind or Mind of State?"[1]

> The price tag for our panic about overall crime has grown so monumental that even law-and-order zealots find it hard to defend. . . . Panic-driven public spending generates over the long term a pathology akin to one found in drug addicts. The more money and attention we fritter away on our compulsion, the less we have available for our real needs, which consequently grow larger. While fortunes are being spent to protect children from dangers that few ever encounter, approximately 11 million children lack health insurance, 12 million are malnourished, and rates of illiteracy are increasing.
> —Barry Glassner, *The Culture of Fear*.[2]

The title of one of Hollywood's top-grossing films for 2002, *Panic Room*, communicates the magnitude of the word "panic" in current Western cultural discourses. *Panic Room* further suggests its political relevance post-9/11 by depicting the failure of the eponymous room's intended function as a sanctuary from the violence of a home invasion. *Panic Room* conveys contemporary concerns with personal and national security by representing the contradictions and tensions that exist during times of unrest. Filmed before but released after the terrorist attacks of 9/11, *Panic Room* serves to critique both the security industry and the media's "culture of fear."[3] By representing misplaced and confused fears concerning personal safety, *Panic Room* highlights connections between domestic and national security. As with director David Fincher's other films, such as *Fight Club* (1999) and *Se7en* (1995), *Panic Room* depicts a dystopian urban space, imperfect institutions, and an individual's struggle to formulate an independent identity. While *Panic Room* utilizes familiar narratives of terror to endear itself to spectators, it also undermines these conventions by providing resistive subtexts that are intertwined with the themes of Fincher's other films. On the surface, *Panic Room* appears to defy the commodity industry's argument that security can be bought. However, *Panic Room*'s ultimate narrative dependence on the reliability of New York's police force undermines this critique by suggesting that America's institutional forces are proficient agents in the ongoing "war against terrorism."

The analysis of Hollywood films as either industrial products or works of art has a rich history within the field of genre theory. Much early genre criticism contends that Hollywood films uniformly express dominant ideological concerns. Such theories also acknowledge that the presence of a strong personality in a film, usually the director, allows ideological tensions to develop between the conventions of genre and the intentions of an author. Many pioneering genre theorists believed that this gave Hollywood films the potential for social critique.[4] While early genre critics asserted that horror films eventually offer the restitution of institutional knowledge, academic work on horror and thriller films made after the sixties refutes this contention. Tony Williams and Carol Clover, among others, have argued that contemporary horror and thriller films can effectively provide arenas for the reassessment of conventional gender roles and the expression of cultural anxieties.[5] While as industrial commodities Hollywood films might address conflicts in a simplistic and reactionary way, on another level, as texts shaped by collaborations between authors, they can reveal social tensions.

Beneath the suspense and spectacle of *Panic Room* there is evidence of the capitalist tensions that exist in a Hollywood product in which the contribution of an author is prevalent. While the marketing tactics used to promote *Panic Room* (particularly the film's trailers and taglines) capitalized on the economic, social, and political climate post-9/11, its content reflects the director's interest in the role violence and terror play in social institutions and in the construction of gendered identities.[6] Additionally, that *Panic Room* was written and for the most part shot before 9/11 indicates there were already growing anxieties regarding domestic security and home invasion in America. Given the film's setting in New York, these anxieties add a further dimension to the film's post-9/11 relevance.

A number of recent texts argue that America's popular obsession with violence and security has continued to grow since the events of 9/11.[7] Joe Lockard's "Social Fear and the Commodification of Terrorism" studies the patriotic, consumer-oriented language that characterized media responses to 9/11. His description of the post-9/11 social landscape explains the political logic of the consumer culture to which *Panic Room* contributes. Here, capitalism needs the fear that breaches of national security produce in order for the manufacture and consumption of security commodities to increase:

> The post-September 11 economy of the United States has become a fear-infested and sober landscape. National security and security-related corporations are providing the major visible economic growth. Corporate sectors without any discernable claim on security products nonetheless work to integrate a national security consciousness into their corporate images. Grim, determined, and upbeat patriotism is being used to sell any product. . . . This fear-intensive economy elides a central truth of economic life: social fears are a constant source of profit. Without fear and insecurity, capitalism would not have the economic sanctions that make it profitable.[8]

Identifying processes that occur in the wider consumer culture, Lockard argues that the security industry makes the threat of foreign hatred manageable by encouraging consumers to invest in their personal safety. In this sense, the commodification of fear reflects the methods used to exploit the entertainment value of terror within the horror and thriller genres. By representing the home as a prime target that must be defended, consumer culture specifically encourages the purchase of commodities, such as guns and security systems. As Lockard puts it, "buying a gun is simply the opposite of submission."[9]

Frank Ferudi also insists that the communications industry is obsessed with producing unfounded fears. In *Culture of Fear* he explains that there is rarely a direct correlation between actual social risk and the kinds of anxieties that are expressed in post-9/11 media culture: "Society today seems preoccupied with the dangers that people face. The past decade has seen a veritable explosion of new dangers. Life is portrayed as increasingly violent. Children are depicted as more and more out of control. Crime is on the increase."[10] While images of crime, violence, and terror proliferate in the news media, security commodities attempt to provide responses to threats that are largely unsubstantiated. Fears about crime are most vociferously expressed in public panics concerning personal security.

Writing three years before Ferudi and Lockard, Barry Glassner contends that Americans have a compulsion to entertain personalized and unfounded fears about crime, drugs, and violence, fears that obfuscate very real areas of social concern. Unusual and isolated acts of violence are seen as captivating the public imagination and generating unfounded paranoias and panics. "When we are not worrying about deadly diseases we worry about homicidal strangers. Every few months for the past several years it seems we discover a new category of people to fear."[11] Government spending on unfounded anxieties disguises the lack of attention to areas that should be of real concern. For instance, while crime indeed seems to reflect disproportionate distributions of wealth, the media will rarely depict fictional or nonfictional murder as the product of such socioeconomic gaps. Disseminating fears to do with violence is immensely profitable for the media and, as Glassner suggests, this displaces other more serious problems. "The short answer to why Americans harbor so many misbegotten fears is that immense power and money await those who tap into our moral insecurities and supply us with symbolic substitutes."[12] In a circular pattern, then, it is the media's fascination with violence as a cause of death that shapes public opinions about what is to be feared. Promotional trailers for *Panic Room* suggest this by connecting collective fears concerning home invasion to America's climate of terror post-9/11.

The trailer for *Panic Room* that is included with the film's DVD package reveals these connections explicitly.[13] As the camera focuses on a list of items contained in a "survival kit," this "teaser trailer" describes the panic room as follows:

> It took three months to design, five more to build. Its flesh, seven tons of poured concrete. Its bones, one thousand linear feeds of steel girder. Two miles of cable connect sixteen surveillance cameras to eight recordable monitors. It has a separate buried phone line. Its only door is reinforced steel, secured by solid core dead bolts and a motion sensitive closing system. The room has one purpose: to keep people out.

This excerpt from the trailer's voiceover might seem to suggest that the panic room is impenetrable, however because the room's fallibility is the focus of the film we know it is not. That this description gives the room human characteristics, such as flesh and bones, is further significant: the vulnerability of the human body was painfully apparent to the American public after 9/11. Because the panic room is given human features here it is portrayed as permeable and weak. The trailer's explanation for the room's purpose—"to keep people out"—establishes further links between *Panic Room*'s marketability and America's "culture of fear." Since two of the three intruders are nonwhite (one is black and another Hispanic), the racial dimension to the threat posed by those the panic room is built to "keep out" is accentuated. The terror of a home invasion is ultimately implied in this trailer's concluding image, where the film's title hovers ominously in blood red as the screen fades to black.

David Fincher and Terrorism

Edward Buscombe explains that the popularity of a film depends on a combination of novelty and familiarity. He defines familiarity as an audience's expectations of a genre and novelty as that which arises during the production process. Drawing on auteur theory, Buscombe assumes the dominant production input to be that of the director. According to Buscombe, the conventions of genre, when used effectively by good directors, allow Hollywood films to become accessible and significant cultural artifacts.[14] This can be said of David Fincher's *Se7en*, *Fight Club*, and *Panic Room*, all of which rely on certain generic conventions in order to communicate with audiences. Fincher's filmmaking techniques can also be characterized by certain prevailing themes and visual components. By representing dark and oppressive environments that allow the perpetrators of terror to remain invisible, Fincher follows the dystopian postmodern city and the violence that urban landscapes foster. In Fincher's films, characters representative of metropolitan institutions are powerless against the passion and intellect of terrorists, who are nurtured by cities that provide a kind of camouflage for evil.[15]

While it is obvious that postmodern terrorists commit multiple murders, Fincher's early film *Se7en* capitalizes on this established notion by representing serial killer John Doe (Kevin Spacey) as a grotesquely eloquent and intelligent terrorist. *Se7en* satirizes Hollywood's fascination with the stereotyped Islamic terrorist by representing John Doe as a Christian extremist. Like the fictitious Arab terrorists that have captivated the Western imagination for decades, John Doe is a religious fanatic, believing he is performing God's will and "setting an example" that will be remembered. According to Philip Simpson's definition, John Doe is a demonic messenger, a punisher of an urban society's sins and transgressions.[16] As *Se7en*'s moral locus, Detective Somerset (Morgan Freeman) also believes that contemporary cities are full of sinners and depravity, though he does not express his disgust through murder. Somerset wishes to escape the decadent and corrupt metropolis he inhabits in order to experience a dream that is lodged in America's imaginary past.

The mise-en-scène of *Se7en*'s concluding scenes depicts the obsolescence of Somerset's desire to exist in a fantasy world where serial killers and terrorists do not exist. Overhead shots portray high-tension power pylons menacingly impinging upon a desolate and parched countryside. The sole occupants of the deserted landscape through which Somerset's unit travels are a dirty caravan and the rusting carcass of an early model car. While the power pylons signify the failure of technology and communication in a world where serial killers and terrorists can exist, as outmoded symbols of an industrial past, the car and caravan represent the disintegration of the purportedly sinless era in American history that Somerset and John Doe dream of. Though the world free from depravity that Somerset pines for perhaps never really existed except in the dreams of extremists, the urban world of *Se7en*, where it always rains and where violence subsists effortlessly, is potently real. Detective Mills (Brad Pitt) argues that John Doe is insignificant because he is just a "movie of the week" or a "T-shirt," however, he is not. Mills' account of the media persona that John Doe is cultivating reveals the extent of the commodification of terror within Fincher's corrupt postmodern metropolis.

While an imaginary sinless world captivates Somerset in *Se7en*, vandalism and terrorist acts of destruction give protagonists' lives meaning in *Fight Club*. Central characters in *Fight Club* recount their feelings of disempowerment as they search for meaning within their existences as workers and consumers in a large, anonymous city. The men in *Fight Club* connect this disempowerment to their perceived paternal abandonment, and subsequent reliance on the emotional and economical support provided by mothers. During one scene Tyler Durden (Brad Pitt) and the unnamed narrator (Edward Norton) discuss how they are representatives of a generation raised by mothers. Having not enjoyed what he considers to be a necessary paternal form of nurture as a child, the narrator of *Fight Club* initially searches for meaning in the purchase and accumulation of consumer items. When Durden enters his life they instead come to seek "enlightenment" through participating in the terrorist destruction of symbols for consumerism. The men experience a sense of community by destroying items linked to large conglomerates, including a computer shop window display, a piece of corporate artwork, and a franchise coffee store. Their "enlightenment" is also accomplished through the rejection of bourgeois notions of cleanliness, fashion, and beauty. This is most significantly related to their contemptuous and misogynistic rejection of women. Durden's business is founded on the sale of soap to beauty counters at department stores. The soap is made from bags of fat stolen from liposuction clinics, and Durden proudly explains that they are therefore selling the waste products of vanity back to women.

The exclusion of women from this search for a defining masculine identity achieved through acts of violence is tinged with homoeroticism. "Fight Club" members battle each other bare-fisted and unclothed from the waist up in a demonstration of excessive masculine physicality and prowess. The homoerotic aspect of this is most compellingly asserted when the narrator fights a "pretty" blonde member of "Fight Club" in whom Durden has earlier shown an intense interest. After smashing the blonde's face into a bloody pulp, the narrator appears satisfied to have destroyed the thing that has aroused Durden's desire.[17] The men's exclusionary homosocial community eventually culminates in the formation of a collective of terrorist cells founded with the intention of destroying large skyscrapers where banks store credit records. Their organization undertakes this act of terrorism, Durden explains, in order to wipe out all records of capitalist hierarchies. *Fight Club* concludes with the reassertion of the narrator's "macho" heterosexuality as he shoots Durden, reconciles with his girlfriend (Helena Bonham Carter), and watches skyscrapers tumble around him. The ending of *Panic Room*, where millions of dollars worth of bank bonds flutter in the wind and are lost forever, is a comparable expression of the destruction of abstract and intangible wealth.

Domestic Security and Self-Defense in *Panic Room*

> Panic is our national pastime. . . . The much heralded individualist
> spirit of American society relies on nurturing a fear of other people.
> Fear of public spaces . . . in turn supports the proliferation of private
> property and restricted access locations. . . . The rhetorical necessity
> of slogans such as "United We Stand" are countered by the ongoing
> national zeitgeist of "Leave Me and My Family Alone." The impli-
> cation embodied in "United We Stand" is that we have some (un-
> American) Other to be united against. . . . Panic inspires pre-emptive
> attacks on whatever violates the sanctity of private life.
>
> —Kevin Carollo, "The New World Disorder."[18]

> I do not agree with the columnists who attribute September 11 solely
> to the anger of bin Laden and his troops toward the excessive greed
> and irresponsibility of global capitalism and its white supremacist
> ways. Nor did September 11 happen simply because the global econ-
> omy is displacing men from their earlier livelihoods. These explana-
> tions are valid, but September 11 must also be viewed in relation
> to the way that male patriarchal privilege orchestrates its hierarchi-
> cal system of domination. The age-old fear and hatred of women's
> sexuality and their forced domestication into womanly and wifely
> roles informs all economies.
>
> —Zillah Eisenstein, "Feminisms in the
> Aftermath of September 11."[19]

While the methodologies of auteurism and genre contribute advanta-
geously to an analysis of the films of David Fincher, evaluating *Panic
Room* itself as a commodity necessitates considering Jodie Foster's
star image. *Panic Room*'s appraisal of motherhood, family, and gender identity is primarily expressed though the character Meg Altman,
played by Foster. Actors perform a significant role in the capitalist
economy of Hollywood and make important donations to films'
meanings.[20] Foster's accomplishments in her previous films, such
as *Taxi Driver* (Martin Scorsese, 1976), *The Accused* (Jonathan
Kaplan, 1988), and *Silence of the Lambs* (Jonathan Demme, 1991),
contribute to the meanings in her performance as Meg Altman in
Panic Room. Perhaps the most central of these meanings is evidenced
in the intersections between her star persona and roles in these films.
As a child star, Foster grew up portraying hardened young urbanites
(for instance, her character in *Taxi Driver*), all the while nurturing an

off-screen persona as a dedicated and diligent performer. By the time *Panic Room* was released she was also famously known as a hard-working mother.[21] Foster frequently plays tough female protagonists who rebel against established misogynistic practices and institutions. Meg Altman's resistance to the panic room's function as a security commodity is informed by Foster's previous performances as capable and quick-witted women who fight institutionalized violence and patriarchal structures. Bearing in mind Eisenstein's interpretation of the links between patriarchal politics, women's sexuality, and war, it is particularly significant that Foster plays Meg Altman in *Panic Room*. The film's critique of gender roles and global capitalism would not have been imbued with the same meanings had another actress played the role of Meg.[22]

News coverage of the release of Private Jessica Lynch's book, *I Am A Soldier, Too*, further confirms the current importance of resilient women in media narratives of courage. Significantly, media coverage of Private Lynch's rescue has been compared to the staging of a Hollywood production. Dr. Anmar Uday, a member of the medical team that cared for Lynch during her ordeal in Nassiriya, commented that her rescue was "like a Hollywood film." "They cried, 'Go, go, go,' with guns and blanks and the sound of explosions. They made a show—an action movie like Sylvester Stallone or Jackie Chan, with jumping and shouting, breaking down doors," alleges Anmar.[23] News reports frequently rely on the headline "Saving Private Lynch" to accompany coverage of the young woman's experiences in Iraq, which implies that her story has become a carefully constructed media narrative. This reference to a popular Hollywood product, *Saving Private Ryan* (Steven Spielberg, 1998), was also utilized as the title for a made-for-television movie (directed by Peter Markle), a narrative that is supposedly based on the "true story" of Lynch's rescue.[24] There have also been connections made in the media between Lynch's ordeal and another Hollywood action film, Jerry Bruckheimer's *Black Hawk Down* (2001).[25]

In a famous interview with Dianne Sawyer, Lynch herself suggests the gender politics at stake in media coverage of war stories. Lynch comments that she does not see herself as a "hero," and her feelings on her capture and rescue are evident in the following excerpt from the interview:

I'm ashamed. . . . But yet I was proud. I was proud to be there, I was proud to serve with every one of those in that vehicle. . . . Everyone in that vehicle was a fighter. I knew that they were there in my vehicle fighting for me, because I had no ammunition, I have a weapon that was jammed. . . . I don't look at myself as a hero. My heroes are . . . the soldiers that are over there, the soldiers that were in that car beside me, the ones that came and rescued me. I'm just a survivor.[26]

Here Lynch modestly insists that she is a "survivor" and that the "heroes" were those men who came to "rescue" her from behind enemy lines. Lynch further explains to Sawyer that she felt "afraid" to "let it all out," to show emotion while "captured" in an Iraqi hospital. "Because I was afraid, OK, if I do that, they're going to see that I'm so terrified of them that, you know, they're going to win," she tells Sawyer. Holding back her emotions, Lynch asserts, allowed her to survive.

Like Private Lynch, Meg Altman in *Panic Room* is not portrayed as a "hero" in the same sense that male protagonists might be depicted as in films such as *Black Hawk Down*. Just as Private Lynch has modestly presented herself as a "survivor" to the American public, Meg's emotional resilience and resourcefulness during her home invasion suggests that she too is a "survivor." Moreover, Meg's salvation in *Panic Room* necessitates the intervention of men in uniform. It is precisely this institutional involvement that denies Meg's agency in her own survival and that therefore lessens the threat that her capabilities pose to classic masculinity.

Speculation over whether or not Lynch was raped during her captivity also provides insight into the gendered representation of Meg Altman in *Panic Room*. As Eisenstien proposes, "September 11 must also be viewed in relation to the way that male patriarchal privilege orchestrates its hierarchical system of domination."[27] Lynch's reputed rape indicates the extent to which women's sexuality becomes the focal point of wartime propaganda. Popular narratives describing Lynch's time in captivity place her injuries within the context of sexual violence and therefore express the intersections between gender, sexuality, and race in media coverage of war. Though a very real "preexisting sexual hierarchical order" indeed permits rape to become a powerful weapon in warfare, Lynch's struggle against military doctors' insistence that her injuries were a result of a sexual assault suggests her desire to retain agency in her "survival." By asserting that Iraqi medics treated her with respect and care, and by denying any memory of the alleged rape, Lynch attempts to resume control over her own capture-narrative. Lynch's resistance to the popular sexualized characterization of her time spent in captivity is implied in her apparent discomfort at the media attention she has received.[28]

The racial aspect to the rape allegations that surfaced after Lynch's rescue is noteworthy and again might be compared to *Panic Room*'s representation of black and Hispanic characters. Hollywood studios have always relied upon the stereotyping of exotic "others" to rationalize America's imperialist politics. As Jack Shaheen establishes, Hollywood has fostered particular genres that are popular because they ease public anxieties over the treatment of various ethnically and racially marked "others."[29] The vilification of Native Americans in the classic Western, for instance, allowed white America to feel that its history of genocide and land-theft was justified because a "race" of "primitives" was gifted the benefits of "progress" through the realization of this "Manifest Destiny."[30] The representation of African American stereotypes such as the "black beast rapist," "the mammy," and "the happy sambo" during Hollywood's early years donated popular justifications for segregation and racist violence in America. In cinema today, the stereotyping of Arabs as terrorists and the parallel heroism of white American hypermasculinity contribute to an environment of fear. Furthermore, the threat the Arab poses in multitudes of Hollywood products is frequently a sexualized one, as Shaheen maintains. Where military doctors assert against Private Lynch's personal recollections that she was raped, they play into an extensive media history of damaging racist stereotypes.

While Lynch's capture narrative utilizes and feeds into negative stereotypes, the relationship between Meg and Burnham (Forest Whitaker), the black man who invades her home in *Panic Room*, helps to alleviate public concern about the implied homogeneity of America's "war against terrorism." Because Burnham is black, it is particularly significant that he is the only intruder who is sympathetic to Altman's plight. Burnham's decision to return to the house to assist the women in their struggle against his sadistic cohort Raoul (Dwight Yokam) mitigates any of the home invasion's racist implications. This uneasy relationship between a wealthy white woman and working-class black man in *Panic Room* asserts the homogenizing premise that America will only vanquish its invisible and incomprehensible enemies if the fight is a "united" one. This assertion must surely contribute to the elimination of communal anxieties about the underlying racism of the Bush administration's interference in Iraq.

While the character Meg Altman in *Panic Room* might be compared with constructions of femininity in the news media's coverage of Private Jessica Lynch's rescue, she is also preceded by a number of strong women in the horror and thriller genres. Feminists writing on horror films made during the seventies, eighties, and nineties point out that they not only reveal anxieties about social change, but also provide legitimate (albeit problematic) arenas for the expression of feminist principles.[31] As protagonists, women are not always victims in postmodern horror and thriller films; they can be "survivors" who resourcefully subdue (though admittedly rarely kill) monsters. *Panic Room* utilizes horror conventions to depict Meg Altman's attempts to overcome the men who invade her home, terrorize her family, and take her daughter hostage. Like Carol Clover's "final girls," who fight inventively in order to subdue the threat that faces their communities, Meg is smart and has foresight.[32] Meg is going back to school at Columbia and is the only client to notice the space that the home's hidden panic room takes up. She expresses concerns about the home's security systems during her first visit, when she calls the panic room a "safety hazard." Despite the vendor's allegation that it is perfectly reliable because it has motion detectors "like an elevator," Meg is proven to be correct to have expressed reservations about the panic room when one of the villains later has his hand caught in the heavy steel door. Just as female protagonists in slasher films have the unique ability to sense the violence to come in their communities, Meg has an uneasy sense of the troubles that this room will cause her.

Clover additionally suggests that horror films provide one of the few popular opportunities for women to express culturally taboo anger about violence. In this sense, *Panic Room* allows Meg and Sarah to articulate repressed rage. Sarah conveys that it is their anger that ensures their survival when she explains to the intruders that it is her father who is rich and that her mother is "just mad." Because Meg is at once a hero and a grieving single parent, audiences viewing *Panic Room* post-9/11 would perhaps have additionally read references to those widowed after the terrorist attacks. The film's opening scenes, where Meg and Sarah are shown around the Manhattan brownstone they will soon inhabit, confirm the possibility for these subtextual meanings. As Meg and Sarah express resentment over the unpleasantness of the divorce they have experienced, their mother-daughter relationship is placed at the film's center. Underneath her adolescent cynicism, Sarah reveals a fondness for her mother and during the home invasion their relationship is characterized by mutual maternal support. Both mother and daughter are struggling to come to terms with the divorce, and it is only once they have survived a home invasion through their combined resources that they are truly comfortable with their new life together and can stop grieving the past. The final scene in *Panic Room* cements this central theme. As Sarah and Meg lounge in Central Park on a bench bathed in sunlight, reading over advertisements for apartments, the film concludes with the suggestion that their mother–daughter bond has been strengthened by their experiences.[33]

Whereas Meg Altman is portrayed as a capable parent who gains the respect of her daughter, her ex-husband, Stephen Altman (Patrick Bauchau), is an impotent patriarch without the capacity to protect his family and defend their home. This is an interesting narrative component of the film, given that America's patriarchal government also failed to protect the "home front" in September 2001. As the burglars hatch their plan to break into the brownstone, they agree to do so because there is no father present to "protect" the occupants sleeping upstairs. Yet it is Meg and Sarah who efficiently defend the home against the invasion, despite the failure of security systems. Though one of the intruders suggests that because "she's a woman" Meg needs "security," she demonstrates that such stereotypes about what women "need" are unconvincing when she steadfastly refuses the men's reassurances that she is safe to leave the panic room. Instead of passively succumbing to the burglars' false encouragements, Meg eventually escapes the panic room and fights them resourcefully. When she does so, she finds her ex-husband tied to a chair, incapacitated: his attempt to save his daughter has been wholly unsuccessful. While Stephen begs Meg to "just do what they ask," and to avoid doing "anything stupid," she perceptively explains that active defiance is their best survival technique.

Stephen further endangers his family by calling the police, who arrive and unsettle the burglars upstairs. It is Meg who must act quickly in order to get the police to leave so that the intruders will not harm Sarah. Though the New York police are smart enough to see through Meg's bluff and later return with a swat team, institutional support only arrives once the intruders have already been subdued by the mother and daughter team. Meg overcomes the intruders through a series of acts of self-defense: she tapes up Stephen's broken arm so that he can hold a gun, smashes the surveillance cameras and leaves broken glass in all routes of escape. Because Stephen misses on every attempt to shoot the intruders, Meg must herself protect Sarah, who also resists creatively when she stabs an intruder with an insulin needle. By fighting in their own defense and by comforting Stephen, Sarah and Meg take on both patriarchal and matriarchal roles in the protection of their family and home.

Where Meg and Sarah convincingly defend their home in *Panic Room*, surveillance and security commodities fail and are instead used by the intruders to intimidate the family. The public equivalent of this surveillance failure can be seen in the post-9/11 use of "protective" surveillance in public spaces, where cameras are often used to intimidate and suppress members of America's population. Horror and thriller films typically represent technologies failing protagonists and placing characters in danger.[34] In *Panic Room*, the commodities of security—guns, surveillance cameras, and the panic room itself—are turned against protagonists and are used by antagonists to generate terror. When they find themselves shut away in the panic room during the first moments of the home invasion, Meg and Sarah discover that the room has a separate phone line from the rest of the house, which Meg has not yet hooked up. From this point on, *Panic Room* suggests that the security the room offers is untenable. Though Meg successfully retrieves her cell phone to call the police, it will not work because of the room's impenetrable steel-cased exterior. Once they manage to hook the cell phone up to a phone-jack they are put on hold by "9-1-1." As Meg's friend Lydia (Ann Magnuson) explains, the panic room's chief function is to provide "security" where the state-run enterprises may no longer be capable. However, it is contended in *Panic Room* that security commodities are as ineffectual in their protective capacities as social institutions.

Meg and Sarah's entrapment is further problematized by the fact that the intruders know the security systems better than they do. The burglars demonstrate that they have ways of terrorizing the home's inhabitants while they are shut in the room and easily use security technologies to their own advantage. Though Meg initially retaliates inventively against the intruders, their safety is increasingly endangered because Sarah is diabetic. The panic room's intended function is reversed when Sarah is locked into the room with the men after her mother escapes to retrieve the insulin supplies they need to survive. Instead of providing the homeowners' security, the room provides the intruders with a space to take hostages. While Meg does discover the intruders' presence by using one of the surveillance cameras, she eventually decides her home's defense systems have been manipulated more to the benefit of the men who are invading her home. By smashing the cameras Meg enacts a final rebellion against her home's security commodities.

New York and the Globalization of Panic

A worldview predicated on various cataclysms—terrorism, nuclear holocaust, killer bees, SARS—encourages panic to become part of the ordinary citizen's reservoir of emotion. . . . One cannot underestimate the power of military ideology to redefine a citizenry. To see the world as a never-ending series of conflicts with other nations and peoples is very narrow-minded—but it's how we teach American history, and how the current government defines the agenda for American foreign policy. It also defines how we view the future of security in general. As we develop greater means by which to treat illnesses and vanquish terrorists, the future should seem brighter— but it can't seem too bright.

—Kevin Carollo, "The New World Disorder."[35]

The women's terrorization in *Panic Room* takes place in a dystopian urban setting that is not fictitious like the worlds of *Se7en* and *Fight Club*. Meg and Sarah's vulnerable domestic environment appears all the more convincing because the home invasion takes place in Manhattan. The city's lonely atmosphere and its generally unconcerned inhabitants are key to the film's ambience and narrative. During Meg's first hours in her new home, *Panic Room* cuts between rainy shots of the brownstone's inner-city exterior and Meg's internal despair as she takes a bath. Just as the gloomy metropolis in *Se7en* is a manifestation of Somerset's inner turmoil, New York's dismal atmosphere serves to accentuate Meg's depression. Once Sarah and Meg are taken hostage in their home, the city's anonymous residents play a significant part in their entrapment. Sarah and Meg initially believe that they might solicit help by calling to their neighbors through a ventilation pipe on the floor of the panic room. However, as this is New York, the street noise and rain muffle their cries for help. Later, when Sarah ingeniously uses this

same pipe to flash SOS calls out to a man in the opposite apartment, her attempt also proves unsuccessful when he simply wakes
and pulls his blinds in annoyance. It is only once the city's police
force is proven vigilant that the film's setting appears less foreboding.
It is probable that *Panic Room*, like *Spiderman* (Sam Raimi, 2002),
was altered post-production in order to capitalize on America's
rekindled interest in "New York's finest."

Spiderman had scenes added post-9/11 that depict New York
citizens banding together to help its hero fight an evil antagonist,
and like *Panic Room* its Manhattan setting accentuated the readings availing to audiences viewing the film in May 2002. Because
Spiderman was penned before the events of 9/11 and by David
Koepp (who also wrote the screenplay for *Panic Room*), it seems
likely that Hollywood studios were keen to tap into the obsessions
with security that were characterizing American society long before
the terrorist attacks of 2001—as Barry Glassner suggests. Like *Panic
Room, Spiderman* capitalizes on the post-9/11 cultural dynamic
that encouraged consumers of Hollywood products to identify with
"heroes." Nickelback's rock-anthem "Hero," which was part of
Spiderman's extensive promotional campaign, indicates to what
extent the film positions its viewers as participants in protagonist
Peter Parker's fight against "evil." The film's widely publicized
tagline, "With great power comes great responsibility," adds further meaning to Peter Parker's heroism. This line is of course easily
read as a reference to America's "duty" to wage an imperialistic
"war against terrorism." The film's mise-en-scène accentuates the
nationalistic implications of Parker's struggle to do "good" by extensively relying on the colors red, white, and blue, which are echoed in
the design of Spiderman's costuming. Just as *Spiderman* invites
spectators to accompany Parker on his vigilante adventures in the
streets of New York, *Panic Room* encourages viewers to identify
with Meg Altman's grief, rage, and determination throughout her
Manhattan home's invasion. The meanings associated with 9/11
therefore add a depth to *Spiderman* and *Panic Room* that allowed
both films to become "blockbusters" by any measure.[36]

Panic Room, then, operates as a primary site for Hollywood's
exploitation of America's social and political climate post-9/11.
A monolithic national identity is conveyed when the Altmans survive their home invasion through active defiance and with help
from New York's "protective" institutions. This ultimately ensured

the film's commercial success, perhaps beyond the bounds that its producer, director, and screenwriter would have envisioned before the events of 9/11 took place. In "L'Sprit du Terrorisme" Jean Baudrillard revealingly describes 9/11 as a "Manhattan disaster film," which "consummately combines the two elements of mass fascination in the twentieth century: the white magic of cinema and the black magic of terrorism."[37] Baudrillard argues that the parallels between filmic violence and real-life terrorist acts are endless in this manner.

> [The] two towers of the World Trade Center were, precisely because of their identicality, the perfect incarnation of [global power]. . . . Countless disaster films have borne witness to these fantasies, and the universal appeal of the images shows just how close the fantasies always are to being acted out: the closer the system gets to perfection or to omnipotence, the stronger the urge to destroy it grows. . . . There is no longer a boundary that can hem terrorism in; it is at the heart of the very culture it's fighting with.[38]

The similarities between terrorism and the social anxieties that horror and thriller films capitalize on are endless: horror and thriller films depict the destruction of domestic security, and terrorism involves the effects of the eradication of national defense; horror and thriller films depict the transgression of boundaries, and terrorism, according to Baudrillard, endeavors to rupture social, political, and economic boundaries.

In "L'Sprit du Terrorisme" Baudrillard also quotes the diary of Columbine "terrorist" Eric Harris. Harris's fantasies suggest further connections between the American "dream" and the acts of terrorism that are supposedly nurtured in the "third world": "If by some weird as shit luck me and V survive and escape we will move to some island somewhere or maybe Mexico, New Zealand, or some exotic place where Americans can't get us. If there isn't such a place, then we will highjack a hell of a lot of bombs and crash a plane into NYC with us inside firing away as we go down. Just something to cause devastation."[39]

This excerpt from Harris's journal implies the potency of devastation in the minds of those compelled to terrorize and expresses how economic centers like New York function in the terrorist imagination. Harris's comments also echo protagonists' homosocial fascination with destruction in *Fight Club*. *Panic Room* turns this anarchic fascination with the destruction of an embodiment of the corrupt wealth of the metropolis, the skyscraper, inwards toward an enclosed and claustrophobic domestic environment.

Harris's comments additionally establish how remote countries like New Zealand function in terrorist philosophies. New Zealand provides economic respite for the Hollywood industry by supplying a cut-price catalog of exotic locations. This suggests a symbolic connection between New York's role as a center for consumer culture and the role of isolated locales as equally commodified landscapes. And just as the film industry affixes a value to "third world" locations, America sells a monolithic interpretation of international politics to these nations. Jennie Bristow's "First Anniversary" examines this globalization of the media's "culture of fear": "It is clearer than ever that the terrorist attacks on New York and Washington did not fundamentally change the world. Rather, they provided a catalyst for a host of pre-existing political and cultural trends to become rapidly, and firmly, entrenched. The dominant response to 11 September in the USA and Europe was the globalization of the culture of fear."[40] The news media's coverage of Private Jessica Lynch's story and *Panic Room*'s portrayal of a Manhattan home invasion both factor in this globalization of America's "culture of fear."

While it does critique the legitimacy of domestic security commodities, in its eventual reliance on the faultless performance of New York's police force *Panic Room* ultimately validates the conservative premise that America may indeed be justified in its "war against terrorism." *Panic Room* at once exhibits traces of Fincher's penchant for social satire and the retrograde political atmosphere that permitted America's disregard for the laws of international governing organizations in the invasion of Iraq. Meg Altman's story of victimization and "bravery" in *Panic Room* contributes to America's "culture of fear" in the same way that media coverage of Private Jessica Lynch's story reaffirms the masculinity of her rescuers and the sexual threat that her captors supposedly presented. However, as the uncomfortable portrayal of excessive heroism in contemporary media products suggests, the heterogeneity of the American public presents an inherent challenge to the homogenizing discourses of the Bush administration's war propaganda.

Notes

1. Jonathan Sterne and Zack Furness, "Panic: State of Mind or Mind of State?" *Bad Subjects*, 64 (2003), www.eserver.org/bs/64/editors.html.
2. Barry Glassner, *The Culture of Fear: Why Americans Are Afraid of the Wrong Things* (New York, NY: Basic Books, 1999), 54.
3. Glassner, *The Culture of Fear*, and Frank Ferudi, *Culture of Fear: Risk-Taking and the Morality of Low Expectation* (London and New York: Continuum, 2002).
4. Two early articles useful for the purposes of examining the intersections between analyzing films as commodities and art are Judith Hess Wright's "Genre Films and the Status Quo" (1974) and Robin Wood's "Ideology, Genre, Auteur" (1977), in *Film Genre Reader II*, ed. Barry Keith Grant (Austin: Texas University Press, 1995).
5. Carol Clover, *Men, Women and Chain Saws: Gender in the Modern Horror Film* (Princeton, N.J.: Princeton University Press, 1992), and Tony Williams, *Hearths of Darkness: The Family in the American Horror Film* (Madison, N.J.: Fairleigh Dickenson University Press, 1996). Other prominent works in this area include Johnathan Lake Crane, *Terror and Everyday Life: Singular Moments in the History of Horror Film Viewing* (Thousand Oaks, Calif.: Sage Publications, 1994); Rhona H. Berenstein, *Attack of the Leading Ladies: Gender, Sexuality, and Spectatorship in Classic Horror Cinema* (New York: Columbia University Press, 1996); Isabela Christina Pinedo, *Recreational Terror: Women and the Pleasures of Horror Film Viewing* (Albany: State University of New York Press, 1997); and Kimberley Roberts, "The Pleasures and Problems of the Angry Girl," in *Sugar, Spice and Everything Nice: Cinemas of Girlhood*, ed. Francis Gatewood and Murray Pomerance (Detroit: Wayne State University Press, 2001), 215–227.
6. Two of *Panic Room*'s promotional taglines clearly capitalize on fears surrounding domestic security: "It was supposed to be the safest room in the house" and "What do you do when your hiding place is their destination?" These taglines, used to sum up the film's audience appeal, reveal much about *Panic Room*'s reliance on communal concerns about the permeability of domestic environments.
7. Preoccupied with social, political, and economic anxieties, the horror and thriller genres were beginning to express these kinds of fears long before the nineties. For example, *The Texas Chainsaw Massacre* (Tobe Hooper, 1974) is for Tony Williams (*Hearths of Darkness*, 1996) a survey of the trauma the Vietnam War caused within American families and communities, and, according to Douglas Kellner (*Media Culture*, 1995), *Poltergeist* (Tobe Hooper, 1980), which was produced during the Reagan era, expresses fears having to do with downward social mobility and losing one's home.
8. Joe Lockard, "Social Fear and the Commodification of Terrorism," *Bad Subjects*, 59 (2002), www.eserver.org/bs/59/lockard.html, 27.
9. Ibid., 30.
10. Ferudi, *Culture of Fear*, 38.
11. Glassner, *The Culture of Fear*, 53.

12. Glassner, *The Culture of Fear*, 53.
13. Another widely circulated trailer for *Panic Room* simply features climactic images from the film played alongside quotes from its screenplay, eventually concluding with Meg's fearful realization, "they're locking us in."
14. Edward Buscombe, "The Idea of Genre in the American Cinema," in *Film Genre Reader II*, ed. Grant, 11–25.
15. A similar kind of fascination with the large and corrupt city as a breeding ground for terrorists is mirrored in crime-investigation television. *CSI, CSI Miami, Law and Order: Criminal Intent, Law and Order: SVU*, and *Without a Trace* testify to the popular belief that large cities like Miami, New York, and Las Vegas reproduce virtually untraceable criminals. Since the events of 9/11 most of these shows have depicted terrorist crimes.
16. Philip Simpson, *Psycho Paths: Tracking the Serial Killer Through Contemporary Film and Fiction* (Carbondale: Southern Illinois University Press, 2000).
17. When it is revealed that Durden is one of the narrator's own "personalities," this jealousy is conveniently displaced as narcissistic rather than homoerotic.
18. Kevin Carollo, "The New World Disorder," *Bad Subjects*, 64 (2003), www.eserver.org/bs/64/carollo.html.
19. Zillah Eisenstein, "Feminisms in the Aftermath of September 11," *Social Text* 20, no. 3 (2003): 81.
20. Richard Dyer's *Stars* (London: BFI Publishing, 1979) analyzes stars' significance as polysemic components of Hollywood's industrial system of production.
21. Foster is also a rumored lesbian and her sexual ambiguity perhaps adds to the characterization of Meg Altman's resourceful self-sufficiency. Meg's daughter Sarah is similarly represented as androgynous and tough. Carol Clover has argued that the slasher genre's androgynous "final girls" are depicted as more capable than their excessively feminized peers (*Men, Women and Chain Saws*, 1992).
22. Foster replaced Nicole Kidman, who was recovering from a knee injury.
23. Quoted in John Kampfner, "The Truth About Jessica," *The Guardian*, May 15, 2003, www.guardian.co.uk/Iraq/Story/0,2763,956255,00.html.
24. In *Saving Private Ryan* American soldiers rescue a comrade from behind enemy lines during World War II.
25. In "The Truth About Jessica" (*The Guardian*, May 15, 2003) John Kampfner alleges that Jerry Bruckheimer had in fact visited the Pentagon in order to pitch a prime-time reality show in the vein of *Cops* that would follow U.S. forces in Afganistan. Coverage of Private Lynch's rescue, Kampfner argues, was staged in a manner "influenced by Hollywood producers of reality TV and action movies, notably *Black Hawk Down.*"
26. Quoted in Rick Hampson, "Lynch Book Tells of Rape by Captors," *USA Today*, November 6, 2003, www.usatoday.com/news/nation/2003-11-06-lynch_x.htm.
27. Eisenstein, "Feminisms in the Aftermath of September 11," *Social Text*: 81.
28. Discussing the ambush that caused her injuries with Dianne Sawyer, Lynch says that, "It hurt in a way that people would make up stories that they had no truth about. Only I would have been able to know that, because the other four people in my vehicle aren't here to tell that story." Reflecting on her time spent in the Iraqi hospital, Lynch tells Sawyer, "From the time I woke up in that hospital, no one beat me, no one slapped me, no one, nothing. I mean, I actually had one nurse, that she would sing to me. . . . I'm so thankful that they helped me in

any way that they could. I'm so thankful for those people, because that's why I'm alive today." Most famously, Lynch comments on her portrayal in the media as follows: "It does hurt that they used me to symbolize all this stuff. Yeah, it's wrong. I don't know why they filmed it, or why they say the things they, you know. All I know is that I was in that hospital hurting. I needed help. I wanted out of there. It didn't matter to me if they came in shirts and blank guns, it wouldn't have mattered to me" (quoted in Kampfer, "The Truth About Jessica").

29. Jack Shaheen, *Reel Bad Arabs: How Hollywood Vilifies a People* (New York: Olive Branch Press, 2001).

30. Interestingly, media coverage of Lynch's capture has been compared to early-American captivity narratives. Just as Lynch's ordeal has been used by the Bush administration to justify imperialist policies and to racialize the threat Iraq supposedly presents to the West, popular captivity narratives, such as Mary Rowlandson's (1682) and Hannah Bradley's (1707) helped to rationalize America's Westward expansion and the consequent confinement of thousands of Native Americans in reservations.

31. Clover, *Men, Women and Chainsaws*; Berenstein, *Attack of the Leading Ladies*; Pinedo, *Recreational Terror*; and Patricia Brett Erens, "The Stepfather: Father as Monster in the Contemporary Horror Film," in *The Dread of Difference: Gender and the Horror Film*, ed. Barry Keith Grant (Austin: Texas University Press, 1996), 352–363.

32. Two frequently analyzed examples of "final girls" are Laurie in *Halloween* (John Carpenter, 1978) and Nancy in *Nightmare on Elm Street* (Wes Craven, 1984).

33. Erens (*"The Stepfather*: Father as Monster in the Contemporary Horror Film," 1996) proposes a similar reading of *The Stepfather* (Joseph Ruben, 1987).

34. In *Poltergeist*, for instance, technological commodities, particularly televisions, become possessed and work according to their own rules.

35. Kevin Carollo, "The New World Disorder," *Bad Subjects*, 64 (2003), www.eserver.org/bs/64/carollo.html.

36. Sony Pictures' web site boasts that "*Spiderman* grossed more than $820 million worldwide and became the fifth highest grossing movie in U.S. history." *Panic Room* also did exceedingly well at the box office, setting an Easter weekend record take of $30.1 million.

37. Jean Baudrillard, "L'Epsrit Du Terrorisme," *Harpers* (February 2002): 419.

38. Ibid., 415.

39. Ibid.

40. Jennie Bristow, "First Anniversary," *Spiked*, September 2002, www.spikedonline.com/Articles/00000006DA29.htm, 136.

Chapter 12
Cynical Nationalism

Thomas Foster

My argument in this chapter is that since the 9/11 attacks there has been a marked shift in the structure of nationalist rhetoric in the United States. That rhetoric no longer seems to need to naturalize itself, as ideological discourses have traditionally been understood to do. But this dispensing with ideological forms of legitimation and mystification has not rendered nationalist arguments more vulnerable to critique and intervention; quite the opposite, in fact. The forms of nationalist rhetoric that have dominated the U.S. public sphere since 9/11 actually seem to preempt traditional forms of left ideology critique, to anticipate, incorporate, and make them irrelevant in advance. This shift in the way nationalism works needs to be understood in terms of the increasing dominance of cynical reason, a term Slavoj Žižek takes from Peter Sloterdijk, precisely in order to redefine the conventions of ideology critique.[1] Lawrence Grossberg's work on the cultural effects of Reagan's anticommunist rhetoric and the forms of media manipulation that emerged during the first Persian Gulf War helps define the historical context for this turn toward cynical forms of nationalism,[2] but in addition I argue that the increasing separation of the national public sphere from the state apparatus, typical of the transformation of the nation-state under the conditions of global capitalism, defines the precondition for cynical reassertions of familiar nationalist rhetoric. My main point, however, is the connection between this historical and epistemological shift in the nature of nationalism and popular responses to 9/11, specifically within the comic book industry and with a particular focus on the Marvel Comics character Captain America.

I believe it's important to try to explain what's new about the post-9/11 resurgence of nationalist and militarist rhetoric, marked as it is by a seemingly familiar insistence on thinking in terms of "us" and "them" and demonizing the enemy as "evil." This last tactic seems to be just the latest version of the historical amnesia that Americanist critics like Michael Rogin have shown to be typical of U.S. imperialism generally, throughout our history.[3] For instance, what struck me about New York mayor Rudolph Giuliani's speech to the U.N. immediately following the attack on the World Trade Center was his insistence that any attempt to contextualize or to explain why the attacks happened had to be understood as mitigating their evil and as an insult to the survivors and their families. President Bush repeated this idea in a speech at the Pentagon on the first anniversary of the attacks, when he declared that "the murder of innocents cannot be explained, only endured." But what I'm interested in here is the paradox involved in the insistence by Giuliani, Bush, and many others that it's necessary to argue for and struggle to secure this act of forgetting—in other words, this is a form of amnesia that is either unable or doesn't need to mystify its own operations, a forgetting Americans don't have to forget but instead can revel in. This dehistoricizing operation openly works to produce the attacks as a traumatic experience that cannot be embedded in any historical narrative of the past, but only as the commencement of a supposedly "new" struggle ("let's roll"). As such, the 9/11 attacks are explicitly represented as unrepresentable and therefore as eliciting only "proper" nationalist sentiment rather than historical knowledge. The incoherence of such claims is in fact the source of their power.

Understood in this way, post-9/11 nationalist discourses and policies pose a basic challenge to the left intellectual tradition of ideology critique itself. The exercise of power no longer seems to need to be justified through the operation of naturalizing and eternalizing the status quo. To cite Rogin again, the real war is still replaced with an imaginary one,[4] but that process of replacement itself is on display in new ways, in direct contradiction of one of the central assumptions of ideology critique—that is, that laying bare the device and exposing operations of mystification are in themselves resistant and adversarial acts of critical reason. In an extension of a process that had certainly already begun with the first Bush president's first Gulf War, we "know" (if knowledge is really the right referent anymore) that this is an imaginary war; we know, for instance, that the U.S. military exercises direct control over the information presented to the U.S. public. The use of "embedded journalists" during the invasion of Iraq precisely exemplifies this shift, to the extent that it created a loss of critical distance and a strategy for generating greater sympathy for war policy by putting journalists in a position to identify more fully with the soldiers fighting the war. At the same time that this breakdown of distinctions between the army fighting the war and the news media representing it enabled greater control over what journalists saw and reported, it also allowed the military and the U.S. government to claim that they were permitting a greater degree of transparency and disclosure. This technique plays on the ambiguity about exactly what these journalists became embedded in, the war or the military arm of the state apparatus.

I want to emphasize here the difficulty this kind of shift creates for the development of an effective left critique of the contemporary form of U.S. nationalism. When Giuliani insisted on the negative effects of *not* demonizing and dehumanizing our national enemies, of *not* refusing to contextualize their actions historically in ways that reveal the implication of past U.S. foreign policy in the development of the terrorism that now seems to confront us from the outside, he was directly responding to Susan Sontag's spectacularly failed attempt to reassert a critical perspective for left intellectuals by reiterating the history of both popular and intellectual critiques of U.S. nationalism, in her brief contribution to the *New Yorker*'s "Talk of the Town" page, on September 24, 2001. Like Sean Penn's open letter to President Bush, published in the October 19, 2002, *The New York Times*, a letter that explicitly takes the president to task for abandoning "all previous lessons of history in favor of following you blindly into the future," Sontag's call for "a few shreds of historical awareness" assumed that the appropriate response to this kind of shortsighted militarism is to demystify its rhetoric, to reveal how it distorts, oversimplifies, and dehistoricizes. But asking why everyone seems to have forgotten that this rhetoric is familiar and has already been critiqued, as Sontag implicitly did, fails to recognize the way in which post-9/11 nationalism presents itself as already demystified and exposes its own ideological mechanisms in advance in order to demand a right to them, thereby preempting the role usually reserved for critical reason.

The contemporary form that nationalist rhetorics and policies take, then, might best be understood as the triumph of cynical reason, to use Sloterdijk's term, more recently elaborated by Slavoj Žižek (most notably in the *Sublime Object of Ideology*), under the formula " 'they know very well what they are doing, but still, they are doing it' "; Sloterdijk calls this condition "enlightened false consciousness," a form of false consciousness or bad faith that knows itself as such, and is therefore "reflexively buffered" in advance against critique of this ideological state of being.[5] In this model of how power works, self-interestedness is acknowledged rather than masked under claims to universality (as in the Bush doctrine, that the United States as sole remaining global superpower has the right to preemptively wage war to protect U.S. interests). At the same time, reasons are found to maintain the mask of universality or national consensus, but explicitly as a mask, an empty form, a rhetorical gesture.[6] This kind of nationalism is like prayer; it's enough to go through the external motions of bowing your head and saying the words, whether you believe or not. The emergence of cynical reason then marks the extent to which the denaturalization and demystification of ideological forms has itself become normative; the key point here is that, in contrast to the assumptions of traditional theories of ideology critique, cynical reason detaches the natural from the normative, so that denaturalization proves not to be incompatible with the reproduction of norms, and therefore the perpetuation of power inequities and social hierarchies.[7] In the cynical denaturalization of nationalism after 9/11, for instance, no one has to believe for this rhetoric to work, including George W. Bush himself. In fact, lies or at least the reiteration of inaccurate information can actually work better, even when they are revealed, since such revelations only encourage further disengagement from the political process in general, thereby giving the state free rein to act. In my view, this is why Sontag or Penn's interventions failed to produce their desired effects, not (or not just) because they were out of touch with popular sentiment or rhetorically clumsy. Bush's notoriously limited affective repertoire in his media performances as a public figure, typically a combination of blank stares and smirks, might be understood as expressing an aggressive and knowing cluelessness (not unlike David Letterman's televisual persona), and this combination, far from undermining his authority, actually makes him a perfect vehicle for the cynical reformulation of nationalist clichés (just as Keanu Reeves's notorious woodenness and affectlessness made him a perfect actor to play Neo in *The Matrix*, a character who is actually only a virtual persona or avatar in most of the film).

I'm suggesting, for instance, that Bush's early declaration that the U.S. would get bin Laden dead or alive was less a slip of the tongue that revealed his ideological fantasies and therefore left him vulnerable to critique, than an effective *preemption* of any critique of how his foreign policy and his ideas about how to fight a war on terrorism might be informed by clichés from Western movies. This gesture makes visible the process of insistent representation that, in the past, normalized abuses of power to the point of invisibility. To exemplify that process of normalization, Rogin cites the example of Ronald Reagan and his use of the Clint Eastwood catchphrase "make my day."[8] But, as a rhetorical strategy, Reagan's quotation of popular narratives gained its power by tapping into the fantasies (of male power) that made the original quotation emotionally compelling to many Americans; in other words, Reagan tried to mobilize belief in the fantasy, a process that would presumably be interrupted if the fantasy became visible as such, rather than being accepted as the truth of the situation. In contrast, Bush's quotation of media clichés seems to gain its power from acknowledging the oversimplification involved but asserting that such oversimplification is justified in order to mobilize action against an immediate threat, rather than to mobilize belief. Bush's quotation retains the quotation marks and acknowledges the clichéd nature of his own rhetoric, so that the critical gesture Rogin performs in relation to Reagan is effectively anticipated.

I find it useful to turn to examples from popular culture in order to get a handle on the problem posed to left critiques by the reemergence of debunked nationalist myths and clichés after 9/11, as more or less recognizably empty or inauthentic forms that are nevertheless presented as necessary and unavoidable, even moving in their very emptiness. One result of such techniques of cynical reason is in fact a weakening of the distinction between culture and politics, as Grossberg suggests in his analysis of how media practices during the first Persian Gulf War tended to produce the "disappearance of politics" and "its encapsulation in everyday life," in the form of lifestyle choices or what Grossberg calls "the disciplined mobilization of everyday life."[9] In the more recent context, we could consider the premature declaration of the death of irony in the aftermath of the attacks as exemplifying these same shifts. Žižek points out that cynical reason should not be confused with popular practices of irony and sarcasm, forms of cynicism that at least remain more politically ambivalent than official forms of cynical reason, since these popular practices indicate dissatisfaction with official discourses even as they encourage forms of quietism and political passivity that can be exploited by those in power;[10] in effect, cynical reason tries to institutionalize that passivity and purge or minimize the critical impulse that generates it. In this light, the immediate post-9/11 calls for a new cultural seriousness that presented themselves as repudiations of popular cynicism can actually be understood as affirmations of it, in a transformed mode.

I would argue, for instance, that David Letterman's seeming transformation from deliberate superficiality and sarcasm to heart-felt sincerity immediately after the attacks should not be interpreted as a welcome return to serious cultural concerns. Instead, this shift is a symptom of the recontainment of popular cynicism and distrust of official culture by a form of cynical reason that has learned to take that distrust into account in advance, to build its strategies on the idea that everyone knows we are being lied to, and tries to convince us that we have no other choice but to affirm the lies anyway. Letterman's sincerity might be understood as a transformation of popular cynicism into an official version rather than a rejection of irony or cynicism in general, or, more accurately, as an indication that Letterman's brand of pop culture cynicism was already a repackaging of popular resistance. The result is to reveal that whatever "cynical distance" a figure like Letterman might have seemed to possess was merely a way of blinding ourselves "to the structuring power of ideological fantasy"—the ways in which "even if we do not take things seriously . . . we are still doing them."[11] Similarly, Mike Davis has pointed to the ironies involved in the way that "professional ironists like Christopher Hitchens [now] police the sacred 'no irony' zone that surround the ruins of the World Trade Center."[12]

The cynicism implicit in this seeming refusal of cynicism and irony is explicitly thematized in a cartoon about Godman, a recurring character usually satirizing superhero comics, in Ruben Bolling's syndicated feature "Tom the Dancing Bug," which appears weekly in the *Village Voice* and online on the Salon site. Demonstrating the possibility of popular self-consciousness about the shift to cynical reason, this cartoon appeared shortly after the 9/11 attacks. (Bolling is the pseudonym for a lawyer and banker named Ken Fisher, whose office was located adjacent to the World Trade Center.[13]) After a panel in which Godman flies off to Afghanistan, the rest of the strip consists of images of his beating bin Laden and various other Arab men who attempt to engage him in a dialogue that he refuses, until one of them asks why "no philosophical banter?," since he's previously been "a character the author uses to make satirical comments on religion and culture." At this point, Godman becomes willing to explain that he's now just "a vehicle for [the author's] wholly un-ironic fantasies of violence and rage," an occasion for the author "to draw someone punching people." Godman ends by wondering "if this helps," and the author intrudes in a caption to reply "not really," even as Godman continues to punch people. This cartoon, I would argue, succinctly captures the impulse to cynically demonize (in this case) Arab others, despite or perhaps because we know this impulse relies on the stereotypes that are typical within orientalist techniques for reducing complex historical relationships to conflicts between good and evil, us and them. While the cartoon's final comment suggests a skeptical attitude of critical distance from the cultural and political situation it represents, the cartoon also seems to dramatize the question of whether knowing what we are doing makes any difference—that is, whether reason has any critical purchase on this situation and whether critical distance doesn't simply reimplicate us in actions we might be skeptical about. This cartoon then thematizes the disjunction, the newly uncertain relation between knowing and doing that Žižek associates with cynical reason.

Instead of lingering over a possible critique of Letterman, I want to pursue the direction suggested by the example of the Godman cartoon and turn to a site of cultural responses to the World Trade Center attacks that has received much less media attention than Letterman, but that both illustrates the dominance cynical reason has gained in our national life and suggests possibilities for resistance by turning the techniques of cynical reason against themselves. One of the first popular texts to memorialize the events of 9/11 was a comic book called *Heroes* published in October 2001 by the Marvel company; the subtitle was *The World's Greatest Superhero Creators Honor the World's Greatest Heroes*—the rescue workers, police, and firemen.[14] Within a year, *Heroes* had gone through three printings and sold over 225,000 copies, making over $700,000 for Marvel's Twin Towers Fund, according to Marvel sources.[15] In the immediate aftermath of the Pentagon and World Trade Center attacks, many of the world's greatest superhero creators found the figure of Captain America irresistible.

Now, for some time, Captain America has seemed a bit out of place in the pantheon of Marvel Comics characters, since the company's reputation was based on its ability to make the superhero genre more realistic and relevant to the youth culture of the 1960s, generally inclined toward an antiwar politics by the end of the

Figure 12.1. CAPTAIN AMERICA TM4 © 2004 Marvel Characters, Inc. Used with permission.

Vietnam period, or at least toward an attitude of distrust for institutional authority and its privileged agents. The revisionist tendency in superhero comics has become much more pronounced in the last two decades, with the emergence (in the mid-1980s) of grim and gritty, film noir–influenced antiheroes like Frank Miller's "dark knight" version of Batman or Alan Moore's *Watchmen*. Captain America has always seemed difficult, if not impossible to revise in this way, despite such efforts as his being teamed with a black superhero, the Falcon, for a while in the 1970s. As one comics writer pointed out, "Cap has to be about America" in a way that Spider-Man, say, doesn't have to be "about spiders."[16] In other words, Captain America's status as a kind of national allegory has made it difficult to characterize him in terms of the skepticism and popular cynicism that is the hallmark of these darker antiheroes. But it is precisely this immediate symbolic burden, this allegorical flatness and lack of psychological depth, and this lack of distance between character and nation, that make Captain America a perfect 9/11 icon for a culture dominated by cynical reason. In turn, the events of 9/11 charge Captain America with the affect and the vulnerability he previously lacked—more accurately, the narrowly patriotic sentiments that constituted practically his entire affective repertoire and, which seemed hopelessly hokey after the 60s, now seem poignant without necessarily seeming any less clichéd or anachronistic (Captain America was of course a WWII hero originally). 9/11 allows a revivification of nationalist sentiment, but in a new, more self-conscious register, which Fred Moten has coined the phrase "the new international of decent feelings" to describe.[17]

One convention of this book is to bring the superheroes down to the same level as the rescue workers, as in an image by Joe Kubert that depicts Captain America's famous shield abandoned against a wall plastered with photos as a memorial to the victims, along with a fireman's ax.[18] Another set of images excludes superheroes entirely, replacing them with rescue workers, while others juxtapose the two in order to acknowledge the rescuers as the greater heroes, as in an image of children replacing posters of Spider-Man and Cap with those of firemen and police.[19]

The book also contains revisionist superhero creator Frank Miller's take on the post-9/11 Captain America, emphasizing his embattlement. This image gains greater depth and ambiguity if we read it as a visual allusion to Al Capp's Fearless Fosdick character from the Lil' Abner comic strip; Fosdick is often depicted as being shot full of holes, like Cap's shield in the Miller image, and Fosdick was Al Capp's satire on Dick Tracy and the image of the incor-ruptible policeman (see figure 12.2). While the Miller image in itself fits into the general representation of Captain America in the *Heroes* book, where

Figure 12.2. CAPTAIN AMERICA TM & © 2004 Marvel Characters, Inc. Used with permission.

he gains iconic power through his newfound bodily and emotional vulnerability, this visual allusion also suggests some continuing skepticism about the very authority figures celebrated as heroes throughout this comic tribute. The skepticism emerges more explicitly in Miller's contribution to a later 9/11 comic anthology. Over the black-and-white icons of a star and a cross, Miller's captions read "I'm sick of flags. I'm sick of God," ending with the words "I've seen the power of faith" printed over an image of the fallen towers. This comic appeared in *9–11: Artists Respond*, a tribute book published later than *Heroes*, in 2002, and containing short narratives by creators from the Dark Horse, Image, and Chaos comics companies. Miller's hardline rejection of faith, whether in religion or nation, our flag or theirs, stands in sharp contrast to an image from the *Heroes* book that features an image of the African character Storm from the X-Men (see figure 12.3), and includes a caption quoting Emerson: "heroism feels and never reasons and is therefore always right," an apt slogan for the era of cynical nationalism. Miller's emphasis on Captain America's vulnerability recurs in other images, including one that shows a kneeling, weeping Cap being comforted by firemen and families of the victims, while other images shift his representation to a different emotional register, of post-rescue relief and affirmation of the resolve of ordinary Americans, celebrated by the superheroes.[20]

I would call special attention to the juxtaposition of images of Captain America's newfound vulnerability and pathos with images like one of Captain America holding up a tattered American flag (Iwo Jima–style), for which the founder of Marvel Comics, Stan Lee, wrote the text. Lee's text shares with Bush and Guiliani the reassertion of a deliberately simplified and dehistoricized moral distinction between good and "naked evil," an assertion that implies there is nothing else to be known, nothing else to be revealed about what happened on September 11, 2001. This deliberate choice not to think historically is emphasized by the collapse of 9/11 into Pearl Harbor, through echoes of Roosevelt's rhetoric, and of today's Captain America with his origin in World War II. Lee's text reads in part, "A day there was of monumental villainy, when a great nation lost its innocence and naked evil stood revealed. A day there was when a serpent struck a sleeping giant, a giant who will sleep no more." I would also emphasize the way in which the use of Captain America as nationalist icon in these memorial tributes tries to have things both ways, in a way characteristic of cynical nationalism. This deployment of Captain America tries to combine the simplified moral conflicts of earlier comics with more recent alternative superhero narratives, which turned to film noir as a model in order to embed superhero characters in fictional worlds that can be marketed as more "realistic" because they are more morally ambiguous and the characters more internally conflicted (the contradictions in

Figure 12.3. CAPTAIN AMERICA TM & © 2004 Marvel Characters, Inc. Used with permission.

this project are commented on by the Godman cartoon). In some ways this use of Captain America suggests an extension of Lauren Berlant's theory of infantile citizenship, which imagines the United States as the ideal "home for a child-citizen protected from the

A day there was of monumental villainy. A day when a great nation lost its innocence and naked evil stood revealed before a stunned and shattered world.

A day there was when a serpent struck a sleeping giant, a giant who will sleep no more. Soon shall the serpent know the wrath of the might, the vengeance of the just.

A day there was when Liberty lost her heart – and found the strength within her soul.

Stan Lee

Figure 12.4. CAPTAIN AMERICA TM & © 2004 Marvel Characters, Inc. Used with permission.

violences of capitalism, class, race, and sexuality."[21] Captain America here figures a simplified moral universe, formerly protected but now embattled and ennobled by the necessity of engaging with a more complex reality, to which he can respond with both straightforward, childlike heroics or emotions and more psychologically sophisticated grief and pain.

The unexpected relevance of revisionist superheroes to post-9/11 nationalism is confirmed by bestselling author Dean Koontz's first post-9/11 novel, *By the Light of the Moon*, published in December 2002. This novel tells the story of a group of ordinary people mysteriously injected with experimental nanotechnology (microscopic computers) in order to modify their bodies, in effect giving them superpowers. More important, the nanomachines produce a "forced evolution of the brain"; specifically, they redesign the main characters' brains so that they are "wired to do the right thing no matter what our preferences, no matter what our desires, regardless of the consequences to us."[22] The novel imagines that everyone is born with "our brains . . . already wired to *know* the right thing, to know always what we ought to do," but the nanomachines build into the main characters a compulsion to act on the "righteous anger" they feel toward "evil"—that is, those who ignore this supposedly innate knowledge.[23] The main target of this anger is a group of white supremacists who try to murder an interracial couple on their wedding day, but these racists are explicitly compared to both street gangs and suicide bombers, in the novel's most direct, though still oblique, reference to 9/11.[24] The ways in which this technologically induced compulsion is conceptualized as a process of bringing comic book superheroes to life is made explicit at the end of the novel, when the characters describe themselves as acting out the "mythology" in which they have all been "marinated," and they note that, "When all is said and done . . . about all we'll be lacking are silly heroic names, cumbersome vehicles full of absurd gadgets, spandex costumes, and an archvillain to worry about between all the ordinary rescues and good deeds."[25]

In effect, the novel imagines the technological installment in its main characters of an inescapable sense of comic book morality, an immediate recognition of and visceral reaction against "evil," a compulsory set of moral distinctions that conflates such historically distinct formations as movements for white racial purity, minoritized inner-city youth gangs, and suicide bombings, regardless of the nature of the conflict in which they take place. The 2003 paperback reprint edition includes a back cover blurb from a review in *Publishers Weekly*, identifying this kind of narrative as "perfectly suited to the mood of America post-September 11" and as an example of novels that "acknowledge the reality and tenacity of evil but also the power of good" and that "celebrate the common man and woman" remade as superhero.[26] The Marvel 9/11 tribute book inverts this narrative strategy, by emphasizing how the attacks remake superheroes as ordinary men and women who retain the superhero comics' sense of clear distinctions between "evil" and "good."

Beginning in April 2002, Marvel began to promote a new "alternative" Captain America in an ongoing title, published monthly,[27] and in this series Captain America gains greater relevance from being forced to fight terrorism within the United States.[28] In other words, 9/11 seems to have solved the representational dilemma that had prevented any real updating of the Captain America character at the end of the twentieth century, and the nature of that representational dilemma and its solution reveals something important about the nature of the event that produced that solution and the cultural work that event is performing. But this ongoing series also demonstrates the difficulty in sustaining Captain America as both national allegory and realistic individual, in sustaining both a framework of moral absolutes and a revisionist narrative of Cap's relevance to the messiness of ordinary life. The writer of this series, John Ney Rieber, had previously worked primarily on DC's alternative Vertigo line (specifically on an urban fantasy title) rather than on superhero comics. (Marvel is currently in the middle of another reinvention of itself, as it generally recruits alternative comics creators to work on its superhero titles, in contrast to DC, which has encouraged alternative creators to work in other genres.) The first issue of the new series references the *Heroes* collection with an opening sequence in which Captain America joins the rescue workers to dig through the rubble of the World Trade Center in search of survivors.[29] He then goes on to prevent an attack on an Arab American by a man whose daughter had been killed in the attack, ending with the Arab American expressing sympathy for the man's loss and Captain America asserting that after the attacks we all have to be America, embody it, as he does, since "we share . . . we are the American dream" (ellipsis in original).[30] This sequence, illustrated with a full-body image of Cap in costume and a close-up of the knife breaking on the stylized American flag of Cap's shield, emphasizes his allegorical embodiment of America as well as asserting the protections (the shield) traditionally afforded by this abstract ideal of citizenship. The same point is made by the covers for the first story arc, which deliberately echo patriotic posters, including ones in which Captain America replaces the figure of Uncle Sam. This first issue ends with Captain America responding to a terrorist takeover of a small Midwestern town, which has been mined with antipersonnel weapons. The resolution of this plotline becomes the focus of issues 1–6 of the comic.

When he first surveys the devastation caused by another attack on American soil, this time on an example of small-town America rather than the metropolis, Captain America's laconic comment is "this is war."[31] But in the context of this story, this phrase ambiguously endorses and criticizes nationalist responses to the 9/11. "This is war" usually means "we have to respond to this atrocity by waging (more) war," but it could also be read as a critical comment on the escalating, shared mutual destruction that has already resulted, depending on where the emphasis is placed: this is *war* or *this* is war. The first reading looks ahead, to retribution, while the second focuses on the lesson of the present effects of violence. After Captain America kills the leader of the terrorists and defuses the immediate crisis, there is a remarkable sequence in which he addresses the television news crews who have descended on the scene, in ways designed to sustain this same ambiguity. The panel borders imitate Cap's public mediation through the televisual apparatus, his framing by the TV screen, and thereby call attention to his status as a representation or allegory. Within this frame, Cap tells us that he doesn't see war or hate, but instead "men and women and children dying," because of hate that is "blind enough to hold a nation responsible for the actions of a man."[32] This statement can be read as a critique of Faysal al-Tariq, the fictional terrorist Cap has just killed, and by extension bin Laden and Al Qaeda, who held all Americans responsible for various (real or perceived) affronts to Islam (such as the stationing of troops in Saudia Arabia or policies favoring Israel over the Palestinians), but it can also be read as a critique of the U.S. invasion of Afghanistan and then Iraq, for similarly holding whole nations responsible for bin Laden's actions. Captain America goes on to declare his refusal to be a part of this kind of blind retaliation, and he announces that America didn't kill the terrorist; he did.[33] This example shows the comic simultaneously offering a potential critique of both terrorism and official U.S. responses to it while also dehistoricizing and reducing the conflict to a simpler level, between two men, as Bush tended to do in his "dead or alive" comment. Cynical nationalism, in turn, consists of a refusal to acknowledge any distinction, any incommensurability, between these two gestures, of self-critique and self-aggrandizement. At the very moment when Captain America seems to be rejecting his own status as national icon, he only reproduces the logics of American exceptionalism and individualism, as well as the reassertion that complex historical dynamics can be understood in the simplest moral terms.

Captain America's refusal to stand for the nation is also a refusal of his own status as superhero, in a revisionist gesture intended to make the character more realistic. Captain America's acknowledgment of personal responsibility is accompanied by his removing his mask to reveal his secret identity to the world (see figure 12.5). The comic clearly encodes this gesture as a startling break with superhero conventions (as suggested by the use of a splash page to interrupt the narrative with the spectacle of Cap's naked face); in subsequent issues, this plot turn results in Cap moving to live in an ordinary neighborhood in New York (rather than the Avengers mansion)—that is, this revelation returns him to civilian life and means that he can no longer enjoy existence as a celebrity superhero. It means that he loses the protection afforded him by his anonymous universality. Clearly, then, this revelation that Captain America is Steve Rogers is intended to particularize and de-idealize Captain America (as in any good revisionist narrative), to dethrone him from his allegorical pedestal, so that he can be used to tell a story other than that of the inevitability of the American dream. However, this gesture is undermined by the fact that the image of a blonde, blue-eyed white man is hardly free of idealization; this page in fact only substitutes one abstract ideal, Captain America, for another: the false universality of the normative American citizen (white, straight, and male). The difficulty involved in revising this character in such a way is suggested by the ways that subsequent storylines in fact have tended to reassert more traditional superhero conventions, such as super-powered guest stars, especially since every storyline can't focus on another terrorist attack on U.S. soil. Rieber actually left the series after issue #11, and the monthly Captain America comic is no longer published under the "Marvel Knights" imprint, used to distinguish Marvel's more adult and realistic comics from more traditional superhero offerings.[34]

The problem posed by the way in which both the hero and the person, Captain America and Steve Rogers, embody an overly narrow ideal of America has been addressed in another post-9/11 revision of Captain America, a seven-issue miniseries by Roberto Morales and African American artist Kyle Baker, entitled *Truth: Red, White, and Black*.[35] This series intervenes in Captain America's origin story (Steve Rogers was a sickly young man ineligible for Army service

Figure 12.5. CAPTAIN AMERICA TM & © 2004 Marvel Characters, Inc. Used with Permission.

during World War II, who is turned into Captain America by injection with a "super-soldier serum").[36] Morales and Baker rewrite Cap's transformation by analogy with the Tuskegee syphilis experiments: the super-soldier serum is developed through experiments on black soldiers, most of whom die, and the series in fact suggests that the entire concept of a super-soldier serum results from the ideology of eugenics and racial purity shared by the United States and Germany prior to World War II. The experiments on black soldiers produce one success, Isaiah Bradley, so that it turns out the first Captain America was black, but this fact is suppressed by the military, who prefer that the only Captain America publicly acknowledged as such be a white man, for propaganda purposes. One striking image shows Isaiah Bradley parachuting into Germany on a suicide mission to free death camp inmates, having defied his orders and stolen and dressed himself in a (variant) Captain America costume and shield.[37] In later issues, it is revealed that the story we have read is being discovered by Captain America for the first time, and he takes it upon himself to return the stolen uniform to Isaiah Bradley; the series ends with this image (see figure 12.6).[38]

The metaphor of the black man who can represent America only through an act of theft and who therefore ends up shredding the image of America he wears offers a clear enough critical commentary on the allegorical character of his white counterpart and the negative effects of the false universality of the norms Cap is capable of embodying. This reading returns us to the vulnerability of the "empty" or "inauthentic" nationalist messages promulgated by forms of nationalism structured by cynical reason. If those messages, those claims to speak for the nation, are understood to be false or at best partial, then there is room for alternative messages. This same instability in the national allegory of Captain America is demonstrated in the third story arc of the monthly comic (written by Chuck Austen now), entitled "Ice," in which it is revealed that another part of Captain America's backstory that fans have always accepted as true may be the result of government manipulation of the media. Cap is supposed to have been accidentally frozen in a glacier at the end of World War II, to be revived in the 1960s and adopted by members of the Marvel superhero team the Avengers. In "Ice," it is revealed that the government actually staged this accident and implanted false memories in order to get rid of Captain America, fearing that he would not be willing to go along with the bombing of Hiroshima and Nagasaki.[39]

My analysis of cynical forms of nationalism in the aftermath of the World Trade Center attacks has emphasized their capacity to preempt traditional modes of resistance, but I have also tried to suggest, at least briefly, how resistance remains possible within such a transformed political and cultural context. To reinforce this point, I will return to an image from the *Heroes* tribute book, one that

Figure 12.6. CAPTAIN AMERICA TM & © 2004 Marvel Characters, Inc. Used with permission.

stands out as sharply uncharacteristic in that context. The text of this two-page spread was written by British comics writer Alan Moore, along with Frank Miller one of the originators of the 1980s genre of revisionist superhero stories. Illustrated by Dave Gibbons, this piece depicts a fireman standing in front of the falling towers, with the smoke above them containing the appalled faces of victims of other bombings, victims from a wide range of different cultures and historical moments. This image conflates the attack on the World Trade Center with the bombing of Baghdad during the Gulf War, the Blitz on London, the atomic bombing of Japan, and the firebombing of Dresden during World War II, ending with the assertion that we're all together now in Guernica.[40] What I want to briefly suggest is that this representation, this mode of memorializing the attacks, mobilizes the post-9/11 conventions of dehistoricizing and decontexualizing events in order to undermine the nationalist assertion of our essential difference from our evil enemies and prevent the consolidation of a selective, official image of America, like the one promoted by the comparison of the World Trade Center attacks to Pearl Harbor. This image mobilizes the rhetoric of trauma against its official use as a justification for demonizing other peoples and cultures as nothing but the agents of our victimization; it reminds us that no one has a monopoly on historical traumas of these kinds. This final example also suggests what popular culture has to teach us about critically inhabiting a thoroughly denaturalized political world.[41] Moore and Gibbons's contribution to the *Heroes* tribute book indicates how popular cynicism might be marshaled against the state rather than exploited to allow the state a free hand to create policy and wage war in our names.

The rest of this essay will unpack the theoretical implications of the analyses I have performed and their relevance to current political discourse in the United States. The denaturalized circulation of exploded nationalist myths that I have referred to as cynical nationalism can be explained in part by the increasing separation of nationalist imaginaries and state power, as "the hyphen that links" nation and state begins to seem "less an icon of conjuncture than an index of disjuncture," to quote Arjun Appadurai.[42] As Eva Cherniavsky has argued, a significantly weakened relation between nation and state challenges the very basis of middle-class hegemony and the modern liberal-democratic state, as understood by Antonio Gramsci.[43] Gramsci argues that capitalist democracies are to be distinguished from "previous ruling classes" that were "essentially conservative in the sense that they did not tend to construct an organic passage from the other classes into their own," in order to "enlarge their class sphere 'technically' and ideologically."[44] The existence of such an "organic passage" is the precondition for the assimilative function of the modern nation and its definition of abstract—that is, generally available—citizenship and upward mobility. Gramsci emphasizes the role of national culture in producing this middle-class "ethical" state, which thus takes on the role of " 'educator.' " Though Gramsci does not spell this out, Cherniavsky points out that the implication is that the distinctive feature of the traditional bourgeois state is the interweaving of national culture and self-definitions with access to the state apparatus; Gramsci's organic passage is the hyphen that conjoins nation and state. The disruption of that (supposedly) easy, organic passage between them, however phantasmatic or idealistic it may have been and however unequal access to that mobility actually was, also disrupts the connection between public sphere and state policy, public opinion and state power. It is this detachment of the operations of the repressive state apparatus, such as the military, from the fictions of national community that recontextualizes nationalist rhetorics within the model of cynical reason. This analysis might help to explain the way that rhetorics of national security were evoked to justify the war in Iraq, the decision for which seems to have originated in the state apparatus itself, specifically in the neoconservative policy advisors staffing the Bush administration, for entirely other reasons (such as neo-imperial ambitions to exploit the United State's status as the world's only remaining superpower or economic interests in Iraq's oil reserves). These developments contradict Žižek's argument that it is only in totalitarian societies that we see the triumph of cynical reason, along with the replacement of hegemonic consent by coercion;[45] the pressures placed on the nation-state under conditions of globalization promote similar shifts in democratic societies.

The controversy that resulted from the failure to discover evidence of Iraq's alleged weapons of mass destruction, the primary justification offered the American public for the invasion of Iraq, provides an occasion to exemplify and test my argument here about new forms of cynical nationalism, in which nationalist rhetorics gain power from their explicit inauthenticity, from the fact that they do not have to possess truth value, and so circulate in an already denaturalized or demystified form. One early focus of this controversy was a specific claim made in President Bush's State of the Union Address: that the Unites States had acquired intelligence indicating that Iraq had attempted to purchase 500 tons of uranium from Niger, and that Iraq therefore posed a potential nuclear threat to the United States. The documents on which this claim was based turned out to be forgeries, and apparently rather obvious and clumsy ones at that, somehow accepted at face value by United States officials. As a result, questions were raised about the credibility of the president and his administration (largely forgotten in the general failure to find weapons of mass destruction in Iraq after the war). At the time, the administration indeed seemed concerned to demonstrate that there was no intent to deceive the American public, with staff members and CIA officials stepping forward to take responsibility for the "error" of including the reference to the uranium purchase in Bush's address to the nation. On the one hand, this concern over being caught in a lie might seem to contradict the assumptions of cynical reason as I have defined them, and to indicate the continued effectiveness of investigative journalism and critical demystifications. This specific controversy was generally subsumed within the larger issue of the failure to turn up weapons of mass destruction in Iraq, and in that form it persisted as an issue in the 2004 presidential election, though it was largely deflected by debates about whether the United States should have continued to pursue bin Laden in Afghanistan instead of opening another front in Iraq. On the other hand, I'm not so sure that these revelations will have the more fundamental effect of democratizing state power and making it more responsive to and dependent on public opinion. For instance, during the presidential campaign, President Bush seemed to have considerable success in replacing questions about the rationale his administration offered for going to war with the question of whether the consequences (the removal of Saddam Hussein from power) weren't laudable, whether or not the reasons we were offered were inaccurate, overstated or even fabricated, as it turned out in this one case. In this context, holding public officials accountable for what they say in public seems to me curiously limited in its political effectiveness, in ways that the model of cynical reason might explain.

It also seems to me that the debate about Bush's credibility has, at least to date, actually functioned to recontain and limit critiques of his administration. The debate and whatever damage it might cause to the Bush administration's power to achieve its agenda have been limited to the question of whether or not he lied or bent the truth. There has been no attempt in the national press to raise questions about why this statement might have been included even if it was known in advance to be false (if it was)—that is, what particular interests would be served by making this claim? What function does it serve, despite or perhaps because of its falsehood, in making possible the exercise of power? These questions remain obscured by the still-dominant assumption that demonstrating the falsehood, exposing the lie, is enough to delegitimate power and demystify nationalist ideology, and these are the questions that the framework of cynical reason foregrounds.

At any rate, it is important to note that if cynical nationalism involves a breakdown in the seemingly natural connection between the state apparatus and the national public sphere, as I have argued, that does not mean that the media and public speech become irrelevant to those in power. As Grossberg's example of the first Gulf War suggests, what happens under these conditions is that it is necessary for the state to saturate the public sphere with its message, even or especially if that message is explicitly presented as such, as a particular spin, and not as "the truth." This implies a potential vulnerability of cynical nationalism. If it is a matter of insuring that public discourse is saturated with a message that doesn't have to be authentic or grounded in fact, then that lack of grounding means that it always remains possible for such a message to be relativized and contested, if a dissenting message can gain some air time (Alan Moore and Dave Gibbons's contribution to the Marvel's *Heroes* book is one example of this kind of contestation). This strategy of saturation is distinct from the bourgeois state's traditional project of gaining hegemony through consent; the whole point of cynical nationalism's saturation of public discourse with empty rhetoric and exploded nationalist myths is to bypass the need to obtain the people's informed consent. The goal is not to convince, but to make persuasion and public debate seem irrelevant, if not positively unpatriotic. One example might be the repeated assertion by public officials before the war that there is a link between Iraq and Al Qaeda, even as the administration was forced to admit that there was no evidence of such a link. But such a strategy tends to yield more transitory and unstable results for those in power than more traditional techniques of persuasion, since it depends not on gaining a particular political commitment but on producing a disengagement from politics in general.

Bush's critics have noted that Secretary of State Colin Powell omitted references to this African uranium purchase, when he made the case for an invasion of Iraq to the U.N. However, State Department fact sheets still listed the allegations about Iraq's attempted purchase of this uranium as late as December 19, 2002, just one month prior to the State of the Union Address. More important, in closed hearings before the Senate Foreign Relations Committee, on September 24, 2002, Powell reportedly repeated these allegations. When news of the forgeries became public in July 2003, Powell argued that the inaccuracy of the uranium claim did not undermine the overall perception that it was necessary to remove Saddam Hussein from power. Defense Secretary Donald Rumsfeld reportedly suggested to the Senate Arms Services Committee that we did not go to war because of any direct or "dramatic" new evidence, but instead because we interpreted the evidence in a "dramatic new light," through the "prism" of the 9/11 attacks (see the *Chicago Tribune* for July 10, 2003). Similarly, it is common now to displace the question of how the war was justified, through invoking Iraq's threat to the United States, onto the question of whether it wasn't a good thing to remove Saddam Hussein from power, a strategy followed by President Bush in the 2004 presidential campaign, when he challenged John Kerry to affirm that the means did indeed justify the ends and that the war in Iraq was justified on the basis of its effects, regardless of the truth value of the prewar rationales. Deputy Defense Secretary Paul Wolfowitz has stated that the administration's emphasis on Iraq's weapons programs as the "core reason" for going to war had "a lot to do with the U.S. government bureaucracy"; it was, he told an interviewer from *Vanity Fair* magazine in May 2003, something "we settled on" as "the one reason everyone could agree on." These kinds of statements seem to me symptomatic of the dominance of cynical reason in contemporary American politics. Wolfowitz tries to assert the immunity of the state apparatus, the bureaucracy, from public norms of credibility and authenticity.

The reason why it doesn't matter whether evidence for going to war is true or not is suggested in the first speech in which Bush presented to the public his reasons for wanting to invade Iraq. This speech was delivered in Cincinnati, Ohio, on October 7, 2002. At one point in this speech, after arguing that there is intelligence supporting the claim that Iraq is a direct threat to the United States, Bush goes on to suggest that "Iraq could decide on any given day to provide a biological or chemical weapon to a terrorist group or individual terrorists. Alliance with terrorists could allow the Iraqi regime to attack America without leaving any fingerprints." What does this statement mean? We must attack Iraq now because, if we don't and there is another attack on U.S. soil, we may not be able to prove, to know, that Iraq had anything to do with it? In other words, both the presence and the absence of evidence that Iraq is a threat are reasons to attack.[46] This statement exemplifies the separation of knowing and doing Žižek defines, as well as the refusal to acknowledge that the abandonment of universality as a legitimation strategy in favor of naked self-interest means that the actions the administration has decided to take, evidence or not, will appear self-evidently justified only to ourselves.

It is important to note, I believe, that this post-9/11 triumph of cynical nationalism is also a function of the intellectual history of left and New Americanist critiques (like Rogin's or Donald Pease's work on postnational American studies).[47] I'm arguing that this is not simply a return to nationalism, and therefore an indication that our critiques haven't taken somehow, haven't been effectively communicated to the American public, or that the project of critique and demystification simply hasn't run its full course and all we need to do is keep on plugging away. Instead, I think this new denaturalized or cynical nationalism marks the success of those critiques; nationalism, especially in its American exceptionalist form, cannot continue to operate as it has in the past. That's the good news. The Susan Sontag controversy is instructive on this point, since much of the negative response focused on the supposed elitism of her tone, which wearily suggested that we've already heard this nationalist rhetoric and are all aware of the critiques, or should be, at least. For Sontag's critics, this meant she could only be addressing herself to an audience of ivory-tower, normative left-wing intellectuals, and the lack of a groundswell of objections to Bush or Giuliani indicated how out-of-touch with the public such an audience must be. I think the assumptions of Sontag's critics are just as wrong as her own assumption that traditional forms of intellectual demystification are still effective responses to abuses of power. It's wrong to conclude that only intellectuals like Sontag or myself are aware of these critiques and they haven't filtered down to the popular level yet. I think they have filtered down, and by doing so have changed the conditions under which nationalist rhetorics can circulate and therefore the conditions for critiquing their continued circulation.

The bad news is that nationalist war-mongering seems to have found a pretty successful way to sustain itself under these new conditions, one that our dominant traditions of left and intellectual critique in general have great difficulty getting any leverage on. The problem isn't that nationalist myths haven't been exposed and exploded, at least in part through the critical work of intellectual and academic movements like American Studies. The problem is that they have been exploded, and still manage to dominate public debate, perhaps even more effectively than before. To the extent that this analysis is valid, it raises basic questions about the place of dissent and intellectual work in the contemporary United States, or the lack thereof. The relevance of comics like the ones I have cited above by Ruben Bolling or Alan Moore and Dave Gibbons results from the extent to which not only culture but politics have been equally denaturalized.

In this respect, it is important to emphasize Žižek's point about the complex relations between cynical reason and popular practices of resistance that take cynical forms; these popular practices still express a desire for an alternative cultural position from which to evaluate official statements.[48] It is precisely this utopian impulse that is evacuated by cynical reason as it exploits the collapse of referentiality and the disjunction between official discourse and social reality, to imply that it doesn't matter if nationalist rhetoric has any truth value or not (welcome to the desert of the real, indeed, a phrase Žižek appropriates from the film *The Matrix* [which appropriated it from Baudrillard]) Žižek, however, seems to feel that 9/11 constitutes a challenge to this disjunction rather than its extension, so that for Žižek 9/11 constitutes the return of a repressed reality that requires "America" to look beyond its own virtual fantasies and to engage with how other cultures perceive us).[49] As I suggested above, cynical reason tries to turn popular cynicism away from utopian possibility and into taking for granted the absence of any positive alternative. Moreover, cynical reason actually tends to break down the distinction Žižek makes between a "prevailing ideology . . . of cynicism," in which people simply "no longer . . . take ideological propositions seriously," and the more "fundamental level of ideology," which is "not that of an illusion masking the real state of things but that of an (unconscious) fantasy structuring our social reality itself" and what we do, rather than what we say.[50] Cynical nationalism demonstrates how the distinction Žižek asserts, between ideology as mystification or masking of an underlying truth and ideology as constitutive of experience, tends to disappear (in *Dead Cities*, Mike Davis similarly reads the 9/11 attacks as uncanny, in the sense of blurring the distinction between imagination and reality[51]). Žižek distinguishes these two concepts or levels of ideological work in order to privilege the unconscious structuring of reality over theories of ideology as false consciousness and to dismiss the challenge posed to theories of ideology by cynical reason. The best example of Žižek's investment in this separation is found in *The Sublime Object of Ideology*, when he argues that his definition of this more fundamental level of unconscious fantasy implies that anti-Semitism has nothing to do with Jews.[52] The post-9/11 discourse of "evil," as an explicit technique of policing what can and cannot be intellectually analyzed, relegates the 9/11 attacks to the level of unconscious fantasy or traumatic kernel of the Real in order to control how that trauma structures our social reality, at the same time that it makes that process of exclusion visible.

I'm arguing that something more is going on here than Sontag recognized, when she criticized the replacement of politics by psychotherapy and "grief management" in public discourse after 9/11, leading to her infamous comment, "Let's by all means grieve together. But let's not be stupid together." But I'm also arguing against Žižek, who claims that "cynical reason, with all its ironic detachment, leaves untouched the fundamental level of ideological fantasy."[53] Because he believes this, he can therefore argue that, despite the prevalence of cynicism and the lack of ideological seriousness or commitment, we are far from being a "post-ideological society," since the "fundamental level of ideology . . . is not of an illusion masking the real state of things but that of an (unconscious) fantasy structuring our social reality itself."[54] For Žižek, in other words, both popular cynicism as a mode of resistance and cynical reason, as a strategy for preempting and manipulating that resistance, remain relatively superficial and therefore fail to effect real change in the ways that either power or dissent can be articulated. Indeed, for Žižek, there ultimately seems to be no real difference between popular and official forms of cynicism, since in both cases "cynical distance is just one way . . . to blind ourselves to the structuring power of ideological fantasy: even if we do not take things seriously, even if we keep an ironical distance, *we are still doing them.*"[55]

The specific forms that nationalist responses to 9/11 have taken suggest otherwise, to my mind. The demonizing of America's enemies as evil, and the policing of any attempts to understand the historical processes that produced people willing to commit suicide attacks, suggests precisely an attempt to manipulate the fantasies that Žižek insists always remain unconscious and therefore prior to cultural processes as such. In other words, the unconscious fantasies that Žižek wants to absolutely distinguish from ideological illusions or constructions turn out to be social constructions of particular social groups or acts as evil, monstrous, unrepresentable, incomprehensible, inscrutable (this is similar to the critique Judith Butler makes of Žižek, in the "Arguing with the Real" chapter in Butler's *Bodies that Matter*[56]). Cynical nationalism consists of an active, conscious refusal to construct our enemies in any other way, even though we realize it is possible to do so. While Žižek reads the aftermath of the 9/11 attacks as "the unique time between a traumatic event and its symbolic impact,"[57] in fact post-9/11 forms of cynical nationalism demonstrate the failure of this gap to be maintained, as the very trauma of the attacks is perpetuated and used to elicit support for national policies informed by specific meanings and interpretations—that is, symbolic structures. I agree, therefore, with Fredric Jameson's comment on how the "new inauthenticity" of national sentiment he associates with 9/11 "casts no little doubt on all those theories of mourning and trauma that were recently so influential, and whose slogans one finds everywhere in the [news] coverage."[58]

I would also argue that Grossberg's analysis of the resurgence of popular conservatism in the Reagan period, in his book *We Gotta Get Out Of This Place*, defines the context out of which this cynical nationalism emerges, well before the Gulf War. Rogin identifies the Reagan presidency as a moment when the distinction between spectacle and secrecy began to break down, in ways that have become characteristic of cynical reason, which typically flaunts and owns up to its own misrepresentations, thereby preempting any critical exposure of them.[59] Grossberg elaborates on this suggestion when he locates Reagan's success in his ability to redeploy the rhetoric of anticommunism by "rendering" it so "irrelevant" as an intellectually coherent political ideology, in part through sheer stubborn repetition, that he "made it possible again to affectively invest in it," in anticommunism as rhetoric or collective ritual, not as a rational political analysis.[60]

It is this shift that Grossberg refers to as the "disciplined mobilization of everyday of life," which results in the replacement of politics by lifestyle choices.[61] This analysis historicizes what Sontag oversimplified as the replacement of politics by psychotherapy after 9/11. Where Grossberg differs from Sontag is in his recognition that there is a core of genuine popular resistance in such lifestyle practices, in which "everyday life has become [a] site of empowerment." The recontainment of this resistance comes when lifestyle practices become not just *a* site of empowerment but "the only place where one can find the energy to act in any way against the grain of social tendencies."[62] His argument, then, is that sometimes the personal is not political enough, and his main example is the ecological movement, which he sees as having been displaced from global issues of policy and economics to micropolitical issues of everyday consumerism and recycling. In the context of the Gulf War, Grossberg suggests, this disciplined mobilization of everyday practices of resistance means that "images of the war were articulated and deployed into people's lives so as not to disrupt or break into the closed space of everyday life. Instead, the war was absorbed into its rhythms, tempos and intensities, into its mattering maps," with the result that it became difficult to protest the war without also seeming to undermine the everyday "forms of empowerment" that people legitimately feel invested in, against state power and control.[63] This saturation of everyday life with media images of the war specifically made it difficult to protest the war without also implicitly threatening the genuinely empowering if limited forms of agency embedded (and contained) at the microlevel of Americans's everyday consumer practices (that is, it became difficult to contest particular images without also seeming to contest the entire commodity form in which those images were presented).[64] I have turned to cartoons and comics to exemplify how this process has been extended and intensified after the 9/11 attacks, but also to locate some examples of resistance within the commodity form itself.

Notes

1. Slavoj Žižek, *The Sublime Object of Ideology* (New York: Verso, 1989), 28–33; Peter Sloterdijk, *Critique of Cynical Reason*, trans. Michael Eldred (Minneapolis: University of Minnesota Press, 1987) (originally published as *Kritik der zynischen Vernunft*, 2 vols [Frankfurt am Main: Suhrkamp Verlag, 1983]).
2. Lawrence Grossberg, *We Gotta Get Out of This Place: Popular Conservatism and Postmodern Culture* (New York: Routledge, 1992), 256–262, 301–309.
3. Michael Rogin, " 'Make My Day': Spectacle as Amnesia in Imperial Politics [and] the Sequel," in *Cultures of U.S. Imperialism*, eds. Amy Kaplan and Donald E. Pease (Durham, N.C.: Duke University Press, 1993), 499–534.
4. Ibid., 525.

5. Žižek, *Sublime Object*, 29; Sloterdijk, *Critique,* 5. For another important application and explanation of the relevance of Sloterdijk's concept, see chapter 4, "The Art of Cynical Reason," in Hal Foster, *The Return of the Real: The Avant-Garde at the End of the Century* (Cambridge, Mass.: MIT Press, 1996), especially 118–124.

6. Žižek, *Sublime Object*, 29.

7. See chapter 2 in Lisa Nakamura, *Cybertypes: Race, Ethnicity, and Identity on the Internet* (New York: Routledge, 2002), for an example of another, perhaps more familiar site where there is a similar disarticulation of nature and norm: online practices of identity performance or what Nakamura calls "identity tourism." Nakamura notes that in online contexts, passing, whether racially or sexually, becomes the norm, since there are no physical bodies present to naturalize identity claims. Nakamura points out, however, that this denaturalization of identity does not prevent the reproduction of orientalizing racial stereotypes (though it may more successfully denaturalize gender and sexual assumptions). As a result, Nakamura argues, the saturation of online discourse and social interaction with these denaturalized performative acts has the effect of establishing acceptable norms for anyone, of whatever race, who wishes to define themselves as "Asian" or "black." Denaturalization allows a very narrow definition of acceptable racial performances.

8. Rogin, " 'Make My Day,' " 504.

9. Grossberg, *We Gotta Get Out of This Place*, 304.

10. Žižek, *Sublime Object*, 29–30.

11. Žižek, *Sublime Object*, 33.

12. Mike Davis, *Dead Cities and Other Tales* (New York: New Press, 2002), 9.

13. For more information about Bolling, and especially his cartoons on the 9/11 attacks, see Kent Worcester, "The Ruben Bolling Interview," *Comics Journal* no. 247 (October 2002): 54–72.

14. *Heroes* 1, no 1 (New York: Marvel Comics, December 2001).

15. Michael Dean, "9/11, Benefit Comics, and the Dog-Eat-Dog World of Good Samaritanism," *Comics Journal* no. 247 (October 2002): 11. For reviews of the range of other 9/11 comics published, see also R. Fiore, "A Moment of Noise," *Comics Journal* no. 247 (October 2002): 46–52.

16. Mike Cotton, "We Will Not Forget," *Wizard: The Comics Magazine* no.133 (October 2002): 54.

17. Fred Moten, "The New International of Decent Feelings," *Social Text* 20, no. 3 (Fall 2002): 189–199.

18. *Heroes*, 4.

19. Ibid., 6.

20. Ibid., 19, 23.

21. Lauren Berlant, *The Queen of America Goes to Washington City: Essays on Sex and Citizenship* (Durham, N.C.: Duke University Press, 1997), 21.

22. Dean Koontz, *By the Light of the Moon* (New York: Bantam, 2002), 273, 397.

23. Ibid., 396.

24. Ibid., 388.

25. Ibid., 428, 430.

26. Dean Koontz, *By the Light of the Moon* (New York: Bantam, 2003), back cover.

27. In September 2002, Marvel also published a hardcover collection of Captain America stories, *Captain America: Red, White, and Blue*, mostly new stories by

alternative creators, including some who had never worked on superhero comics before, most notably Peter Kuper, one of the mainstays behind the New York–based radical political comic *World War III Illustrated* (Kuper's two-page story depicts a dream of Captain America's in which Cap takes off his mask to find that he is Hitler, and ends with him being kissed by his arch-enemy, the Nazi villain Red Skull). This collection also republishes some classic, earlier stories, including one Stan Lee/Jack Kirby example and one by Jim Steranko, who in the early 70s attempted to reimagine Captain America as a James Bond–style Cold War covert agent, as Steranko had already done with Nick Fury.

28. On the ways in which this revision of Captain America has been controversial, see Cotton, "We Will Not Forget," 54. In issue #3 of the new monthly series, Captain America breaks the neck of a terrorist who has launched an attack on a small Midwestern town, and then reveals his secret identity on live national TV. Cotton quotes the writer of the comic, who argues that "the real battle wasn't the fight between Cap and al-Tariq [the terrorist], it was the questioning, the moral struggle that Cap put himself through as he crossed the battlefield" (Cotton, "We Will Not Forget," 54). My argument is that it is only the events of 9/11 that make it possible to apply this psychologizing move (typical in other revisionist superhero narratives) to Captain America. Cotton's article also notes that a relaunch of Captain America was already planned prior to 9/11 ("We Will Not Forget," 52), but I believe that 9/11 provided a context that enabled the success of this revision.

Note also that Jim Steranko (one of the more well-known writers and artists who worked on an earlier version of Captain America in the early 70s) used 9/11 as an occasion to launch an attack on the morbidity of contemporary superhero comics, attacking their creators as "cultural terrorists." Steranko went on to produce a limited edition print, depicting a collage of Captain American and other World War II–era heroes and villains, as part of a charity effort (Dean, "9/11," 14).

29. John Ney Rieber and John Casaday, *Captain America* 4, no. 1 (New York: Marvel Comics, June 2002): 4–11.

30. Ibid., 18–20, 24.

31. Ibid., 32.

32. John Ney Rieber and John Casaday, *Captain America* 4, no. 3 (New York: Marvel Comics, August 2002): 20–21.

33. Ibid., 21–22.

34. However, I should note that Roberto Morales, the writer for the "Truth" miniseries discussed in the next paragraph, subsequently wrote a five-part story arc for the monthly Captain American comic, entitled "Homeland," in which Captain America is asked to serve on a military tribunal sitting in judgment on detainees at Guantanamo Bay, a storyline that returns the new alternative Captain America to a more direct engagement with the aftermath of 9/11; Roberto Morales, Chris Bachalo, and Tim Townsend, *Captain America* 4, nos. 21–25 (New York: Marvel Comics, February-June 2004).

35. Roberto Morales and Kyle Baker, *Truth: Red, White, and Black* nos. 1–7 (New York: Marvel Comics, January-July 2003).

36. For a reading of Captain America's origin as the "first 'cyborgian' " superhero, see Mark Oehlert, "From Captain America to Wolverine: Cyborgs in Comic Books: Alternative Images of Cybernetic Heroes and Villains," in *The*

Cybercultures Reader, eds. David Bell and Barbara M. Kennedy (New York: Routledge, 2000), 112–113. In effect, Captain America literalizes the argument that the "real attraction of abstract citizenship" resides in the way that "the citizen conventionally acquires a new body," a universal or typical body, "by participation in the political public sphere"; Lauren Berlant, "National Brands/National Body: *Imitation of Life*," in *Comparative American Identities: Race, Sex, and Nationality in the Modern Text*, ed. Hortense J. Spillers (New York: Routledge, 1991), 113. The specificity of Captain America's origin as a masculine fantasy resides in the way in which it produces this abstract idea, in effect short-circuiting the structure of "national manhood" that Dana Nelson defines, in which the "imagined fraternity" of American masculinity requires the absence of its phantasmatic ideal. Captain America is the living presence of the "uniform, brotherly state of unity and wholeness" that Nelson argues informs national manhood only in a nostalgic and melancholic form, as something lost that never truly existed; Dana D. Nelson, *National Manhood: Capitalist Citizenship and the Imagined Fraternity of White Men* (Durham, N.C.: Duke University Press, 1998), 205. In that sense, through these techniques of literalization and materialization, Captain America can be understood as putting some critical pressure on these abstract ideals. However, Captain America can also be read as demonstrating that the refusal of nostalgia and melancholy is not necessarily progressive or transformative, either.

37. Morales and Baker, *Truth: Red, White, and Black* no. 4, 21.

38. Morales and Baker, *Truth: Red, White, and Black* no. 7 (New York: Marvel Comics, July 2003), 23.

39. Chuck Austen and Jae Lee, *Captain America* 4, nos. 12–16 (New York: Marvel Comics, June-October 2003).

40. *Heroes*, 31.

41. It is possible to argue that the comics medium is itself particularly suited for an exploration of what it means to understand the world as denaturalized. In his influential graphic novel about the nature of comics, Scott McCloud argues that one of the key features of the medium is what he calls "closure," or the juxtaposition of sequential images to create a narrative that explicitly lays bare its own fissures or suturing processes, in the form of the gutters separating the panels; *Understanding Comics* (Northampton: Tundra, 1993), 63–64. McCloud in fact contrasts comics to film on this point, citing Godard's famous line about how films give us reality at twenty two frames a second (*Understanding Comics*, 65). In contrast, comics refuse to produce the illusion of reality and narrative continuity produced by film's persistence of vision. Similarly, McCloud cites comics' dependence on cartooning techniques, or what he calls "iconic abstraction" (that is, abstraction intended to communicate meaning rather than for pure aesthetic enjoyment), as an example of how comics make ideas visible (*Understanding Comics*, 41), how they represent a visible world visibly informed by our ways of seeing it (31). The allusion to John Berger's book *Ways of Seeing* is significant, since for Berger such ways of seeing are ideologies. In this sense, then, comics is a medium that lays bare its own fictional and ideological devices, that makes ideology visible, without necessarily contesting ideological norms, just as is the case with cynical reason.

42. Arjun Appadurai, *Modernity at Large: Cultural Dimensions of Globalization* (Minneapolis: University of Minnesota Press, 1996), 39.

43. See Cherniavsky's forthcoming book *Incorporations: Race, Nation, and the Body Politics of Capital* (Minneapolis: University of Minnesota Press, 2006), especially chapter 2; I am indebted to her for calling this passage from Gramsci and its implications for the current status of the nation-state to my attention.

44. Antonio Gramsci, *Selections from the Prison Notebooks*, trans. Quintin Hoare and Geoffrey Nowell Smith (New York: International Publishers, 1971), 260.

45. Žižek, *Sublime Object*, 30.

46. For a similarly convoluted logic, see the September 10, 2002, column by former Chicago Tribune writer Bob Greene (section 2, page 1), "The day that infamy pulled a vanishing act," which imagines what would have happened if, after the Pearl Harbor attacks, Japan had made no further aggressive actions toward the United States or even public statements about the attacks. The point of this thought experiment (and the assertion that Pearl Harbor is still a valid analogy, no matter how different the 9/11 attacks are) is to interpret the lack of subsequent attacks as a kind of threat in itself, to the extent that it encourages the "dangerous" emotion of relief. The claim here is that America is threatened by terrorists whether they attack us or not, that we are at war whether there is ever another attack or not, whether or not there is actually a conflict in process.

47. Don Pease, ed., *National Identities and Post-Americanist Narratives* (Durham, N.C.: Duke University Press, 1994).

48. Žižek, *Sublime Object*, 29–30.

49. Slavoj Žižek, "Welcome to the Desert of the Real!," *South Atlantic Quarterly* 101, no. 2 (Spring 2002): 385–389.

50. Žižek, *Sublime Object*, 33.

51. Davis, *Dead Cities*, 6.

52. Žižek, *Sublime Object*, 48.

53. Ibid., 30.

54. Ibid., 33.

55. Ibid.

56. Judith Butler, *Bodies that Matter: On the Discursive Limits of "Sex"* (New York: Routledge, 1993), 187–222.

57. Žižek, "Welcome to the Desert of the Real!," 389.

58. Fredric Jameson, "The Dialectics of Disaster," *South Atlantic Quarterly*, 101, no. 2 (Spring 2002): 299.

59. Rogin, " 'Make My Day,' " 499–500.

60. Grossberg, *We Gotta Get Out of This Place*, 256.

61. Ibid., 304.

62. Ibid., 304–305.

63. Ibid., 304, 305.

64. Ibid.

Contributors

MICK BRODERICK teaches Media Analysis at Murdoch University in Perth, Western Australia. He is author of *Nuclear Movies* (McFarland, 1991) and editor of *Hibakusha Cinema: Hiroshima, Nagasaki and the Nuclear Image in Japanese Film* (Kegan Paul, 1996) and Associate Director of the Centre for Millennial Studies at the University of Sydney.

MOLLY HURLEY DÉPRET is a student in the Anthropology Ph.D. Program at the CUNY Graduate Center in New York, NY. Her dissertation Fieldwork will be set in Belfast, Northern Ireland, and will Focus on memory, experience, and political violence.

THOMAS FOSTER is Professor of English at the University of Washington. He is the author of *Transformations of Domesticity in Modern Women's Writing: Homelessness at Home* (Palgrave Macmillan, 2002) and *The Souls of Cyberfolk: Posthumanism as Vernacular Theory* (University of Minnesota Press, 2005).

FRANCIS FRASCINA is John Raven Professor of Visual Arts in the Department of American Studies, Keele University, Staffordshire. He is the author of *Art, Politics, and Dissent: Aspects of the Art Left in Sixties America* (Manchester University Press, 1999) and editor of *Pollock and After: the Critical Debate*, Second Edition (Routledge, 2000).

MARK GIBSON is Director of the Centre for Everyday Life at Murdoch University and editor, with Brian Shoesmith and Ian Hutchison, of *Continuum: Journal of Media and Cultural Studies*. He has published widely on television, everyday life, and Australian cultural politics and is currently completing a book on the concept of power.

WILLIAM HART is Founding editor of Intercultural Relations.com. In addition to his work on intercultural relations he writes on U.S.

media responses to 9/11, including studies of editorial cartoons, television, and popular music. He currently teaches a course on communication and 9/11.

DANA HELLER is Professor of English and Director of the Humanities Institute and Graduate Program at Old Dominion University, Norfolk, Virginia. She is the author of *The Feminization of Quest Romance: Radical Departures* (University of Texas, 1990), *The De-Oedipalization of Popular Culture* (University of Pennsylvania Press, 1995), and editor of *Cross-Purposes: Lesbians, Feminists, and the Limits of Alliance* (Indiana University Press, 1997).

JOE LOCKARD is Assistant Professor of English at Arizona State University and an editor of *Bad Subjects: Political Education For Everyday Life*, a journal to which he frequently contributes. He teaches early American and African American literatures, and directs the online Antislavery Literature Project. He is co-editor with Mark Pegrum of the forthcoming volume *Brave New Classrooms: Educational Democracy and the Internet*.

BIANCA NIELSEN is currently preparing to submit her Ph.D. dissertation in the American Studies Department at the University of Canterbury, Christchurch, New Zealand. Her dissertation title is "Girls, Women and Communities of Women in the Contemporary Horror and Thriller Genres." She also works as an Assistant Lecturer in Communications at the University of Otago, Dunedin, New Zealand.

JENNIFER SCANLON is Associate Professor and Director of Gender and Women's Studies at Bowdoin College in Maine. She is the author of *Inarticulate Longings: The Ladies' Home Journal, Gender, and the Promises of Consumer Culture* (Routledge, 1995), editor of *Significant Contemporary American Feminists* (Greenwood, 1999), and *The Gender and Consumer Culture Reader* (NYU Press, 2000).

YONEYUKI SUGITA is Associate Professor of American History at the Osaka University of Foreign Studies in Osaka, Japan. He is a specialist in American foreign policy and the U.S.-Japanese relationship. He is the author of *Pitfall or Panacea: The Irony of US Power in Occupied Japan, 1945–1952* (Routledge, 2003).

LYNN SPIGEL is a Professor in the School of Communications at Northwestern University. She is the author of *Make Room for TV: Television and the Family Ideal in Postwar America* (Chicago, 1992) and *Welcome to the Dreamhouse: Popular Media and Postwar Suburbs* (Duke, 2001). She also has edited numerous anthologies on media and culture, including *Television After TV: Essays on a Medium in Transition* (Duke, 2004).

JAMES TRIMARCO is a student in the Anthropology Ph.D. Program at the CUNY Graduate Center in New York, NY.

ØYVIND VÅGNES teaches American literature and is a Ph.D. candidate at the Department of English, University of Bergen, Norway. His doctoral dissertation, *Kennedy Dying: Quoting Zapruder's Film*, will be completed in 2006. His second novel in Norwegian, *EKKO*, has just been published in Norway.

Index

(Numbers in bold indicate figures within the text)